Media, Religion and Gender

Media, Religion and Gender presents a selection of eminent current scholarship that explores the role gender plays when religion, media use and values in contemporary society interact. The book:

- surveys the development of research on media, religion and culture through the lens of key theoretical and methodological issues and debates within gender studies
- includes case studies drawn from a variety of countries and contexts to illustrate the range of issues, theoretical perspectives and empirical material involved in current work
- outlines new areas and reflects on challenges for the future.

Students of media, religion and gender at advanced level will find this a valuable resource, as will scholars and researchers working in this important and growing field.

Mia Lövheim is a professor in Sociology of Religion based in the Faculty of Theology at Uppsala University, Sweden.

Media, Religion and Culture
Edited by Stewart M. Hoover, Jolyon Mitchell and David Morgan

Media, Religion and Culture is an exciting series which analyzes the role of media in the history of contemporary practice of religious belief. Books in this series explore the importance of a variety of media in religious practice and highlight the significance of the culture, social and religious setting of such media.

Media, Religion and Gender

Key issues and new challenges

Edited by
Mia Lövheim

Routledge
Taylor & Francis Group
LONDON AND NEW YORK

First published in 2013
by Routledge
2 Park Square, Milton Park, Abingdon, Oxon OX14 4RN

Simultaneously published in the USA and Canada
by Routledge
711 Third Avenue, New York, NY 10017

Routledge is an imprint of the Taylor & Francis Group, an informa business

British Library Cataloguing in Publication Data
A catalogue record for this book is available from the British Library

Library of Congress Cataloging in Publication Data
Media, religion and gender : key issues and new challenges / edited by Mia
Lövheim.
p. cm. -- (Media, religion and gender)
1. Mass media in religion. 2. Mass media--Religious aspects. 3. Women and
religion. 4. Sex role--Religious aspects. 5. Sex role. 6. Mass media. 7. Religion.
I. Lövheim, Mia, 1968-
BL638.M425 2013
201'.7--dc23
2012042997

ISBN: 978-0-415-50472-0 (hbk)
ISBN: 978-0-415-50473-7 (pbk)
ISBN: 978-0-203-52174-8 (ebk)

Typeset in Sabon
by Taylor and Francis Books

MIX
Paper from
responsible sources
FSC
www.fsc.org   FSC® C013056

Printed and bound in Great Britain by
TJ International Ltd, Padstow, Cornwall

Contents

Notes on contributors

Alexandra Boutros is Assistant Professor in Communication Studies and Cultural Studies at Wilfrid Laurier University, in Waterloo, Canada. Her research is generally concerned with the intersection of media, technology and identity within the context of religious, social and cultural movements. Recent publications include *Circulation and the City: Essays on Urban Mobility* co-edited with William Straw (McGill-Queens University Press 2010) and "Gods on the Move: The Mediatization of Haitian Vodou," in the journal *Culture and Religion* (2011).

Grace Chiou is a Ph.D. student at the Joint Program in Religious Studies at University of Denver/Iliff. Her research interests include the cultural production of sacred space, urban forms, material and visual culture, and religion and popular culture.

Lynn Schofield Clark is Associate Professor and Director of the Estlow International Center for Journalism and New Media at the University of Denver, where she teaches participatory courses in journalism, media, and culture as well as in qualitative research methods. Clark is author of *The Parent App: Understanding Families in the Digital Age* (Oxford University Press 2012), *From Angels to Aliens: Teenagers, the Media, and the Supernatural* (Oxford University Press 2005). She is also co-author of *Media, Home, and Family* (Routledge 2004), and editor of *Religion, Media, and the Marketplace* (Rutgers 2007).

Curtis D. Coats is Assistant Professor of Communication Studies at Millsaps College in Jackson, MS. In 2011, Coats and Stewart M. Hoover published "The Media and Male Identities: Audience research in media, religion and masculinities" in the *Journal of Communication* (61,5) and Coats published "The Melodramatic Structure of New Age Tourist Desire" in *Tourist Studies* (11, 3).

Mary E. Hess is Associate Professor of Educational Leadership at Luther Seminary, in St. Paul, Minnesota. Her most recent books include *Teaching Reflectively in Theological Contexts: Promises and Contradictions* (with

Stephen D. Brookfield, Krieger 2008), and *Engaging Technology in Theological Education* (Rowman & Littlefield 2005). She contributes frequently to the journal *Religious Education,* and has been president of the Religious Education Association. She consults widely with US theological school faculties on topics of distributed learning and pedagogy, has written the blog *Tensegrities* since 2003, and is the editor of Storyingfaith.org.

Stewart M. Hoover is Professor of Media Studies and Religious Studies at the University of Colorado at Boulder, where he directs the Center for Media, Religion, and Culture. From 2006 to 2009, he directed a major research project on media, religion, and masculinities. Hoover is author of *Religion in the News: Faith and Journalism in American Public Discourse* (Sage 1998) and *Religion in the Media Age* (Routledge 2006), and co-author of *Media, Home and Family* (Routledge 2004).

Pamela E. Klassen is Professor in the Department for the Study of Religion at the University of Toronto. Her recent books are entitled *Spirits of Protestantism: Medicine, Healing, and Liberal Christianity* (University of California Press 2011) and, co-edited with Courtney Bender, *After Pluralism: Reimagining Religious Engagement* (Columbia University Press 2010). She is currently writing a book on "confessional production" and forms of mediation in early twentieth-century colonial encounters among Christian missionaries and First Nations.

Kathryn Lofton is the Sarai Ribicoff Associate Professor of Religious Studies and American Studies at Yale University. Her first book, *Oprah: The Gospel of an Icon* (University of California Press 2011), used the example of Oprah Winfrey to explore the formation of religion in modern America. She is currently working on several projects, including a study of sexuality and religion; an analysis of parenting practices in twentieth-century America; and a religious history of Bob Dylan.

Mia Lövheim is Professor in Sociology of Religion, University of Uppsala. Her research focuses on performances of religious and gender identity among youth, particularly on the Internet, and on representations of religion in Swedish daily press. Her work has appeared in the journals *Nordicom Review*; *Information, Communication and Society*; *Feminist Media Studies*; *Culture and Religion*; and *Nordic Journal of Society and Religion*. She is the editor, with Stig Hjarvard, of *Mediatization and Religion: Nordic Perspectives* (Nordicom 2012).

Anna Piela is a researcher at the University of Leicester, UK. Her research interests include gender, sexuality, media, and Islam. Her Ph.D., conducted at University of York, focused on Muslim women's contemporary readings of Islamic sources conducted online. In addition to the monograph *Muslim Women Online: Faith and Identity in Virtual World* (Routledge 2011), she has published articles in the *Journal of Muslim Minority Affairs*, *Contemporary Islam*, and *CyberOrient*. She is currently editing a volume entitled *Muslim Women's Digital Geographies*.

Line Nybro Petersen, Ph.D., is a research assistant at the Department for Film and Media Studies at the University of Copenhagen. Her Ph.D. dissertation *Wicked Angels, Adorable Vampires!* analyzes changes in religious representations in American audiovisual serial fictions and religious imaginations in Danish teenagers. Recent publications include "American Television Fictions Transforming Danish Teenagers' Religious Imaginations" in *Journal of European Communication Research* and "Danish *Twilight* Fandom: Transformative Processes of Religion" in *Mediatization and Religion: Nordic Perspectives* (Nordicom 2012).

Michele Rosenthal is a lecturer in the Department of Communication at the University of Haifa. She is the author of *American Protestants and Television: Responses to a New Medium* (Palgrave 2007) and *Mediating Religion, Sanctifying Media: Exploring the Nexus of Media Practice and Contemporary Religious Revival in Israel* (De Gruyter forthcoming). She is currently working on a research project with Rivka Ribak entitled "Unplugged: Media Ambivalence and Avoidance in Everyday Life."

Joyce Smith is Associate Professor of Journalism at Ryerson University in Toronto, and director of the school's graduate program. She has worked as an editor for the digital arm of Canada's *The Globe and Mail* as well as at *The Toronto Star*. Her research focuses on the representation of religion in secular news sources in South Africa, Canada, and the United States. She has contributed to a forthcoming book on securitization, radicalization, and religion in Canada (University of Toronto Press) and *Key Words in Religion, Media and Culture* (Routledge 2008).

Diane Winston holds the Knight Chair in Media and Religion at the University of Southern California. A historian of American religion and a former religion reporter, Winston has most recently authored and edited *The Oxford Handbook on the American News Media and Religion* (2000), *Small Screen, Big Picture: Television and Lived Religion* (Baylor University Press 2009), and *Red Hot and Righteous: The Urban Religion of the Salvation Army* (Harvard University Press 2000).

Chapter 1

Introduction

Gender – a blind spot in media, religion and culture?

Mia Lövheim

At the beginning of 2011 the whole world watched the events of what has been termed the "Arab spring" in Tunisia, Libya, Egypt and other countries of the Middle East. These events have been seen as symbols of the recent "resurgence" of religion in international politics and in the media, and hailed as a sign of the power of digital grassroots media with Facebook, YouTube, Twitter and mobile phones playing a key role. But equally significant is the prominence of gender in the media representations and mediated practices of these events. One example is "the girl in the blue bra" story, initiated by an amateur video shoot on December 17, 2011, showing a young woman being beaten and dragged through the streets by uniformed soldiers during a protest in Cairo. In the turmoil, her clothing is ripped and her blue bra is clearly displayed. The image spurred an outrage nationally and internationally against the violence of the Egyptian military during the protests, but also against the systematic degradation of women in the country. In the coverage of this story, images of women protesters with and without veils, standing side by side, are prominent (Higgins 2011). Another example rooted in these events concerns the reporting on the role of young Muslim women in the protests. In 2011 the Nobel Peace Prize was awarded to three women for "their non-violent struggle for the safety of women and for women's rights to full participation in peace-building work" (Nobel Peace Prize 2011). One of them was Tawakkol Karman from Yemen, founder of the network "Women Journalists Without Chains," and one of several young female journalists and bloggers who have been hailed for raising their voices against military violence and dictatorship, but also against religiously informed social and political structures upholding inequality and oppression of women's rights and values. Remarkably, the picture chosen to represent Karman among the revolving images on the head banner of the Nobel Peace Prize website shows her looking into a mirror and adjusting her veil.

Gender is a concept with several meanings, which are connected but also deeply contested during the history of feminist politics and research. A simple working definition of gender would be as a social construct defining the attributes, behavior and roles that are generally associated with men or women.

Gender is thus derived from but different than biological sex. However, as the later history of feminist theory has shown, gender can hardly be "defined" once and for all but is rather constructed in the relation between biological genitalia and hormones defining male and female bodies, the socially and culturally constructed values and norms attached to these physical markers, and the individual and social identities and actions enacted out of these. Gender, thus, is also constructed by the social and political implications of ascribing men and women certain positions, characteristics and value based on biological sex. According to Swedish historian Yvonne Hirdman (1990) gender as a social and cultural system is structured according to two fundamental logics: that there are two categories – men and women – which are fundamentally different, and that one of these categories – men – is superior to the other. Feminist politics and research has challenged primarily the second of these. Queer theory and politics challenges the first, and thereby has drawn gender studies into new and challenging questions.

All of these complexities make it clear, first of all, that gender is at the heart of culture, conceived as the way and forms through which human beings make meaning out of their social and material existence (see Hall *et al.* 1980). As pointed out by Pamela Klassen (2009: 2–3) gender is simultaneously a funda-mental source for structuring identities, traditions, values and rituals within religious traditions *and* an unstable and contested category questioning these distinctions. Gender also deeply informs the production of media texts, the symbols circulated through media and popular culture, as well as the uses of these texts (see Gill 2007, Gauntlett 2002). But as the examples above from the Arab Spring show, the ways in which gender is represented and interpreted in media texts and practices are becoming more complex. Not least when these representations also involve religion. Both of these examples highlight how stereotypical conceptions of gender, religion, power and oppression – here of Muslim women as oppressed and veiled – on the one hand are reproduced in news reporting. On the other hand, they become challenged with the intro-duction of new media technology which is ascribed a key role in fighting social and political structures upholding inequality and oppression of women's rights and values. The outcome is, as both examples show, ambiguous and complex. What is changing, and what is not? What is the meaning of this combination of images and texts representing women's agency and exploitation as connected to a powerful religious symbol such as the veil? What are the implications for analyzing the potentials of new media technology for critical and multiple articulations of religion, not least if we add also the heritage of colonialism and the powers of commercial global media actors to the question? There are no given answers on how to analyze and interpret these questions. However, they clearly show how gender as a dimension of media representations and media practice can no longer be ignored if we are to understand the interplay between religion, media and culture in late modern society. As gender highlights the complexities of bodies, social relations, cultural conventions and individual agency in mediations of religion, why should gender not be important and make a difference in our studies?

Media, religion and culture

The research field media, religion and culture was initiated in the mid 1990s in order to facilitate and develop cross-disciplinary research between sociology of religion/religious studies, media and communication studies and cultural studies (Hoover and Lundby 1997a). Since the early 1990s, research undertaken within the field has been crucial in placing religion on the agenda of media studies, and media on the agenda of religious studies (see Engelke 2010). Furthermore, there has been an exponential growth of academic literature in the field. However, a review of the published works over the first decade of the new field (1997–2007) reveals that gender, by and large, has remained a neglected theme. The international, biennial conferences on Media, Religion and Culture (CMRC), initiated in Uppsala, Sweden in 1993, have been of central importance for the formation of the field.[1] Presentations and publications emanating from these conferences as well as the series "Media and Religion" (published by Routledge) can, arguably, be seen as the main public expressions of the subject matter. A review of the edited conference volumes, papers and panels, as well as related journals, showed that publications that explicitly discuss gender and/or use theories with a gender perspective are scarce (Lövheim 2008). *Rethinking Media, Religion and Culture* (Hoover and Lundby 1997b), published in 1997, includes one chapter by Clare Badaracco, aptly entitled "A Utopian on the Main Street," which introduces new approaches within feminist theology. *Practicing Religion in the Age of the Media* (Hoover and Clark 2002), published in 2002, has no chapter that explicitly focuses on gender issues. However, both Diane Winston's chapter on the performed religion of the Salvation Army 1880–1920 and Erica Doss' chapter on popular religious practices of belief in Elvis brings out the significance of gender in these processes and practices. While *Mediating Religion: Conversations in Media, Religion and Culture* (Mitchell and Marriage 2003) has no chapter that analyzes gender, *Implications of the Sacred in (Post) Modern Media* (Sumiala-Seppänen *et al.* 2006) includes a gendered analysis of the film *As in Heaven* (Hammer 2006). The collection *Religion, Media and the Public Sphere* (Meyer and Moors 2005), closely related by theme, also includes one chapter discussing gender and politics in Palestinian family law (Moors 2005). Turning to more recent publications in the series "Media, Religion and Culture," the volume *Keywords in Media, Religion and Culture* (Morgan 2008) features no chapter explicitly addressing gender, while *Religion, Media and Culture: A Reader* (2011) includes one chapter by Diane Winston on the dynamics of religion, media, gender and commodification in the Salvation Army.

In 2002 the first issue of the quarterly *Journal of Media and Religion* was published. A search for keywords on the website of the journal from 2002 to

2007 shows 13 hits for articles on "gender" and "women."[2] In nine of these articles, gender is included as a factor in the analysis of survey data on media use and media attitudes (see e.g. Haskell 2007). Only two of the articles explicitly discuss gender: Hillary Warren's (2002) analysis of depictions of race, gender and authority in the children's video series *Veggie Tales*, and Claudia Schippert's (2007) analysis of gender and sexuality in the sanctification of the priest and 9/11 victim Mychal Judge. During the same period, the online *Journal of Religion and Popular Culture* published seven articles focusing on gender: for example, Rebecca Barrett's article on what women gain from reading Christian romance novels (2003). In a parallel review of articles in the *Journal of Communication and Religion* during 1999–2009, Helen Sterk (2010) concludes that the intersection of gender, communication and religion remains an undeveloped area in the journal's publication history. During these 10 years, 43 articles were written by women or included some form of gender analysis. However, only nine conducted gender-based analysis and seven used categories from feminist research to frame or theorize findings and arguments. The amount of publications from women scholars had increased during the period but was still only 30 percent of the contributions.

These reviews make clear that gender has been a marginal issue in central publications presenting research on media, religion and culture. However, as the reviews in the next two chapters show important research on media and religion inspired by gender perspectives has been carried out within the field, and more publications including gender perspectives have begun to appear during recent years. Nevertheless, there is yet no publication that explicitly addresses the significance of gender in the production, circulation and daily use of mediated religion.[3] The aim of this volume is to fill this gap.

Marginalizing gender: reasons and concerns

Why, then, is research that focuses on the experiences of women or analyzes the interplay between media, religion and contemporary culture from a gender perspective so invisible in the field? There are, of course, several possible and interconnected reasons for this situation. The historical legacy of gendered rules and traditions structuring the positions of men and women within academic life plays an important part, as well as conceptions of gender and the place of feminist studies within dominant discourses of particular scholarly disciplines. Without forgetting the complexity of the question, it seems relevant for the purpose and focus of this book to address the last of these reasons, meaning the place of gender within the disciplines that were once brought together to form the new field of research: studies of "media," "religion" and "culture." To survey these disciplines in all their depth and complexity is, needless to say, a task that would take several books of their own (see Klassen, Goldberg and Lefebvre 2009). Therefore, the following discussion will necessarily be brief and limited to a few significant points that reveal some of the reasons for the lack of gender analysis in the field.

Media and gender

In their critical agenda for "rethinking media, religion and culture" Stewart Hoover and Knut Lundby (1997a: 6, 9) argue that a shift in media studies is needed from research that focuses on media as institutions and the symbolic production of messages toward processes of consumption and interpretation. This argument shows how the new field emerged alongside a "culturalist turn" in media studies from the 1980s and onwards (Hoover 2002, White 1983). This shift implied a critique of theories and methods drawing on a transmission model of the media and focusing on the "effects" or the persuasive power of the media in shaping values and relations. In short, it instigated an emphasis on the contexts and situations of meaning construction, thus, on the complexity of the meaning of media texts, and a focus on reception and on media use as embedded in everyday lived experiences.

Although this shift opened up more complex and nuanced understandings of the role of media in meaning making, and of the significance of the particular social and cultural context of media consumption, gender has for the most part remained an "add on" dimension, and few studies have so far ventured beyond a descriptive level of gender differences in media use (see, further, the chapters by Lövheim and Clark and Chiou). A thorough and more critical analysis of how gender shapes representations of religion in media as well as individual use of the media in everyday religious practice is necessary to understand, for example, if and how the mediatization of religion, meaning the shift from religious institutions to popular culture and the media as the prime channels, language and arenas for religion (Hjarvard 2008), can challenge patterns of authority and normative boundaries established by traditional religious discourses (see Byerly and Ross 2006).

Religion and gender

Hoover and Lundby (1997a: 8) also argue for a shift of focus in studies of religion from the forms and doctrines of institutional religion to the meaning making practices of everyday life. This argument echoes the debate in sociology of religion and religious studies about the thesis that modernization necessarily implies a secularization of society, and the subsequent call for a "new paradigm" for studies of transformations of religion in late modern societies (Davie 2007). The focus on institutional religion has implied a bias concerning, first, the location of religion in modern society. As argued by James Beckford, although religion in late modern western societies is still to a large extent practiced through institutions, it has increasingly "come adrift from its former points of anchorage and become a cultural resource" (1989: 170). This shift has been a main concern in previous work in media, religion and culture exploring how media and religion increasingly have come to occupy a "common turf" of "the everyday world of lived experiences" (Hoover 2006) and form temporal "sacred spaces" for the negotiation of meaning, identities and social relationships. Research on "lived religion" (Orsi 1997, McGuire 1997, Ammerman 2007), where religion is seen as "a form of cultural work," has also contributed to an understanding and analysis of religious meaning as constructed in the practices of media use (see Hoover *et al.* 2004, Clark 2003) or in the act of seeing (Morgan 2005) rather than encoded in texts.

This development has meant that a broader variety of expressions of religion, such as embodied, affective and aesthetic aspects of religious life, have been included in the analysis (Lynch *et al.* 2011: 3). However, as pointed out by Meredith McGuire (1997: 96), the understanding of religion and religiosity underpinning western, academic discourse is largely modeled after the experiences and interests of a male, religious elite. The experiences and practices of women and other groups that have traditionally made up the silent majority in religions have largely been left out of the picture (Woodhead 2001).

Thus, even though research in media, religion and culture has problematized several of the assumptions of sociology of religion and religious studies, a shift of focus toward religion as a cultural resource for meaning making might not be enough to challenge this bias. A critical analysis of gendered values and relations also within these forms of religion, and how media contribute to uphold or challenge these, is needed in order to better understand for whom and with what consequences religion is changing in contemporary society.

Culture and gender

As pointed out above, the "culturalist turn" has been of significant importance for shaping the media, religion and culture research field. This turn might rather be seen as several, interconnected theoretical and methodological movements influenced by the developments of the field known as cultural studies (Hoover 2002: 25). In Hoover and Lundby's (1997a) agenda for the new field, placing religion and the media in the context of "the cultural dynamics of modernity" is seen as key to the rethinking of previous attempts to study these interactions. Of crucial importance, here, has been the analysis of culture as a way to critically interpret the social and political implications of modernization, as developed by British cultural studies (see Hall *et al.* 1980), but also the challenge of post-modern thinking to core ideas of modernity such as linearity and grand narratives (Lyotard 1984), the notion of the unified, rational subject (Bauman 1996), and the mixing and blurring of distinctions between "high" and "popular" culture (Featherstone 1991).

As shown by Lynn Schofield Clark and Stewart Hoover (1997, cf. Lynch 2007), these debates and influences have indeed offered new perspectives, concepts and methods for rethinking narrow conceptions of media and religion. But cultural studies also has its blind spots and biases. The critique toward elitist notions of art and literacy opened the way for cultural expressions and dimensions previously deemed trivial, inferior or harmful. Nevertheless, for a long time the field was dominated by studies of the popular culture of young men, which by its more public character and overt challenge of hegemonic values in society captured political and scholarly attention (cf. Hall *et al.* 1980). It was not until the 1980s that young women's culture was also included (Women's Studies Group 1978). This gender bias has also shaped the analysis of late modern culture within media, religion and culture, expressed in a certain preoccupation with media cultures that are public, in the sense of extrovert, challenging the conventional, and "new" with reference to media technology. As men so far primarily perform and consume these media forms, studies of more everyday, home-based and "traditional" mediations of religion, which have been the domain of girls and women's culture, remain as a minority. Also, more attention has thus far been paid to how the blurring of boundaries between religious and popular culture opens possibilities for exploring and playing with stereotypical and narrowing conceptions of gender than, for example, a critical analysis of the ambiguity of sexualized and commercialized models of femininity and masculinity in a "post-feminist" media culture (Gill 2007: 249). The essays collected in *Religion, Media and the Marketplace* (Clark 2007) show an emerging concern with analyzing the commodification of religion in media and popular culture. This underlines the need for further reflection on the kinds of popular culture that is focused on in the field, and for a critical gendered analysis of religious representations in popular culture.

This discussion brings out how the field of media, religion and culture needs to be approached as a historical and social construction with a particular narrative. The main focus of the field during its first decade was to raise awareness and arguments against ignorance and prejudice in other fields, concerning the relation between religion and media in modern society (Hoover and Lundby 1997a). When establishing a new research field, the risk of making some shortcomings in received scholarly discourses more important than others is unavoidable, but without a critical awareness of this risk it may also mean overlooking and reproducing other "blind spots." One consequence is, perhaps, the lack of analysis of power in the field. Of the three major forms where the dynamics of media, religion and culture can be observed, as outlined by Hoover and Lundby (1997a: 7–8), a development from a concern with the primarily instrumental relationship of institutional religion to the media ("rallies") toward situations where media consumption takes on "quasi-religious" functions ("rituals") is visible. However, an analysis of "resistance," meaning negotiations or struggles between different social groups over truth, value and meaning in readings of media texts largely remains to be explored. With their longstanding concern for the experiences of women and other marginalized groups, feminist and gender perspectives can contribute to open our eyes for a critical analysis of the distribution of power and resources as well as forms of resistance in the production and use of mediated religious and cultural values.

The aim of the book

Against this background, the aim of this volume is to show the relevance of focusing on gender for researchers working within the field of media, religion and culture. The chapters of the book review how feminist and gender perspectives and methods have contributed to developing the field, as well as present case studies that illustrate how this is done in practice. In this way the volume highlights work that has been done but which remained in the margins of mainstream research in the field. However, the purpose is not merely to "add gender" as one significant issue among others that needs to be included in order to understand media and religion in contemporary society. As feminist scholars have pointed out, "adding women" does not suffice to address the concerns of feminist studies to critically analyze the causes and consequences of gender blindness in previous research. Thus, this volume aspires to contribute to a development that goes beyond a practice of "adding women" toward "add gender *and stir* ... " (cf. Hutchison 1993), meaning to initiate a critical discussion on the state of research within media, religion and culture as well as on crucial issues for the future (Aune *et al.* 2008).

Before introducing the chapters of the volume, the use of the concept gender here needs some clarification. As pointed out in the introduction, gender can be analyzed on several, interconnected levels. The history of feminist research underlines that there can be no single or privileged perspective from which to approach these issues. Furthermore, research during the last decades shows how the category of gender needs to be problematized through addressing differences among women due to age, ethnicity, class and sexuality, as well as including the experiences of men. In line with this complexity the authors of the chapters use various definitions of and approaches to gender. However, some common points of departure can be found. All chapters share the aim to problematize and nuance stereotypical understandings of gender, particularly "woman" and "femininity," but also "masculinity," in media texts and cultures. Furthermore, they share an intention to highlight and, to various extents, critically analyze, social, cultural and religious structures that assign women and men different positions, value and agency, thus, contributing to patterns of inequality, domination and oppression. Finally, all contributors seek to reveal and strengthen signs of empowerment, as well as discuss the intersection of gender, ethnicity, class, age and sexuality in the representations, identities and practices they study.

The interdisciplinary character has been and still is one of the strongest features of gender studies as well as research in media, religion and culture. In keeping with this tradition this volume includes contributors from different disciplines, regions and academic positions. Furthermore, the chapters provide examples from several religious settings and media forms and genres. Through presenting and exploring a variety of ways in which religion is mediated, and how religious individuals and groups respond to this, from a gender perspective, the book might also generate insights and new issues for researchers familiar with gender perspectives.

Introducing the chapters

The first two chapters of the book cover the purpose of surveying the development of research on media, religion and culture through the lens of key theoretical and methodological issues and debates within gender studies. In this way, these chapters set the scene for the case studies in the proceeding part of the book.

In "Media and religion through the lens of feminist and gender theory," I survey research about media, religion and gender since the end of the 1990s. Starting from three shifts in theoretical paradigms within contemporary feminist media studies – from structuralism to post-structuralism, the culturalist turn and the challenging of the concept of gender – the chapter reviews how the issues raised by these debates have influenced five salient themes in research so far. The review shows how a focus on gender has enhanced critical analysis of religious and gendered stereotypes in the media and a broader variety of perspectives in the analysis of media and religion. Nevertheless, a further engagement primarily with issues raised by post-colonial feminist, queer and post-feminist theories would be fruitful to address the complexity of the interplay between religion and media in contemporary society.

In "Feminist orientations in the methodologies of the media, religion, and culture field," Lynn Schofield Clark and Grace Chiou critically survey the influence of feminist research on the methodologies of the field. Drawing on a trajectory of traditional, interpretive and participatory approaches to methodology and knowledge production, they show how feminist methodologies have challenged traditional approaches and shaped the research agendas formulated within the field. This review also reveals lingering questions concerning, not least, what phenomena and approaches that come to be included or not. Thus, when considering feminism's role in studies of religion and media moving forward, questions of how our methodologies address agency, advocacy and underrepresentation are crucial.

The second and main part of the book consists of a number of case studies that illustrate how the issues and debates lifted in the first two chapters are addressed and developed in current research. In the first of these chapters, "Material witnesses: women and the mediation of Christianity," Pamela Klassen and Kathryn Lofton describe how Christian women in twentieth- and twenty-first-century North American contexts have used new media formats, from printing press to blogs, to articulate their testimonies. Across time and medium, women's bodies have played a key role in this mediation, at once a source for their authority *and* exclusion as legitimate witnesses of faith. This analysis brings out the importance of situating previous and contemporary mediations of religion in the material, embodied conditions of its production and its producer.

Joyce Smith, in her chapter "Occupying pews, missing in news: women, religion and journalism," surveys the ways in which women are represented in Canadian news reporting about religion, as well as how women as journalists report on religion. Drawing on the history of beat reporting, she suggests that changes in the so-called "softer" news reporting and current trends of digital and transmedia journalism present new opportunities for stories about women and religion. By showing how media representations of women and religion connect and collide with broader trends in news journalism this chapter speaks to researchers as well as media professionals working with media, religion and gender.

In "Danish female fans negotiating romance and spirituality in *The Twilight Saga*," Line Nybro Petersen analyzes young women's fascination with the themes of romance and eternal love with a particular focus on how the transcendental and emotional qualities of the *Twilight* series contribute to this process. She argues that through the conjunction of the supernatural content and the fan culture these young women participate in, the series offers a unique space that allows room for engaging in intense and uncompromising emotions, which simultaneously connect to and transcend their everyday life experiences and identities. Through digital media, young female fans also become active participants in the narratives they engage in, which invites negotiations of gender interactions, values and norms they encounter in other contexts.

In the chapter "*Lwa* like me: gender, sexuality and Vodou online," Alexandra Boutros analyzes cross-cultural collisions and negotiations of gender, sexuality and religion among Haitian practitioners and newcomers to the religion within online discussions of the deities (the *lwa*) of Haitian Vodou. Drawing on perspectives from transnational feminism, this analysis asks new questions about what happens to conceptions of gender and sexuality, and especially their connection to religion as a source for authenticity and identity, in a context of global mobility of people, images, signs and symbols, as well as in the context of online media practices that are at once representational and participatory.

Michele Rosenthal presents a case study of the mediated ritual practice emerging around the lectures of a popular orthodox Jewish rabbi. In her chapter "Infertility, blessings, and head coverings: mediated practices of Jewish repentance," she discusses the connection between mediation and religious socialization as ritual practices of obedience, mediated through the bodies of those who attend the meetings, becoming re-mediated through visual media. The subsequent screening of these films in meetings simultaneously performs a didactic and miraculous function, teaching and reinforcing for future audiences the connection between gender, adoption of a devout lifestyle and practice, and divine blessing.

Contemporary online spaces as arenas for the interpretation of Islamic texts is the focus of Anna Piela's chapter "Claiming religious authority: Muslim women and new media." The novel feature of these groups, she argues, is the potential to bring together women representing different religious and political attitudes in a joint project of learning about and interpreting Islam in the context of their own lives rather than according to formal authorities. Through these online spaces Muslim women can claim authority over their own religious lives, thus contributing to challenging conventional media stereotypes of "women in Islam" as well as to a shift in power in the Islamic context of gender relations.

In the chapter "Meanings and masculinities," Curtis Coats and Stewart Hoover address the US cultural discourse about media, masculinity and religion. Starting from a critical discussion of current understandings of masculinity, media and religion in previous research and popular discourse, they propose an alternative approach that seeks to uncover how men use various media in reflexive and constructive ways. Comparing the experiences of evangelical and mainline Protestant men, they show how religious and secular media provide symbolic resources that allow men to understand their masculine identity in contemporary US society, but also how these reflections are shaped by the gender discourse of various religious traditions.

Diane Winston, in her chapter "*Saving Grace*: television with 'something more'," explores how new media forms, such as niche cable television, may change representations of religion and gender. The series *Saving Grace*, aired by TNT, portrays alternative female characters with ambiguous lives and spiritual struggles. She argues that, on the one hand, the commercialization inherent in the entertainment media calls for conventional representations of women and religiosity that appeal to consumers. On the other hand, by challenging categorical boundaries of religious women, *Saving Grace* invites viewers to reflect on their own experiences and attitudes toward female sexuality and religious themes such as sin and salvation.

In the final case study, "Digital storytelling: empowering feminist and womanist faith formation with young women," Mary Hess addresses gender in the formation of religious identity among young people. Focusing on three elements of religious identity that are shifting particularly rapidly due to new media cultures – authority, authenticity and agency – she discusses what new opportunities and challenges this brings not only for the young women themselves, but also for feminist faith formation. These concerns are important not only for those working within faith communities, but also for educators and for researchers interested in the broader issue of how participatory and emancipating research intersects with gender awareness and religious values.

In the concluding chapter, Mia Lövheim draws together themes presented in the case studies and reflects on what they show about where the field of media, religion and culture is going, and outlines some challenges for further analysis and theoretical elaboration of the issues and debates addressed in this book.

Notes

1 During the 8th International Conference in Eskesehir, Turkey, July 8–12, 2012, the International Society for Media, Religion and Culture (ISMRC) was founded.

2 Six articles include "gender" and 12 "women." Four of these articles overlap the categories.
3 The closest equivalent would be *Sex, Religion, Media*, edited by Dane S. Claussen in 2002.

Bibliography

Ammerman, N.T. (2007) *Everyday Religion, Observing Modern Religious Lives*, Oxford, NY: Oxford University Press.

Aune, K., Sharma, S. and Vincett, G. (eds) (2008) *Women and Religion in the West, Challenging Secularization*, Farnham: Ashgate.

Badaracco, C.H. (1997) "An Utopian on Main Street," in S.M. Hoover and K. Lundby (eds) *Rethinking Media, Religion and Culture*, Thousand Oaks: Sage, pp. 246–262.

Barrett, R.K. (2003) "Higher Love: What Women Gain from Christian Romance Novels," *Journal of Religion and Popular Culture*, 4 (summer), www.usask.ca/relst/jrpc/art4-romancenov-print.html (accessed August 2008).

Bauman, Z. (1996) "From Pilgrim to Tourist – or a Short History of Identity," in S. Hall and P. duGay (eds) *Questions of Cultural Identity*, London: Sage, pp. 18–36.

Beckford, J.A. (1989) *Religion in Advanced Industrial Society*, London: Unwin Hyman.

Byerly, C.M. and Ross, K. (2006) *Women and Media. A Critical Introduction*, Malden, MA: Blackwell.

Clark, L.S. (2003) *From Angels to Aliens, Teenagers, the Media, and the Supernatural*, Oxford: Oxford University Press.

Clark, L.S. (ed.) (2007) *Religion, Media and the Marketplace*, New Brunswick, NJ: Rutgers University Press.

Clark, L.S. and Hoover, S.M. (1997) "At the Intersection of Media, Religion, and Culture," in S.M. Hoover and K. Lundby (eds) *Rethinking Media, Religion and Culture*, Thousand Oaks, CA: Sage, pp. 15–36.

Claussen, D.S. (ed.) (2002) *Sex, Religion, Media*, Rowman & Littlefield.

Davie, G. (2007) *The Sociology of Religion*, Sage: London.

Doss, E. (2002) "Believing in Elvis, Popular Piety in Material Culture" in S.M. Hoover and L.S. Clark (eds) *Practicing Religion in the Age of the Media, Explorations in Media, Religion and Culture*, New York, NY: Columbia University Press, pp. 63–86.

Engelke, M. (2010) "Religion and the Media Turn," *American Ethnologist* 37(2): 371–379.

Featherstone, M. (1991) *Consumer Culture and Post-Modernism*, London: Sage.

Forbes, B.D. and Mahan, J.H. (eds) (2005) *Religion and Popular Culture in America*, Berkeley: University of California Press.

Gauntlett, D. (2002) "Introduction," in *Media, Gender and Identity: An Introduction*, London and New York: Routledge, pp. 1–18.

Gill, R. (2007) "Gender and the Media," in *Gender and the Media*, Cambridge: Polity Press, pp. 7–42.

Ginsburg, F., Abu-Lughod, L. and Larkin, B. (eds) (2002) *Media Worlds, Anthropology on New Terrain*, Berkeley: University of California Press.

Hall, S., Hobson, D., Lowe, A. and Willis, P. (eds) (1980) *Culture, Media, Language*, London: Hutchinson.

Hall, S. and Jefferson, T. (eds) (1976) *Resistance Through Rituals: Youth Subcultures in Post-War Britain*, London: Hutchinson.

Hammer, A. (2006) "As in Heaven, Dionysian Ritual on the Big Screen," in Sumiala-Seppänen, Lundby and Salokangas (eds) *Implications of the Sacred in (Post) Modern Media*, Gothenburg: Nordicom, pp. 177–195.

Haskell, D. (2007) "News Media Influence on Nonevangelical Coders' Perceptions of Evangelical Christians: A Case Study," *Journal of Media and Religion* 6(3): 153–179.

Higgins, M. (2011) "Police Beating of 'Girl in Blue Bra' Becomes New Rallying Call for Egyptians," National Post, Online, http://news.nationalpost.com/2011/12/20/beating-of-blue-bra-woman-reignites-egyptian-protests/ (accessed May 17, 2012).

Hirdman, Y. (1990) *The Gender System: Theoretical Reflections on the Social Subordination of Women*, Uppsala: Maktutredningen.

Hjarvard, S. (2008) "The Mediatization of Religion: A Theory of the Media as Agents of Religious Change," in *Northern Lights*, vol. 6, Bristol: Intellect Press.

Hoover, S. (2002) "The Culturalist Turn in Scholarship on Media and Religion," *Journal of Media and Religion* (1)1: 25–36.

——(2006) *Religion in the Media Age*, New York, NY: Routledge.

Hoover, S.M. and Clark, L.S. (eds) (2002) *Practicing Religion in the Age of the Media, Explorations in Media, Religion and Culture*, New York, NY: Columbia University Press.

Hoover, S.M. and Lundby, K. (1997a) "Introduction: Setting the Agenda," in S.M. Hoover and K. Lundby (eds) *Rethinking Media, Religion and Culture*, Thousand Oaks, CA: Sage, pp. 3–14.

Hoover, S.M. and Lundby, K. (eds) (1997b) *Rethinking Media, Religion and Culture*, Thousand Oaks, CA: Sage.

Hoover, S.M., Clark, L.S. and Alters, D. (2004) *Media, Home and Family*, New York, NY: Routledge.

Hutchison, E.Q. (1993) "Add Gender and Stir? Cooking up Gendered Histories of Modern Latin America," *Latin American Research Review* 38(1): 267–287.

Journal of Media and Religion, volumes 2002–2007, Online, www.informaworld.com/smpp/title~content=t775648133~db=all (accessed August 2008).

Journal of Religion and Popular Culture, volumes 2002–2007, Online, www.usask.ca/relst/jrpc/index.html (accessed August 2008).

Klassen, P. (2009) "Introduction," in P. Klassen, S. Goldberg and D. Lefebvre (eds) *Women and Religion: Critical Concepts in Religious Studies, Volume I*, Abingdon: Routledge, pp. 1–8.

Klassen, P., Goldberg, S. and Lefebvre, D. (eds) (2009) *Women and Religion: Critical Concepts in Religious Studies*, Abingdon: Routledge.

Lynch, G. (ed.) (2007) *Between Sacred and Profane, Researching Religion and Popular Culture*, London: Tauris.

Lynch, G., Mitchell, J. and Strhan, A. (2011) *Religion, Media and Culture: A Reader*, London and New York: Routledge.

Lyotard, J.F. (1984) *The Postmodern Condition: A Report on Knowledge*, Manchester: Manchester University Press.

Lövheim, M. (2008) "Gender – A Blind Spot in Media, Religion and Culture?" Paper presented to the 6th international conference on Media, Religion and Culture, São Paulo, Brazil, August 11–14, 2008.

McGuire, M. (1997) *Religion: The Social Context*, Belmont, CA: Wadsworth.

McRobbie, A. (2000) *Feminism and Youth Culture* (2nd edn), New York: Routledge.

Meyer, B. and Moors, A. (eds) (2005) *Religion, Media and the Public Sphere*, Bloomington: Indiana University Press.

Mitchell, J. and Marriage, S. (eds) (2003) *Mediating Religion: Conversations in Media, Religion and Culture*, Edinburgh: T.&t. Clark/Continuum.

Moors, A. (2005) "Representing Family Law Debates in Palestine: Gender and Politics of Presence," in B. Meyer and A. Moors (eds) *Religion, Media and the Public Sphere*, Bloomington: Indiana University Press, pp. 115–132.

Morgan. D. (2008) *Keywords in Media, Religion and Culture*, London and New York: Routledge.

Morgan, D. (2005) *The Sacred Gaze: Religious Visual Culture in Theory and Practice*, Berkeley: University of California Press.

Nobel Peace Prize (2011) "The Nobel Peace Prize 2011: Ellen Johnson Sirleaf, Leymah Gbowee, Tawakkol Karman," Online, www.nobelprize.org/nobel_prizes/peace/laureates/2011/ (accessed January 7, 2013).

Orsi, R.A. (1997) "Everyday Miracles, The Study of Lived Religion," in D. Hall (ed.) *Lived Religion in America: Toward a History of Practice*, Princeton, NJ: Princeton University Press, pp. 3–21.

Schippert, C. (2007) "Saint Mychal: A Virtual Saint," *Journal of Media and Religion* 6(2): 109–132.

Sterk, H.M. (2010) "Faith, Feminism and Scholarship: The Journal of Communication and Religion, 1999–2009," *Journal of Communication and Religion* 33(2): 206–216

Sumiala-Seppänen, J., Lundby, K. and Salokangas, R. (eds) (2006) *Implications of the Sacred in (Post) Modern Media*, Gothenburg: Nordicom.

Warren, H. (2002) "The Bible Tells Me So: Depictions of Race, Gender, and Authority in Children's Videos," *Journal of Media and Religion* 1(3): 167–179.

Winston, D. (2002) "All the World's a Stage: The Performed Religion of the Salvation Army 1880–1920," in S.M. Hoover and L.S. Clark (eds) *Practicing Religion in the Age of the Media: Explorations in Media, Religion and Culture*, New York, NY: Columbia University Press, pp. 113–137.

White, R. (1983) "Mass Communication and Culture: Transition to a New Paradigm," *Journal of Communication* 33(3): 279–301.

Women's Studies Group, Centre for Contemporary Cultural Studies, University of Birmingham (1978) *Women Take Issue: Aspects of Women's Subordination*, London: Hutchinson.

Woodhead, L. (2001) "Feminism and the Sociology of Religion: From Gender-blindness to Gendered Difference," in R.K. Fenn (ed.) *The Blackwell Companion to the Study of Religion*, Oxford: Blackwell, pp. 67–84.

Chapter 2

Media and religion through the lens of feminist and gender theory

Mia Lövheim

Although gender comes out as a marginal theme when reviewing the mainstream publications in media, religion and gender so far, it would be wrong to say that research within the field has not been influenced by insights from and issues raised within feminist and gender theory. Nevertheless, this contribution to the narrative of the field largely remains to be revealed. Against this background, the aim of this chapter is to provide a review of research about media and religion that has focused on gender. As pointed out in the introduction an analysis of gender can be conducted in several ways. The next chapter by Lynn Schofield Clark and Grace Chiou will focus on feminist orientations in the methodologies of previous research. In this chapter, the focus will be on theoretical approaches to gender.

Epistemology, or questions about the nature and production of knowledge, has been a core concern of feminist research since its beginnings. Starting from the experiences of women, feminists have argued that knowledge is not neutral but situated (Hartsock 1983). Knowledge is produced by individuals in particular personal, social and historical situations and in positions with more or less ability to act and make their voices heard. Furthermore, feminists argue that gender is one of the key factors shaping these situations and positions. Thus, knowledge is deeply connected to identity, social relations and to power and agency. This concern has shaped the ways in which feminist researchers approach theory, as theories are concerned with defining, structuring and explaining empirical phenomena or life as we experience it. Thus, theory shapes how we make sense of and explain the social world as well as perceive our position and ability to act in it.

In line with this concern this chapter will highlight conceptions of gender and ways of accounting for gendered patterns in media representations and practices in previous studies. Following a feminist concern with analyzing enduring gender inequalities and the causes and consequences of these a key concern has been to look for studies that go beyond describing gender differences toward an analysis of relations between gender and power, value and agency (see Gill 2007: 8, 25). The review is based on a survey of books and articles from the mid 1990s until the completion of this volume.[1] This period parallels the establishment of media, religion and culture as a research field. The early 1990s also marks an important shift in feminist media studies through the introduction of new theoretical approaches following the enhanced diversity of representations of gender in the media (Gill 2007: 19, 38, Gauntlett 2002: 90). The chapter starts out with a short recollection of some key debates and concerns actualized by these developments, followed by a review of previous work on gender, media and religion focusing on how these issues have been addressed. The concluding part summarizes tendencies in theoretical approaches used for analyzing media, religion and gender so far, and points to some issues that are still in need of further consideration.

Key issues and debates in feminist media studies

Feminist theory can and should not be approached as a monolithic body of research but consists of many perspectives. Earlier accounts of feminist studies were often structured along the lines of liberal, Marxist, radical, psycho-analytic, socialist and post-modern theoretical foundations (see Tong 1993). More recent accounts rather refer to first, second and third wave feminism and the various approaches to research they have introduced (cf. Gill 2007: 26, Kroløkke and Sørensen 2006: 1). While the concerns of first and second wave feminism were how women's particular position and experiences were excluded from and could reshape theoretical perspectives and models in various disciplines, the concern of third wave feminism has been how to approach the increasing complexity of the core concepts of gender and sex/sexuality, as well as their connection to identity, knowledge and power. This chapter will, following Gill (2007) and Kroløkke and Sørensen (2006), focus on three shifts in theoretical approaches that, following current influences from masculinity studies, queer perspectives and post-feminist theories, have shaped feminist and gender theory since the end of the 1990s.

The first theme concerns the shift from *structuralism to post-structuralism* as a foundation for theories of gender and communication (Kroløkke and Sørensen 2006: 34). While structuralism as a paradigm for understandings of reality and knowledge assumed the unified and stable character of identities and meaning, the dialectic interaction between social structures, and the definite character of explanations, the works of post-structural scholars such as Michel Foucault and Jacques Derrida emphasized the instability of meaning and identity, and complexity and contingency in the relation between individual agency and the power of social structures and ideologies. This critique came to have a huge impact on the understanding of gender, and challenged many core concerns and assumptions of particularly second wave feminist media scholars. Second wave feminism consists of a broad variety of theoretical approaches based in an understanding of gender that emphasizes the particularities of women's position in society in relation to men. Standpoint theory, as one of the most prominent approaches of second wave feminism, starts out from an understanding of women's position as suppressed but simultaneously a privileged perspective from which to criticize male dominance (Harding 2004). This has meant a focus in research on women's experiences and on enhancing women's agency. The influence of post-structural theories challenged this focus on the commonality of women's situation and initiated the discussion about the complexity of and differences within women's experiences that saturates third wave feminism.

With regard to the analysis of gender and media, the implications of the shift toward post-structuralism can be seen in studies of representation of women in media. Starting from the theory of representation as the process by which signifying elements of media texts – symbols, metaphors and images – form our understanding of social reality and, furthermore, are connected to relations of dominance and inequality (cf. Hall 1997), a main concern in feminist media studies has been to critically analyze the often demeaning or patronizing stereotypes through which women are represented. The influence of post-structuralism challenged two core ideas in the dominant approaches used in this analysis: semiotics and ideological analysis. The first concerned the understanding of media as powerful agents controlling and reproducing ideological values in society. The second concerned the understanding of the relation between representations and reality in the critique against stereotypes as distortions of women's experiences. Both of these ideas were based on the structuralist belief in the possibility to identify stable and unified gender identities, experiences and relations of power challenged by post-structuralism.

Post-structuralist approaches to analyzing gender in media texts have come to focus on how gender is constructed through media representations rather than how media representations "mirror" pre-existing meanings of masculinity and femininity (Gill 2007: 12). This has implied a shift from a concern with stereotypes to a focus on diversity in media representations of gender, and subsequently the introductions of new theoretical approaches, among those performance theory which will be described further on. However, there is also a large degree of overlap and dialogue between earlier approaches such as standpoint theory and feminist post-structuralist perspectives (Kr{\o}l{\o}kke and S{\o}rensen 2006: 33), in which the focus on women's particular situation is combined with an awareness of the complexity of their experiences. The use of feminist psychoanalytic theories to analyze the multiple and contradictory meaning of gendered subjectivities in feminist film analysis is one example of such approaches (Gledhill 2006), and also the use of critical discourse theory to account for how gendered subjectivities are shaped by shifting and intersecting discourses (Wodak 1997). As underlined by Gill (2007:13), the emphasis in post-structuralism on meaning and subjectivity as polysemic, shifting and contradictory also introduced an ongoing debate within feminist media studies about the possibility of identifying oppressive or empowering media representations.

The second theme concerns the change in media analysis referred to as "the culturalist turn" in the 1980s (Hoover 2002). This shift was enhanced by the post-structuralist critique of textual determinism inherent in ideology analysis, and also intersected with increasing critique against "transmission models" (van Zoonen 1994) of the media, in which these where conceived as agents of social control conveying ideological messages for largely passive audiences to uncritically absorb (Gill 2007: 17). Of utmost importance in this shift is, thus, the emphasis of individual agency in meaning making processes. The development of audience studies as a consequence of this approach is an important part of the culturalist turn that will be covered more extensively within the chapter by Clark and Chiou. Here, I will focus more on the theoretical implications for feminist media studies. As described above, the influence of post-structuralism inspired a turn from uncovering the realities of women's experiences behind the media stereotypes to analyzing *how* individuals and groups construct gender through symbols, values and other resources in a particular cultural context. The focus on culture as a (contested) site of meaning making, inspired by research on the multiple "encoding" and "decoding" of media messages (Hall 1992), brought out the complexities in how media texts are given meaning in people's lives. These complexities actualize three related issues for further studies: first, what kind of media texts should be included in the analysis; second, the significance of location, competences and situation for the construction of meaning; and, third, how to interpret and value the various meanings people construct out of media texts. The "turn to pleasure" in feminist media studies in the mid 1980s illustrates these issues well with Janice Radway's (1984) seminal study of women's reading of romance fiction, and Ian Ang's (1985) study of the audiences of *Dallas* as prominent examples (Gill 2007: 13, 18). The focus on pleasure illustrates the influence of the debate about the distinction between high and popular culture within cultural studies, which in feminist media studies paved the way for an inclusion of genres enjoyed by female audiences that had previously been deemed too trivial. These studies also showed the significance of, for example, class, ethnicity and age, as well as the uses of media in everyday domestic life for analyzing relations between gender and media. However, the focus on pleasure also complicated the evaluation of the various meanings that audiences make out of media texts; when and how are they to be seen as conservative, escapist, compensatory or oppositional (Gill 2007: 19–21)?

These last two issues intersect strongly with the critique toward second wave feminist theory voiced by black and third world feminist scholars starting in the mid 1980s (see hooks 1984, Spivak 1998). This critique, directed toward the assumed universalism of women's experiences in first and second wave feminism, ushered in an emphasis on differences among women due to social location – in the form of ethnicity and race but also class, age and disability – which had previously to a large extent been ignored. This called for a critical rethinking of the privileged position of white, western and middle class feminist scholars, building on post-colonial theory and its focus on exposing and disrupting binary oppositions between center and periphery, the "West" and the colonized "other." This focus on difference and on intersections between different systems of oppression is a core concern of "third wave feminism" (Kroløkke and Sørensen 2006: 12f). However, the consequences of this critique against earlier feminist approaches also initiated the current broadening of feminist research to gender studies (Gill 2007: 25).

The third theme concerns precisely the *diversity and complexity of gender as a category* characterizing the contemporary period of research. This shift builds on and continues the issues and debates actualized by the influences of post-structuralism and the culturalist turn, but includes new issues and approaches drawn from intersectionality theory, queer theory, studies of masculinities and post-feminist perspectives (Gill 2007: 29f). A strong tendency in contemporary research has been the use of "performance" as a concept and theoretical position (Kroløkke and Sørensen 2006: 123). Introduced by gender theorist Judith Butler (1990), performance theory implies a new way of conceptualizing and analyzing gender. Butler presents a radical understanding of gender as not merely reflected in or affected by communication, but as an effect of communicative practice (Kroløkke and Sørensen 2006: 36). Gender is seen as a "regulatory social practice" that is enacted through repeated, stylistic citational practice. Through the focus on how this practice reinscribes but also reconstructs this regulatory framework, performance theory addresses the stability as well as the instability of gender. The interest in performance theory has also meant a destabilization of the assumed relation between sex, gender and sexual desire within feminist theory. Queer theory, in particular, has brought out the significance of hetero-sexuality as normative in media texts, and of queer as a strategy of performing gender that contributes to destabilizing the heteronormative order through, for example, parody or mimicry (Gill 2007: 70, Kroløkke and Sørensen 2006: 130).

Another significant influence comes from masculinity studies and the problematization of representations of men in media. The development of "critical men's studies" (Connell 2000) follows the tendencies within contemporary gender research in emphasizing the extent to which masculinity must be understood in relation to heteronormative patriarchy in public and private gender relations, of recognizing "multiple masculinities," and seeing masculinity as a process of active negotiation of meaning, often through practices of consumption (see Gauntlett 2002). Finally, third wave feminism has meant the introduction of more self-assertive, playful but also provocative forms of feminism. Approaches such as "Girl feminism" (Walker 1995) seek to reclaim and play with stereotypes of femininity, such as sexual attraction and fashion, in order to explore their potential for resistance and empowerment. A similar strategy inspires "post-feminist" analysis where, for example, the potential of TV series such as *Sex and the City* is discussed as promoting women's entitlement to sexual pleasure and satirically playing with norms of bodily control and beauty. However, post-feminism has also caused a debate over whether the ideals of individual choice and sexual competence as connected to consumption and self-regulation in these series introduce new gender regimes rather than enhance women's agency (Gill 2007: 249f).

The new perspectives described in this theme have been crucial in adding theoretical concepts and tools for exploring the complex, diverse and paradoxical ways in which gender and sexuality are represented in contemporary media cultures, and the variety of ways in which people engage with them. However, they also underscore the tensions and questions of feminism as an analytical project noted earlier. While some feminist media scholars embrace the complexity and ambiguity of the present "transversity" of approaches (Krøløkke and Sørensen 2006: 23), others are concerned with the challenges implied for the critical feminist concern with analyzing "enduring gender inequalities and injustices" (Gill 2007: 25, 37), where gender still structures women's lives and possibility of agency in other ways than for men.

Salient themes in previous studies of media, religion and gender

The survey of research engaging with gender in media, religion and culture from the mid 1990s to the present shows that some themes clearly dominate, followed by a few strong sub-themes.

Representations of religion and gender in news media

The concern with confronting stereotypes and highlighting variety and complexity is a strong tendency in studies of how news media portray women's religiosity and their role in religion. Most studies have focused on women and Islam, even though a few studies of women in the Christian press can also be found (see Kaylor 2010). Several of these studies focus on uncovering the frames of reference used in news media to portray gender and religion. Elisabeth Klaus and Susanne Kassel's (2005) analysis of the representation of gender in news reports on the wars in Afghanistan is one example. By extending the concept of media logic or the process where media present and transmit information through the use of certain formats (Altheide and Snow 1979) to include a gender logic, defined as a symbolic construction of male and female as a dichotomy, and a logic of war based on a similar dichotomy between perpetrators and victims, they show how the interconnectedness of these logics leads to a specific representation with the purpose to legitimize the western military intervention in Afghanistan. Key in this process was the use of the veil as a symbol – following the gender logic – of women as mute victims of oppression (Klaus and Kassel 2005: 345). The veiling of women was again used in the logic of war to construct the Taliban as perpetrators and as opponents to the ideals and freedoms of western civilization. Finally, images of unveiled women following the defeat of the Taliban regime were used as proofs of their liberation and the success of the war (Klaus and Kassel 2005: 347).

This study is an example of the use of feminist theories about the hierarchical construction of gender to show how a particular media discourse that

media utilized veiled
women as symbol of
oppressed victim → justification for military force in
Feminist and gender theory 21 Afghanista

involves religion, here news reporting on western military intervention in the Muslim world, contributes to produce a certain kind of subjectivities and social relations. Klaus and Kassel's analysis contributes to media studies by showing how the theory of media logic can be developed through taking into account the cultural and social factors shaping the content of media texts, here gender and religion. Their analysis shows how the intersection of these logics contributes to the stereotyping of women, and also how media interest in the issue of women's rights can be used for other purposes than enhancing women's agency. Furthermore, their analysis illustrates the use of post-structuralist, primarily post-colonial, theories to analyze how gender and religion become used for constructing an ideal of gender equality and individual autonomy as characteristic of western culture. A representation that hides the diversity and complexity of women's voices and experiences – in the Middle East as in the West (see also Brown 2011).

As pointed out by Myra MacDonald, the feminist analysis of representations of Muslim women in the media can, however, become inhibited by a fixation on veiling. In addition to the use of gender and colonial stereotypes and dichotomization in news media she points to how western post-feminist perspectives that equate agency and women's bodily self-expression risk ignoring other expressions of feminist subjectivity. Therefore, a focus on the plurality of Muslim women's voices in the media following the events of 9/11 can possibly open up a different, more varied understanding of Muslim femininity (see MacDonald 2006). Another example of this kind of analysis is Anna Korteweg's (2008) study of different representations of agency in Canadian newspapers' reports on discussions of Sharia law. Korteweg applies the concept of "embedded agency" used by post-colonial feminist scholars to argue that women's capacity to act cannot only be approached as resistance to forces of domination (2008: 437, cf. Mahmood 2005). Through focusing on connections between agency and religion in these reports, she shows how these display a variety of interpretations, where some connect resistance to religiously upheld domination, while others present agency as possibly embedded in religion. These studies can be seen as indications of a move "beyond the hijab debates" toward addressing "the interconnectedness between religion, media, conflict, gender and race" (Vis 2011: 176) and how this contributes to various forms of agency among Muslim women.

Gender and religion in popular culture and entertainment media

The largest theme in research published so far is studies of representations of gender and religion in popular culture and entertainment media. Some of this research can be found in the *Journal of Popular Culture and Religion* and in edited collections such as *Religion and Popular Culture in America* (Forbes and Mahan 2005) and *Small Screen, Big Picture: Television and Lived Religion* (Winston 2009). The strong influence from "the culturalist turn" is noticeable, for example, in the emphasis on gender but also religion as constructed out of the symbols and narratives circulated through popular culture (Winston 2009: 3–4, cf. Hoover 2006).

Research within this theme is dominated by film and television series produced within US cultural discourse. This also means a dominance of Christian (Protestant) religion and spirituality. Several studies analyze representations of gender and religion primarily on a textual level – focusing on the meaning constructed within the text through symbols, metaphors, narratives and characters. One example is Jennie Knight's study of representations of femininity in *The Da Vinci Code* and *The Secret Life of Bees* (2005), where she relates the popularity of the novels to their potential to offer new myths of a divine femininity within a Christian symbol system (see also Briggs 2009). Other studies seek to take the analysis a step further in exploring media representations as cultural practice, meaning how representations of gender relations in media connect with debates about gender relations and negotiations of gender identities in wider culture and society. Among these, the gender dynamics of popular media produced within the context of US conservative evangelical Christian discourse is a common topic (see Frykholm 2005, Frank 2011).

Kristy Maddux's (2010) analysis of gendered civic identities in popular Christian media is an example of how gender perspectives in later years have come to saturate the analysis in a more explicit way. Starting from the premise that popular media offer discursive resources for individual and collective interactions with the wider society, she analyzes how models of civic participation in these texts are connected to different ideologies of gender, and how they intersect with contemporary disputes over gender in theology and politics: for example, in her analysis of *The Passion of the Christ*, how the coding of the three main characters as feminine presents female submission as an exemplary model of discipleship within an oppressive social and political context. Thus, gender becomes a lens for a critical analysis of representations of human agency and divine will, clearly connected to power relations in religious communities and the wider society (see also Hendershot 2009).

Anthea Butler and Diane Winston's (2009) analysis of understandings of spirituality, sexuality and power within the TV series *Saving Grace* and *Battlestar Galactica* show how studies published in the last decade incorporate influences from third wave and post-feminist media analysis. Their analysis shows how the mix of conventional male codings of sexuality and power (violence, physical strength, recklessness), and female vices (softness, friendship, love) in the representation of female characters challenge the gendered, religious dichotomy between the "whore" and the "Madonna," as when female characters are portrayed as both spiritual leaders and sexually active beings. At the same time other traditional norms of femininity remain, such as beauty and sexual attraction, and the women in these series are largely portrayed as in need of salvation and redemption through spiritual intervention – in both series revealed in the male form. As this example shows, representations of women and spirituality in contemporary entertainment media can be interpreted as subversive but simultaneously as a reapplication of gender stereotypes in religion (Butler and Winston 2009: 274).

This kind of analysis takes studies of gender and religion in popular media beyond the question of *how* gender and religion are represented to a discussion of how these representations relate to experiences of power and agency in the lives of individual women and men (Winston 2009: 8, see also Lelwica 2005). These examples also testify to the increasingly complex, paradoxical and uncertain meaning of religious and existential values, as well as gender representations, in late modernity, and to the challenge of how to critically analyze and evaluate these.

Despite the dominance of Christianity and the US cultural context, studies from other national and cultural contexts have become more prominent during the last five years. The significance of the work of Purnima Mankekar (1993) for introducing post-colonial and Third World feminist theories and methodologies is further discussed in the chapter by Clark and Chiou. Several of the studies that apply these theories focus on uncovering orientalist conceptions of gender and religion, where representations of men as fanatics and terrorists and women as either exotic sexual objects or victims of patriarchal religion are salient (Ramji 2003). One example of popular cultural representations of Islam as challenging such stereotypes is Canas' (2008) analysis of the Canadian television comedy *Little Mosque on the Prairie*. Drawing on post-colonial and performance theory, she argues that the series seeks to provide a counter-hegemonic narrative through satire, mimicry and personalization that questions prejudices of gender roles in Islam. Nevertheless, the selection of religious characters in the series also shows that this alternative narrative is structured by a dominant liberal conception of multiculturalism. This analysis shows how perspectives from post-colonial feminist theory can contribute to a critical reflection on the consequences of the focus on US-produced media in the field. Is there a tendency to highlight the liberating potentials of representations of religion in western popular media while deeming representations of Third World women as traditionalist and submissive?

New, digital media – connection, participation and performance

Starting around the year 2000 studies on religion and digital media emerged as a sub-area within religion, media and culture. In accordance with the development of this area (Campbell and Lövheim 2011), a first wave of research focused on how the blurring of boundaries between body, technology and gender opened up by new media technology provided opportunities for deconstructing gender stereotypes in Christian theological discourse. Elaine Graham's article (1999) "Cyborgs or Goddesses? Becoming Divine in a Cyber Feminist Age" represents an early example of this discussion.

Research in the more empirically oriented, second phase downplayed the focus on new techno-cultures as spaces for parody, irony and playful gender performances (Kroløkke and Sørensen 2006: 141) and rather focused on the potentials of new computer technology to enhance women's authority, community and reflexivity with regard to religion. Helen Berger and Douglas Ezzy's (2009) study of young Australian and America witches shows that for young women in particular, the internet provides possibilities to explore and present one's own version of religion, and even to access positions as authorities in online religious communities. Anna Piela's work (2011) shows how online forums for Muslim women facilitate personalized, grass root and multi-vocal discourses on gender and religion, and enhance the potential for collaborative formulations of these.

Over the last few years, publications across the themes described above, more often than not, includes an analysis of the reception of older forms of media texts in online discussion groups, blogs, social networks and video sharing sites. These studies connect to the new phase of studies on digital media focusing on the convergence of media forms and online–offline life. A key question here is an analysis of if and how digital media might enable users to participate more actively in critical reflection and in the creation of alternative readings of media texts.

Anna Stewart's (2011) analysis of personal and communal worship practices among Christian charismatic women shows how the transmission to digital texts has the potential to disrupt the conventions of gendered speech associated with offline ritual genres. In their analysis of Muslim women's responses to the anti-Islam film *Fitna*, Farida Vis, Lisbeth van Zoonen and Sabina Mihelj (2011) show how YouTube offers an alternative space to express opinions in different formats than those of mainstream media coverage. Furthermore, these women's uploaded videos enable alternative representations of Islam that challenge the dominant orientalist discourse in mainstream media. These studies show how digital media spaces can become arenas for the construction of new forms of female subjectivity, where women in a previously male-dominated public sphere act as agents, presenting their own interpretations of religion.

Darnell Moore's (2011) analysis of teachings of Pentecostal preachers posted on YouTube shows the other side of the coin, that is, how new media tools can also serve as catalysts for the reproduction of traditional and problematic understandings of male dominance and female subordination. Inspired by black feminist theologians, this study discusses new media as "terrains of conflict" (Moore 2011: 270) with the potential to produce and share both empowering and unjust conceptions and practices of gender. This analysis follows earlier studies on gender differences in uses of online discussion forums (Lövheim 2004), where young women experienced marginalization and discomfort with the kind of culture developing in these discussions. Thus, these studies contribute to the debates within feminist media studies of how gender is not absent from communication in digital media, but rather re-enacted in ways that highlight the ambiguous relation between bodies, technology and social context.

Religion and gender in early mass media

Despite the general "presentist" bias in studies on media, religion and culture, several examples of analyzing media representations of gender and religion before 1960 can be found. Two of these are Kerith Woodyard's (2008) analysis of the reception of Elizabeth Cady Stanton's *The Woman's Bible* in 1895, and Lisa Maria Hogeland's (1999) analysis of the case of the early whistle-blower Victoria Woodhull in the 1870s. Both these studies show how controversies and tensions between different agendas within the early feminist movement affected the common goal of advancing women's presence and concerns. As pointed out by Hogeland (1999: 98) these "tendentious histories and multi-plicitous heroines" connect clearly to contemporary debates about tensions between different feminisms, and add an important historical perspective on "our allegedly post-feminist historical moment."

Rebecca Sullivan's (2005) analysis of the presence of nuns in film, television, popular music and magazines in the 1950s and 1960s along with Mary Ellen Davis' (2007) analysis of representations of Mary in the magazines of Roman Catholic devotional organizations during the same time period, complicate simplistic assumptions about gender images and behavior within "traditional" forms of religion (see also Winston 2011). In highlighting complexities as well as continuities across time periods, these studies in an important way nuance contemporary analyses and debates on media, religion and gender (see, further, the chapter in this volume by Klassen and Lofton).

Masculinity and queer studies

Despite the recent interest in masculinities in gender and media studies, the scholarly literature on religion, media and masculinities to date is thin. As argued by Curtis Coats and Stewart Hoover (this volume), there is a growing literature on religion and masculinity and media and masculinity, but this largely suffers from reductionist notions of either religion or media.

Previous research on men and religion has primarily focused on representations of masculinity in conservative, Christian evangelical media (Claussen 2000). As argued by Singleton (2004) in her critical content analysis of Christian men's self-help literature, the theme of a "crisis of masculinity" is salient in this genre, in response to competing, especially feminist, critical discourses about men's status in society. However, as shown, by Bartkowski (2007), the patri-archal rhetoric in these media is complex and diverse and evangelical men and women negotiate its meaning in a variety of ways (cf. Frykholm 2005, Frank 2011).

Stewart Hoover and Curtis Coats' (2011) research represents an alternative strand with their focus on reception studies of how the media provide symbolic resources that allow men to situate themselves in religious space. Grounded in "the culturalist turn," they argue that religious men are reflexive in their media use and that they engage with "traditional" as well as "alternative" media representations in constructive ways. Here, the focus on practices of consumption and "self-narrativising" (Gauntlett 2002, Hoover 2006: 94) provides examples of new analytical tools for capturing the changing performance of masculine identities in relation to media narratives (see also Thomas' 2011 analysis of BBC2's reality-TV program *The Monastery* as one of few examples of research outside of the US context).

At present, studies focusing on religion, media and gay, lesbian, bi- and transsexual identities are even scarcer than those on religion, media and masculinities. As religious affiliation as well as sexual orientation are key nodes around which narratives of identity and meaning are spun, research on how these are represented in the media is a matter of considerable importance, not least because of the history of connecting non-heterosexual relations with feelings of shame and sin within religious traditions. Claudia Schippert's (2007) analysis of the sanctification of the New York City Fire Department chaplain Mychal Judge, a victim of the 9/11 attacks, focuses on online constructions and negotiations of sexual, religious and national identities and how these challenges notions of "authentic" religion. Newer studies of online sites for religious lesbian and gay people show how these can provide powerful platforms for finding information, overcoming feelings of isolation and building mutual support networks (O'Riordan and White 2010). However, further research is needed to find out the extent to which the internet also provides a safe space for processes of negotiating heteronormative attitudes and trying out queer performances of religious identity.

Summary

The aim of this chapter has been to highlight how feminist and gender theories have contributed to studies of media, religion and culture by surveying published research in the field that has focused on gender since the late 1990s. What tendencies – in terms of influences from theoretical debates within feminist and gender theory – can then be discerned in work on media, religion and gender so far? As stated in Chapter 1, gender analysis has for the most part remained on a descriptive level in studies of media, religion and culture. The publications highlighted in this review show how insights from contemporary feminist and gender theories in several ways have contributed to a deeper and critical analysis of religion and gender in the media. The studies by Klaus and Kassel (2005) and Brown (2011) show how a combination of second-wave theories of the positioning of women through gender dichotomies and post-colonial feminist perspectives contribute to analyzing how the intersections between religion and gender in media representations can enhance stereotypes of and polarizations between ideals of western and "other" cultures. As pointed out by MacDonald (2006) and Vis (2011) it is, however, important for studies of these issues to move "beyond the hijab debates" and assumptions about oppression of women as connected to the ideals and symbols of certain religions and cultures. The studies by MacDonald (2006) and Korteweg (2008) show that an important learning from these debates is to engage in critical reflection on conceptions of agency and oppression within feminist categories and theories largely developed in a western, Christian scholarly context.

Influences from "the culturalist turn" in feminist media studies brought a focus on the agency of individuals and groups in constructing gender through symbolic resources provided by the media. This turn also implied the inclusion of "popular" media forms mostly produced for and consumed by women, and highlighted how class, ethnicity and location shaped the meanings and identities formed in individual uses of the media. These insights have clearly influenced studies of representations of gender in religious media and in the use of religious symbols within entertainment media. As the review shows, feminist perspectives have contributed through highlighting female characters in films and television series, but also by critically analyzing gender stereotypes in orientalist discourses in film, or dichotomous constructions of feminine submission and male heroism within popular Christian media. Studies that go beyond the textual level to analyze text as cultural practice (Maddux 2010, Butler and Winston 2009, Lelwica 2005) show how feminist perspectives have also contributed to critical analysis of the implications of gender representations and discourse for social relations within religious communities, and for the formation of individual identity as well as for civic participation.

The continued dominance of US-produced popular culture and the focus on Protestant Christian religion in studies so far show that there is still a need for a critical analysis of the significance of location – of the researcher as well as the research subject. The work of Mankekar (1993) and Canas (2008) demonstrates how the critical questions raised by post-colonial and other strands of third-wave feminist theories have much to offer for a further development of this analysis also within entertainment media. The insights from historical studies of religion and gender represent a further contribution to avoiding being too narrow-sighted an analysis of potentials and dilemmas of representations of gender and sexuality in contemporary media cultures.

A crucial issue in contemporary gender studies concerns how to handle questions of agency and power when facing the complex, diverse and paradoxical ways in which gender and sexuality are represented in the media. This is also a challenging theoretical question following the replacement of a structuralist paradigm that located power to certain ideologies, groups and positions in society with theories focusing on intersecting discourses and sites that present multiple and contradictory subject positions and various forms of power and agency. This review shows how these complex questions have also influenced research on media, religion and gender. This is evident in the discussions on variety and tensions in news media representations of women and Islam, in gender discourses mediated through popular culture and religious media among evangelical Christians and the ambiguous connections between (female) agency, sexuality and spirituality in contemporary films and television series. These perspectives also inform the focus on narratives of self, embedded agencies and on variety and complexity in how women and men negotiate these messages in relation to the religious communities and discourses in which they are situated in their constructions of religious and gendered identities and relations.

This question is also a core theme in studies of new, digital media and how the interactive and participatory character of these affects stereotypical and unequal gender positions in media and society. In this debate, feminist perspectives have been important in highlighting the potentials of new media genres and forms for, primarily, women's presence and agency (Berger and Ezzy 2009, Vis *et al.* 2011). However, the complexities of relations between online performances of gender and the embodied social relations of everyday life highlighted by Schippert (2007) and Moore (2011) call for a deeper, critical analysis of these issues.

Although this review has revealed a number of ways in which feminist theory and contemporary debates within feminist and gender media research have influenced research on media, religion and gender, it is not always easy to find explicit references to feminist scholars and discussions about concepts and theories from feminist and gender studies and how these can be applied to or developed in studies of media and religion. This makes it difficult to outline particular trends in the use of feminist theory in the work published so far. However, it seems as though this strand of research is now at a moment where theories and concerns rooted in Second Wave feminist that highlight women's experiences and enhance women's agency are still the strongest influence, combined – as this review has shown – with insights from Third Wave, primarily post-colonial feminist theories. This means that the debates about broadening gender as an analytical category from a focus on women's experiences to include also men and gay, lesbian, bi- and transsexual identities, issues about the consequences of heteronormativity within media and religious discourse raised by queer theory, and post-feminist ideas of acquiring agency through playful and parodic use of gender stereotypes largely remain to be explored. As the history of feminist research shows, these perspectives actualize a critical process of self-examination but also present ways for further theoretical development of a field.

As pointed out in the introduction, a core concern of feminist research has been to show how knowledge and theory is deeply connected to social position, which has implications for our perception of the social world and ability to act in it. This review has shown how insights from feminist theory have contributed in valuable ways to understanding the position and experience of women in studies of media and religion. However, in order to further pursue an analysis of how gender shapes the interplay between media and religion in the contemporary world, a further recognition of and engagement with a broader variety of feminist and gender theoretical perspectives is needed.

Note

1 The survey consisted of a search in the following databases and journals from 1993 to 2011 on the 28–29 of December 2011, based on the search words religion AND media AND gender: SCOPUS, ATLA+ATLAS Religion, Communication and Mass Media Complete, International Bibliography of the Social Sciences (IBSS), *Journal of Media and Religion, Journal of Contemporary Religion, Journal for the Scientific Study of Religion, Critical Studies in Mass Communication, Journal of Religion and Popular Culture, Material Religion, Journal of Communication and Religion*, Brill journals online and SAGE journals online.

Bibliography

Altheide, D.L. and Snow, R.P. (1979) *Media Logic*. Beverly Hills, CA: Sage.

Ang, I. (1985) *Watching "Dallas": Soap Opera and the Melodramatic Imagination*. London: Methuen.

Bartkowski, J.P. (2007) "Connections and Contradictions: Exploring the Complex Linkages Between Faith and Family," in N. Ammerman (ed.) *Everyday Religion: Observing Modern Religious Lives*. Oxford: Oxford University Press, pp. 153–168.

Berger, H. and Ezzy, D. (2009) "Mass Media and Religious Identity: A Case Study of Young Witches," *Journal for the Scientific Study of Religion*, 48 (3): 501–514.

Briggs, S. (2009) "'Elect Xena God': Religion Remixed in a (Post-) Television Culture," in D. Winston (ed.) *Small Screen, Big Picture: Television and Lived Religion*. Waco, TX: Baylor University Press, pp. 173–200.

Brown, K.E. (2011) "Muriel's Wedding: News Media Representations of Europe's First Female Suicide Terrorist," *European Journal of Cultural Studies*, 14 (6): 705–726.

Butler, A. and Winston, D. (2009) "'A Vagina Ain't a Halo': Gender and Religion in *Saving Grace* and *Battlestar Galactica*," in D. Winston (ed.) *Small Screen, Big Picture: Television and Lived Religion*. Waco, TX: Baylor University Press, pp. 259–286.

Butler, J. (1990) *Gender Trouble: Feminism and the Subversion of Identity*. New York: Routledge.

Campbell, H. and Lövheim, M. (2011) "Introduction. Rethinking the Online-Offline Connection in the Study of Religion Online," *Information, Communication and Society*, 14 (8): 1083–1096.

Canas, S. (2008) "The Little Mosque on the Prairie: Examining (Multi) Cultural Spaces of Nation and Religion," *Cultural Dynamics*, 20 (3): 195–211.

Claussen, D.S. (ed.) (2000) *The Promise Keepers: Essays on Masculinity and Christianity*. Jefferson, NC: McFarland and Company.

Connell, R.W. (2000) *The Men and the Boys*. Sydney: Allen and Unwin.

Davis, M. (2007) "Mary as Media Icon: Gender and Militancy in Twentieth-century U.S. Roman Catholic Devotional Media," in L.S. Clark (ed.) *Religion, Media, and the Marketplace*. New Brunswick, NJ/London: Rutgers University Press, pp. 123–153.

Derrida, J. (1981) *Writing and Difference*. London: Routledge.

Forbes, B.D. and Mahan, J.H. (eds) (2005) *Religion and Popular Culture in America* (revised edition). Berkeley: University of California Press.

Foucault, M. (1980) *Power/Knowledge: Selected Interviews and Other Writings 1972–1977*, ed. C. Gordon. New York: Pantheon.

Frank, G. (2011) " 'Ideals of Stability, Order and Fidelity': The Love Dare Phenomenon, Convergence Culture, and the Marriage Movement," *Journal of Religion and Popular Culture*, 23 (2): 118–138.

Frykholm, A.J. (2005) "The Gender Dynamics of the *Left Behind* Series," in B.D. Forbes and J. Mahan (eds) *Religion and Popular Culture in America*. Berkeley: University of California Press.

Gauntlett, D. (2002). *Media, Gender and Identity: An Introduction*. London: Routledge.

Gill, R. (2007) *Gender and the Media*. Cambridge: Polity Press.

Gledhill, C. (2006) "Pleasurable Negotiations", in J. Storey (ed.) *Cultural Theory and Popular Culture: A Reader* (third edition). Harlow: Pearson.

Graham, E. (1999) "Cyborgs or Goddesses? Becoming Divine in a Cyber Feminist Age," *Information, Communication and Society*, 2 (4): 419–438.

Hall, S. (1992/1980) "Encoding/decoding," in S. Hall, D. Hobson, A. Lowe, and P. Willis (eds) *Culture, Media, Language: Working Papers in Cultural Studies, 1972–1979*. Abingdon and New York: Routledge, pp. 117–127.

Hall, S. (1997) *Representation: Cultural Representations and Signifying Practices*. London: Sage.

Haraway, D. (1991) "A Cyborg Manifesto: Science, Technology, and Socialist-Feminism in the Late Twentieth Century", in D. Haraway (ed.) *Simians, Cyborgs and Women: The Reinvention of Nature*. London: Free Association Books, pp. 149–182.

Harding, S. (ed.) (2004) *The Feminist Standpoint Theory Reader: Intellectual and Political Controversies*. New York: Routledge.

Hartsock, N.C.M (1983) "The Feminist Standpoint: Developing the Ground for a Specific Feminist Historical Materialism," in S. Harding and M.B. Hintikka (eds) *Discovering Reality: Feminist Perspectives on Epistemology, Metaphysics, Methodology, and Philosophy of Science*. Boston: Reidel, pp. 283–310.

Hendershot, H. (2009) " 'You Know How It Is with Nuns … ': Religion and Television's Sacred/Secular Fetuses," in D. Winston (ed.), *Small Screen, Big Picture: Television and Lived Religion*. Waco, TX: Baylor University Press, pp. 201–232.

Hogeland, L.M. (1999) "Feminism, Sex Scandals, and Historical Lessons," *Critical Studies in Mass Communication*, 16(1): 94–99.

hooks, b. (1984) *Feminist Theory from Margin to Centre*. Boston: South End Press.

Hoover, S. (2002) "The Culturalist Turn in Scholarship on Media and Religion," *Journal of Media and Religion* (1) 1: 25–36.

Hoover, S.M. (2006) *Religion in the Media Age*. London/New York: Routledge.

Hoover, S.M. and Coats, C.D. (2011) "The Media and Male Identities: Audience Research in Media, Religion, and Masculinities," *Journal of Communication*, 61 (5): 877–895.

Kaylor, B.T. (2010) "Gracious Submission: The Southern Baptist Convention's Press Portrayals of Women," *Journal of Gender Studies*, 19(4): 335–348.

Klaus, E. and Kassel, S. (2005) "The Veil as a Means of Legitimization: An Analysis of the Interconnectedness of Gender, Media and War," *Journalism*, 6 (3): 335–355.

Knight, J.S. (2005) "Re-Mythologizing the Divine Feminine in *The Da Vinci Code* and *The Secret Life of Bees*," in B.D. Forbes and J. Mahan (eds) *Religion and Popular Culture in America*. Berkeley: University of California Press, pp. 56–74.

Korteweg, A.C. (2008) "The Sharia Debate in Ontario: Gender, Islam, and Representations of Muslim Women's Agency," *Gender and Society*, 22 (4): 434–454.

Krøløkke, C. and Sørensen, A.S. (2006) *Gender Communication: Theory and Analyses*. Thousand Oaks, CA: Sage.

Lelwica, M.M. (2005) "Losing their Way to Salvation: Women, Weight Loss, and the Salvation Myth of Culture Lite," in B.D. Forbes and J. Mahan (eds) *Religion and Popular Culture in America.* Berkeley: University of California Press, pp. 174–193.

Lövheim, M. (2004) "Intersecting Identities: Young People, Religion, and Interaction on the Internet" (PhD dissertation). Uppsala: Teologiska institutionen, Uppsala Universitet.

MacDonald, M. (2006) "Muslim Women and the Veil: Problems of Image and Voice in Media Representations," *Feminist Media Studies*, 6 (1): 7–23.

Maddux, K. (2010) *The Faithful Citizen: Popular Christian Media and Gendered Civic Identities.* Waco, TX: Baylor University Press.

Mahmood, S. (2005) *Politics of Piety.* Princeton: Princeton University Press.

Mankekar, P. (1993) "National Texts and Gendered Lives: Ethnography of Television Viewers in a North Indian City," *American Ethnologist*, 20 (3): 543–563.

Moore, D.L. (2011) "Constructing Gender, Old Wine in New (Media) Skins," *Pneuma*, 33 (2): 254–270.

O'Riordan, K. and White, H. (2010) "Virtual Believers: Queer Spiritual Practice Online," in S. Munt, K. Browne and A. Yip (eds) Queer Spiritual Spaces: Sexuality and Sacred Places. Farnham and Burlington: Ashgate Publishing Group, pp. 191–230.

Piela, A. (2011) "Piety as a Concept Underpinning Muslim Women's Online Discussions of Marriage and Professional Career," *Contemporary Islam*, 5: 249–265.

Radway, J. A. (1984) *Reading the Romance: Women, Patriarcy, and Popular Literature.* Chapel Hill: The University of North Carolina Press.

Ramji, R. (2003) "Representations of Islam in American News and Film: Becoming the 'Other'," in J. Mitchell and S. Marriage (eds) *Mediating Religion: Conversations in Media, Religion and Culture.* Edinburgh: T.&t. Clark/Continuum, pp. 65–72.

Schippert, C. (2007) "Saint Mychal: A Virtual Saint," *Journal of Media and Religion*, 6 (2): 109–132.

Singleton, A. (2004) "Good Advice for Godly Men," *Journal of Gender Studies*, 13 (2): 153–164

Spivak, G.C. (1988) "Can the Subaltern Speak?" in C. Nelson and L. Grossberg (eds) *Marxism and the Interpretation of Culture.* Basingstoke: Macmillan Education, pp. 271–313.

Stewart, A.R. (2011) "Text and Response in the Relationship between Online and Offline Religion," *Information, Communication and Society*, 14 (8): 1204–1218.

Sullivan, R. (2005) *Visual Habits: Nuns, Feminism, and American Post-War Popular Culture.* Toronto: University of Toronto Press.

Thomas, L. (2011) "Changing Old Habits? 'New Age' Catholicism, Subjectivity and Gender in BBC2's *The Monastery* and Its Reception," *European Journal of Cultural Studies*, 14 (5): 558–572.

Tong, R. (1993/1989) *Feminist Thought: A Comprehensive Introduction.* London: Routledge.

Van Zoonen, L. (1994) *Feminist Media Studies.* London: Sage.

Vis, F. (2011) "Media, Religion and Conflict/Beyond the Hijab Debates: New Conversations on Gender, Race and Religion," *European Journal of Communication*, 26 (29): 172–176.

Vis, F., van Zoonen, L. and Mihelj, S. (2011) "Women Responding to the anti-Islam Film Fitna: Voices and Acts of Citizenship on YouTube," *Feminist Review*, 97: 110–129.

Walker, R. (ed.) (1995) *To Be Real: Telling the Truth and Changing the Face of Feminism.* New York: Anchor Books.

Winston, D. (2011) "'The Angel of Broadway': The Transformative Dynamics of Religion, Media, Gender and Commodification," in G. Lynch, J. Mitchell and

A. Strhan (eds) *Religion, Media and Culture: A Reader*. London/New York: Routledge, pp. 122–130.

Winston, D. (ed.) (2009) *Small Screen, Big Picture: Television and Lived Religion*, Waco, TX: Baylor University Press.

Wodak, R. (ed.) (1997) *Gender and Discourse*. Thousand Oaks, CA: Sage.

Woodyard, K.M. (2008) "'If by Martyrdom I Can Advance My Race One Step, I am Ready for It': Prophetic Ethos and the Reception of Elizabeth Cady Stanton's *The Woman's Bible*," *Journal of Communication and Religion*, 31 (2): 272–326.

Chapter 3

Feminist orientations in the methodologies of the media, religion, and culture field

Lynn Schofield Clark and Grace Chiou

How do we study media, religion, and culture? Feminist theory has shaped some of the ways in which scholars have thought about knowledge at the intersection of media, religion, and culture, as noted in the previous chapter. But have feminist theories and theories of gender also shaped our methodologies? In this chapter, we will argue that they have, and often in ways that remain unacknowledged. The field of media, religion, and culture has to be seen as a social construction itself, with a particular narrative, a particular history, and specific relationships to place and people. It is inevitable that studies in this field have been informed by the insights of first-, second-, and third-wave feminism as well as queer theory. However, there is also a great deal of room for further research development building on the contributions of feminist methodologies and queer theories. Our aim in this chapter is to trace the relationships between feminist methodological concerns and developments in this field, highlighting studies that have embraced methodological approaches, and point toward approaches that remain unexplored. We then consider some of the challenges that researchers face as they strive to incorporate feminist and gender methodologies into contemporary studies of media, religion, and culture.

Following insights from scholars who are writing about feminist, gender, and queer methodologies, we propose that the field of media, religion, and culture has had at least three different strands of methodology and knowledge production, which we will refer to as *traditional*, *interpretive*, and *participatory*. *Traditional* research refers to that which in the social sciences is survey-based or experimental, and in the humanities refers to the period before historical criticism, when histories were written as unproblematic narratives that reflected the truth (rather than viewed as narratives written in relation to a certain perspective on, and construction of, the truth). The *interpretive* strand grows out of a response to traditional approaches to methodology and knowledge production, and its beginnings are associated with the Chicago School of Sociology and with cultural anthropology of the early twentieth century. Basic to this critique is the idea that knowledge is always situated and that there are multiple perspectives and differing claims to truth, and that researchers make choices within the process of research that are part of a negotiation over meaning that occurs between researchers and their subjects of research. Whereas feminist theory questioned the subject/object nature of the research relationship, queer theory pushed the boundaries of the interpretivist paradigm even further, questioning and challenging all of the taken-for-granted binaries of culture and society. Methodologically, queer theory works to destabilize the categories through which researchers would examine identities and construct accounts (see, e.g., Teresa de Lauretis, Judith Butler, Adrienne Rich, Eve Kosofsky-Sedgwick, all following Michel Foucault). Due to it being largely concerned with issues of language and representation, queer theory's methodologies tend toward using textual and discourse analysis. One of the challenges of queer theory methodologies, however, is that because of the focus on deconstructing subject positions, it is difficult to make arguments for what a "gay" or "lesbian" subjectivity would be; in other words, it destroys the distinctiveness of the same sex identity positions from which it speaks (Green 2002). One direction of post-queer theory has been to address research away from discursive deconstruction and toward the justice concerns of members of same sex communities.

In this sense, then, *participatory* research is related to queer theory and is a further outgrowth of interpretive research. Participatory research refers specifically to efforts that recognize the agency of research participants, and that view research as part of a collaborative effort toward seeking greater justice relations. Research participants can produce their own representations and can co-create new knowledge when given tools for knowledge production such as still or video cameras, drawing implements, or access to music or gaming production facilities, thereby working to challenge and change the limits of existing cultural and discursive positions.

Scholars have employed methodologies rooted in each of these three paradigms toward research supporting the emancipatory projects of feminist inquiry. The influence of feminist theory beginning in the 1960s and 1970s coincided with, and in many ways spurred, the challenges to traditional research and the "interpretive turn" that shaped the following research agendas, and has thus shaped the emergence of current participatory research, as well.

Although research on media and religion started in the mid-twentieth century with the employment of traditional approaches, the bulk of research that remains influential has grown out of frameworks that critique traditional research in the social sciences and the humanities. Yet, we suggest that this has not been a linear progression toward more inclusion of feminist, gender, and queer perspectives and methods over time. Rather, as the field considers its encounters with feminist theories and methodologies, we inevitably raise some lingering and uncomfortable questions. Why have so few studies on media and religion focused on the experiences of women and of gendered relations? Have those studies that have focused on gender been less frequently cited as central to the field than others? Why have we embraced some of feminism's and queer theory's methodological innovations but not others? Why has the field seemed so interested in certain phenomena and not in others? And as we consider feminism's role in the studies of religion and media moving forward, what methodological challenges might we face when striving to address the legacies of colonialism, exploitation, and underrepresentation that have also shaped the mediated religious encounters we so often study? In order to consider these questions, we review the methodologies scholars have embraced as they have moved the feminist agenda forward in studies of media and religion. Because these are questions that raise the intertwining issues of epistemology, research methods, and methodology we begin by offering definitions for each of these terms.

Epistemologies, methods, and methodologies

Feminist research is broadly understood as research that is conducted primarily by and for women (Oakley 1998). It assumes that the concerns and perspectives of women have been overlooked, and that the task of feminist researchers involves working within specific disciplines to embrace "distinctive approaches to subverting the established procedures of disciplinary practice tied to the agendas of the powerful," as Marjorie DeVault (1990: 96) writes. How a researcher goes about creating or following such "distinctive approaches" is a question of feminist methodology, just as how one creates categories of analysis increasingly has been a question of gender and queer theory.

In her groundbreaking work on feminist methodologies, Sandra Harding (1987) has argued that it is helpful to begin any discussion about "method" with clarity about the ways that method, methodology, and epistemology are interrelated. A *method* is a means of gathering evidence. A *methodology* is a theory regarding how research should proceed. *Epistemology* refers to a theory of how knowledge is produced or how it is justified. Harding argues that "this lack of clarity permits critics to avoid facing up to what is distinctive about the best feminist social inquiry." She claims that it also "makes it difficult to recognize what one must do to advance feminist inquiry" (1987: 2). In the previous chapter, Mia Lövheim pointed out that all knowledge is rooted in particular theories of knowledge, and she addressed the differing theoretical approaches that provide a foundation for feminist inquiry as it has occurred in studies of media and religion. In this chapter, we are primarily concerned with methodology, or the assumptions that have guided how research should be undertaken. We explore the questions that have been asked, how researchers have addressed these questions, and the ways in which their claims have been legitimated within the field.

Whereas research methodologies are a common source of discussion among those in the social sciences, they are less frequently discussed in the humanities. Yet all of the fields within the humanities have undergone a similar soul-searching when it comes to questions of how research should proceed, what "counts" as evidence, and how a researcher must work to justify his or her claims to knowledge.

These challenges to knowledge production first arose in relation to the early modernism of the Enlightenment era. Beginning in the sixteenth and seventeenth centuries, thinkers vested great hope in humanity's ability to change and improve social relations through the application of rational thought. The promise of modernity was that such thought could eliminate ignorance and irrationality and thus deliver humans to a state of greater equality and shared just relations. The crisis of modernity, however, was embedded in the discovery that rationality could not produce such progressive and desirable results, and the recognition that instead, rationality had produced, at its worst, the efficiency of the Holocaust and the dropping of atomic bombs on Hiroshima and Nagasaki. In other words, the manifestation of authoritative systems that arose from human reason resulted not in greater justice, but in the continued and perhaps even the deepened expression of unjust power relations around the world. Modernity, thus, ignited both a crisis in representation and a memory crisis, forcing us to recognize that all accounts are constructed narratives and that some are more valorized than others (Terdiman 1993; White 1978; Southgate 1996; Jenkins and Munslow 1991). Histories, for example, are no longer viewed as objective reports of the past, but rather are particular ways of representing the past as a story (White 2001). Such efforts have led feminist and gender researchers to question the absence of women and of marginalized groups and to utilize various methods to gather evidence about those whose stories are missing from taken-for-granted accounts. It is our task here, then, to pick out from these broader influences of feminism the specific innovations in research that have advanced the long-standing feminist commitment to defining and ending the social, economic, and political sources of women's oppression, as such work is a necessary part of the larger quest for social, economic, and political justice.

Traditional inquiry in media and religion

Early studies of religion and media focused on the effects of religious broadcasting on its audience. The methods for studying these audiences drew upon the social psychology of persuasion and public opinion that had emerged in the mid-1930s and had gained prominence through US federal funding of wartime research into propaganda and advertising (Lazarsfeld, Berelson, and Gaudet 1944; Merton 1946). As Jefferson Pooley and Elihu Katz (2008) point out in their review of mass communication research in these early years, the field of media research defined public opinion as "a measurable aggregate of individual attitudes" (2008: 770). Early studies of media and religion were, therefore, interested in the persuasive strength of religious broadcasting, and conceived of gender as an individual attribute which might influence attitudes toward religious media (cf. Buddenbaum 1981; Casmir 1959; Johnstone 1971; Parker, Barry, and

Smythe 1955). Even as recently as the decade of 1997 to 2007, the *Journal of Media and Religion* published nine articles including gender as a variable in the analysis of survey data on media use and media attitudes, demonstrating that this traditional approach to media and religion research continues (see Baker, Randle, Carter, and Lunt 2007; Bobkowski 2009; Haskell 2007; Hoover, Clark, and Raine 2004; Mullikin 2006).

The tradition of attitudinal research shaped studies of televangelism well into the 1980s, when televangelists rose to political prominence and new funding was directed toward research that explored televangelism's role in the political process (Bromley and Shupe 1984; Hadden and Shupe 1988; Hadden and Swann 1981). Some studies of televangelism drew upon emerging interdisciplinary methods, placing televangelism in historical context and questioning television's role in reinforcing conservative political ideologies (Frankl 1987; Peck 1993). This represented a methodological innovation; for the first time, research into religion and media focused attention on how mediated religion maintained power relations and provided support for conservatism in particular. Although these early studies of religion, media, and power did not focus on gender, it is notable that Razelle Frankl and Janice Peck, two women in the field, conducted them independently.

Up until this point, research funding investigating religion and media focused on media's persuasive and propagandistic uses. With the turn to interdisciplinary interests in televangelism, the focus and funding of research shifted away from behavioral scientific methods (Bruce 1990; Hoover 1988; Horsfield 1984). As key foundations such as the Lilly Endowment, the Pew Foundation, and the Ford Foundations supported both applied and basic research into televangelism, researchers began to expand the agenda of religion and media research to include attention to religion and news, and to the role of media and their audiences in shaping religion (Buddenbaum 1998; Clark 2003; Dart and Allen 1993; Hoover 1998; Silk 1998; Stout and Buddenbaum 1996). This opened new opportunities for feminist, gender, and queer research.

The interpretive turn in studies of media and religion

By the mid-1980s, the social sciences and humanities underwent a reexamination of research methodologies, primarily due to the influence of feminism, as noted earlier. Feminist scholars articulated objections to traditional research and directed attention toward studies interested in "taking the women's self-understanding seriously," as Janice Radway has written (1984:14). Feminists in media and in cultural studies, wishing to "give voice" to women's experience, advocated placing analyses of subjective experiences within larger frameworks of social constraint, usually those determined by gender (McRobbie and Gerber 1976; Cirksena and Cuklanz 1992; Press 1991). Feminists Judith Butler (1999, 2009) and Elizabeth Grosz (1994) have urged scholars to take the body seriously as a subject and site for individual lived experience, and scholars in religious studies and sociology of religion began to explore methodologies foregrounding embodiment and personal experience (cf. Spickard, Landres, and McGuire 2002; Orsi 2005). Researchers embracing ethnographic, historical, and feminist cultural analysis began to turn their attentions to religion and media, offering a range of new approaches that influenced the shape of the field in the 1990s and early 2000s, exploring women's experiences and, in some cases, drawing inspiration from efforts countering the perceived influence of the religious Right (Kintz and Lesage 1998).

Feminist scholars exploring personal experiences outside the western world also offered new directions for methodologies and research agendas in the study of media and religion (Spivak 1988). Several of the first of these efforts came from anthropologists and sociologists studying culture, media, and issues related to globalization. Marie Gillespie's (1995) *Television, Ethnicity and Cultural Change*, Purnima Mankekar's *Screening Culture, Viewing Politics* (1999), and Birgit Meyer's *Translating the Devil* (1999) warrant some special attention in this consideration.

In *Television, Ethnicity and Cultural Change*, media sociologist Marie Gillespie contended that by highlighting the small-scale processes of people's perceptions and actions regarding media (in this case East London Punjabis), ethnography enables a "connection between micro- and macroprocesses; between the public and private, the domestic, local, nations and international spheres in contemporary societies; and between 'micro' issues of power in everyday life and 'macro', structural social features" (1995:1). Rather than studying the media produced (as in news or televangelism), Gillespie, following trends in cultural studies audience research, focused on cultures of consumption, thereby foregrounding religion and media in everyday life. Media is "produced in and directed at a variety of distinct places," she argued, and "there is no uniformity of access to the media, or to the cultural and educational resources which are likely to make profound differences to the ways in which people respond to them" (1995:16–17). This enabled her to argue against a common perception at the time regarding the popular television epic, the *Mahabharata*, as many were concerned that this program that fictionalized the history of India exacerbated trends toward Hindu fundamentalism among its audiences. Whereas Gillespie did note that the Hindu nationalist Bharatiya Janata Party had attempted to exploit the program for their own ends, she also argued that most Hindu families found the program useful in communicating traditional religious values and beliefs. Rather than supporting political positions, they found solace and even a practice of devotion. Gillespie's methodology allowed her to call into question the homogeneity of media interpretation, foregrounding the agency of those who self-identify with religious communities in that process (1995:26).

Anthropologist Purnima Mankekar further contributes to considerations of the insider/outsider binary in studies of media, gender, and religion in *Screening Culture, Viewing Politics* (1999). Like Gillespie, Mankekar also draws upon the work of Stuart Hall, who argued that people are shaped by multiple, contesting, and unstable discourses of gender, religion, nation, and family within broader structures of power and inequality (Hall 1981:233). Building upon anthropology's prominent concerns with ethnographic authority, Mankekar challenges her own authority as an ethnographer and offers a model for reflexive scholarship. Noting her own positionality as a conflicted, western-educated, upper-middle-class, Hindu woman with progressive ideas, she considers the narratives her informants had constructed of Mankekar's life. She notes their interpretations regarding her childless state and relationship with her husband and in-laws which caused her to question assumptions regarding her own agency, and also to re-conceptualize the subjectivities of the women with whom she worked (1999:35). Her reflexivity and ability to engage with her participants inform Mankekar's understandings of the female Indian audience. Seeing their capacity to reflect upon and critique the television programs they watch, she claims that audience resistance and compliance are not mutually exclusive. Mankekar delves into these intersections to analyze how *Doordarshan*, state-television epics that were extremely popular, produced or effaced differences among women, and to investigate how women negotiate their positions in the family, religious community, and nation.

Similarly, anthropologist Birgit Meyer drew upon ethnographic traditions in her exploration of how modern filmic representations of Christianity's devil assisted in a reenchantment that brought Ghana's traditional Ewe religion into conversation with Christianity. In the discussion of designing methodology to explore the appropriation of Christianity in Ghana, Meyer wrote that she embraced a translation metaphor because it "implies a turning away from a positivist anthropology which pretends to represent the Other as he or she 'really is.'" Instead, she wrote, she came to

> understand my own fieldwork, which included a lot of practical translation, as an encounter with people or another culture that changed my understanding of established terms (such as religion, the body, and emotion, the family). The point is that, rather than taking translation for granted and subsuming new experiences under established categories ... one should realize the creative meaning-transforming process which is at work whenever people of different cultures meet.
>
> (1999:xxv)

In keeping with the feminist concern regarding context, then, like Mankekar's and Gillespie's work, Meyer's book begins with a historical examination of relevant political, socioeconomic, and religious developments.

In the late 1990s and early 2000s, others within the fields of religious studies and media studies began to explore similar themes considering religion, media, and gender, borrowing from anthropology's methodologies. Scholars in religion challenged their field's focus on institutional religion, turning instead to the practices of religion in everyday life, just as scholars in media studies looked toward media consumption in everyday life and as feminist scholars in a variety of disciplines advocated the study of power's reproduction through the cultural practices of everyday life (Ammerman 2007; Seiter 1999; Press 1991; Hochschild 1993). Among the most influential of these works for sketching out methods for the study of media and religion were those by Stewart Hoover and his colleagues at the University of Colorado.

After his earlier work in audience reception of the religious television program *The 700 Club* and in news coverage of religion, the Lilly Endowment provided significant support to Stewart Hoover and his colleagues, who led several studies of religion and media in everyday life that involved in-depth interviewing and ethnographic observation (Alters 2003, 2004; Clark 2003, 2004, 2007; Emerich 2011; Hoover 1988, 1998, 2006; Hoover and Emerich 2010; Hoover and Park 2004, 2005). These studies aimed to connect the meaning-making practices of individuals to the wider cultural and ideological patterns that contributed both to the stability and instability of institutional religion in the US. Some, such as Clark's (2003) study of teenage religious identity and popular cultural narratives, as well as family case studies completed by Diane Alters (2004), Joseph Champ (2004), and Hoover (2006), foregrounded the experiences of mothers and young women, as the burden of religious socialization continues to fall to women. Gender was not a primary focus in these studies, however, although later work on gender, media, and family studies (Clark 2012) as well as work on masculinity and media (Hoover and Coats 2011) built upon this foundation, particularly as evident in the work on media, gender, and religious identity by Lövheim (2005) and Line Nybro Peterson (this volume). Nevertheless, the support for such long-term and ambitious qualitative research enabled the building of a network of scholars in this area, placing feminist, gender, and queer research methodologies in the forefront of the study of media, religion, and culture in the beginning of the new millennium.

At the same time, scholars in history and American studies were also foregrounding gender and the study of everyday life, beginning with Colleen McDannell's *Material Christianity: Religion and Popular Culture in America* (1998). Rather than studying elite expressions of religion, McDannell explored objects that people invested with religious meaning in their everyday lives, similarly drawing upon foundation and other sources of funding while establishing a research agenda and a methodology for studies that would follow. Angela Zito (2006, 2007) similarly obtained research funding for her interest in the study of women's bodies and their containment in relation to religion and material culture in her study on foot binding in China. Indeed, McDannell's and Zito's initiatives articulate methodological approaches that share some similarities with the more humanities-oriented works of Rebecca Sullivan's *Visual Habits: Nuns, Feminism, and American Postwar Popular Culture* (2005), and Heather Hendershot's *Shaking the World for Jesus: Media and Conservative Evangelical Culture* (2004); both books foreground the body, religion, and mediated discourse. Sullivan's textual analysis of *The Nun's story* and *The Flying Nun* examines how women and religion were negotiated in a similar discursive space in the 1950s and 1960s, linking both the representation of women and social institutions to women's identity and to the social and political conditions of women's everyday lives. As Sullivan wrote, "in a feminist analysis, the context is the relationship of popular culture to the stratification of power and authority in a society that tends to privilege men over women" (2005:13). She argues that a feminist analysis is not limited to studies regarding women, but also the "gender of institutions, systems, and structures and their association with women through similar cultural discourses" (2005:17). Hendershot similarly expands the study of gender, media, and religion to include not only women but also explorations of homosexuality in relation to representations and practices of conservative and liberal branches of Christianity (on paganism, see Hoff Kraemer 2008). These frameworks study religion in relation to its historical, social, and political contexts including gender, social institutions, value systems, and power networks; an approach that is also evident in Diane Winston's study of women and media in the Salvation Army movement (2000), and, later, in Kathryn Lofton's study of religious dimensions within Oprah Winfrey's empire (2011). Winston's (2009) compilation of textual analyses of religion within commercial popular television also speaks to various questions of religion, media, and gender and moves the field forward by introducing this interdisciplinary approach to a new generation of scholars in religion and media studies, just as other work beckons us to consider the relationship between religious worldviews and the rise of commercial industries that profit from them, such as Lofton's (2011) work on Oprah, Monica Emerich's (2011) work on the sustainable and organic food industry, Michele Rosenthal's focus on new televangelisms (forthcoming), and Mara Einstein's work on the marketing of compassion (2011). By veering away from generalizations about the homogenous and timeless "effects" of media on religion and commercial culture, Lila Abu-Lughod likewise argues that her method is "writing *against* culture" (1991). Rather than producing typicality, Abu-Lughod, like many other scholars of media, religion, and gender working in the interpretivist vein, emphasizes the need for actual circumstances and histories of individuals, noting that their relationships are crucial to the constitution of experience (1993:14).

In summary, the field of religion, media, and gender has merged multiple interlocking methods from varying areas, enriching the way we understand the field: ethnography from cultural sociology, textual analysis and reception studies from literary and media studies, discursive analysis from queer theory, and historical analysis foregrounding subjects previously overlooked. Much focus has been on the "other," images and bodies that have been marginalized or invisible, and the ways they are discursively formed and inscribed in relation to systems of power. Specifically, authors have considered how various media representations and practices shape, constrain, and catalyze resistance in different contexts. Each study has deeply engaged a specific population, place, and religion. Accordingly, the conclusions drawn from these studies cannot be easily generalized and applied under the heading of "religion," but instead are rather unique and particular. This is consistent with the contemporary resistance to metanarratives and sweeping claims about religion or media, but a tension remains between constructing thorough and contextualized work and the need for generating applicable theories.

Where do we go from here? Participatory and reflexive research

Although significant areas remain unstudied within the interpretive tradition of research into media and religion, some experimentation is taking place in relation to methodologies inspired by feminist, gender, and queer scholarship. Faye Ginsburg's work is particularly noteworthy in this regard as it charts a course for what we term *participatory* research. Specifically, Ginsburg details the emergent tradition of Aboriginal filmmaking, as an outgrowth of the Australian Labor government's policy of supporting the self-determination of Aboriginal people in the 1970s, and as an important development in anthropological approaches to studying aboriginal cultures (Ginsburg 1995). Significantly, she points to a shift in how we might think about media production in relation to the self-actualization of marginalized groups. Too often, scholars have thought of activities like digital storytelling and video documentary as perhaps idiosyncratic narratives of personal expressions. Yet, she writes:

> Rather than accepting the dominant culture's model of the media text as the expression of an individuated self, [Aboriginal video producers and artists] stress the activities of the production and reception of indigenous media as processes of collective self-making, part of a continuum of social action for Aboriginal empowerment.
>
> (1995:134)

Paying attention to this work offers a perspective that differs from the tradition of ethnographic filmmaking and visual anthropology, as it recognizes the agency of those who construct their own self-representations, and it also recognizes the collective and collaborative nature of such endeavors. Such works can become anchoring narratives for those who construct them (Clark and Dierberg 2012). Projects such as video documentaries and other forms of digital storytelling afford groups the opportunity to tell, listen to, and reflect upon their own stories. Experiments with digital storytelling have taken place in relation to several religious groups and individuals, as documented by Clark and Jill Dierberg (2012) and Birgit Hertzberg Kaare and Knut Lundby (2008; see also Hess 2010).

With reference to the question of whether or not digital and video stories are an enactment of identity, Alan Davis and Daniel Weinshenker (2012) note

the importance of the context in which these stories are viewed and interpreted. They contend that "without the ongoing support of a community, the
self-realizations [digital stories] report and the personal transformations they
testify to are likely to fade from consciousness without translation into action"
(2011:22). Digital storytelling may provide groups with anchoring narratives
that contain significant aspirations; however, they only become catalysts to
support movement toward those aspirations with the support of a community.
Such self-reflective projects can therefore serve as a catalyst for both individual
and collective purposeful action. Scholars who work in partnership with those
creating such projects can, therefore, engage in interesting methods in studying
how individuals and groups experience and initiate change over time. Both
Elizabeth Olson and Giselle Vincett's (2011) study of religion in the use of
video documentary among marginalized youth communities in the UK and
Jason Anthony's (2011) introduction of gaming into ritual offer opportunities
to rethink the nature of knowledge and its role in relation to religion, media,
and gender. But such participatory feminist approaches do not come without
challenges.

Challenges

As we consider the feminist value of encouraging collaborative knowledge in
the politics of transformation that is at the heart of these methodological
approaches, at least three challenges emerge for consideration among all
researchers in media, religion, and gender. First, researchers must consider:
Are there certain communities that are prohibited or limited in their abilities to
"do" media? Just as gender is performed within a range of possibilities and norms
both conditioned and circumscribed by historical conventions, media participation also has barriers to entry and doing. For instance, Karen Zuga (1999)
traces the low representation of women in fields of technology and technological occupations, and writes,

> using feminist, racial, and class theory and critique would give voice to the
> concerns of not only women, but also other underrepresented groups in
> the content of what is taught as technology education … More important,
> the critical discussion of technology and the way in which we, as a society,
> choose to implement technology, especially as a society in which gender
> race and class structures create inequities in power, would give students
> insight into how to subvert prescriptive technologies in favor of developing
> redemptive technologies.
>
> (Zuga 1999)

If this statement is reinterpreted for media and religion scholars, one can see
how participatory research can address the technological divide as well as give
voice to individuals and their religions. This process of giving voice in critical

research both enables subjects to express their values, and allows researchers to utilize media as a tool for agency and advocacy. Yet, it also forces all researchers to recognize that even in a "remix" culture, not all members have equal access to the processes of production.

A second challenge relates to the practicalities of the researcher in the context of publishing demands, as participatory projects (as well as feminist, gender, and queer methodological approaches more generally) face resistance within academia. The co-production of knowledge fits uneasily with the norm of academic objectivity, and such efforts are not always welcomed in a scholarly community that values "findings" over processes of knowledge construction. Nevertheless, we see possibilities in bringing precarious, marginalized communities into the media landscape through scholarly research that is teamed with advocacy. An ethical, participatory method challenges the scholar to contemplate the consequences of her/his research and raises important new questions for others in the field to consider.

Third, since participatory research projects question the scholarly enterprise itself, they also foreground the need for researchers to consider the stakeholders involved in the research of media, religion, and culture. Those engaged in participatory research projects have argued that stakeholders include not only the research community, but also the participants of research and the groups and organizations that constitute their cultural milieu, and these groups shape the ways in which research is written (Clark 2012). In other words, feminist, gender, and queer methodologies demand that researchers consider the intersection of research and advocacy and place themselves within this field. The individual researcher is, therefore, destabilized and decentered, as such projects call into question both the construction of knowledge and the field in which the intended audience interprets and acts upon such constructions.

Those who have experimented with participatory approaches find themselves answering to several different stakeholders, thus, asking themselves questions such as: What difference does it make if the intended audience of such narratives is not the scholarly community but rather the people whose voices are marginalized or those who have opted to participate in a particular game or ritual action? If such cultural work is not meant for "knowledge," but for the empowerment or experience of particular groups, how does that change the relationship between the researcher and the researched? And if such work is funded for the purposes of advocacy rather than research, how does that shape the research that results? Such questions have long been at the center of feminist, gender, and queer methodological inquiry, as feminists have considered the relationship between scholarly work to be activist efforts meant to address societal injustices, and the resources devoted to exploring knowledge construction (Fine 1992). These are questions with which future scholars must grapple, particularly in an era in which resources are dwindling for research and are more targeted to the instrumental interests of social movements and religious organizations. Such changes are bound to present feminist researchers with new ethical challenges as they consider issues of research design, implementation, and data analysis as they continue to seek to address their research to the role of religion and of media in contributing to or ameliorating society's inequities.

Conclusion

This chapter has considered the development of feminist, gendered, and queer thought in relation to the methodologies embraced within studies focused on media and world religions. We have argued that although the field's beginnings were rooted in traditionalist methodological approaches that focused on the attitudes of individuals and tended to conceive of religion as individualistic, this has changed with the introduction of the interpretivist critique. Interpretivist methodological approaches introduced more collectivist sensibilities that challenged this westernized, individualist orientation and foregrounded issues of power and the construction of knowledge. We have argued that feminist, gender, and queer methodologies and epistemologies have had a central role in shaping the field of media and religion since the 1990s. At this moment feminist scholarship embraced a focus on the everyday, just as media studies similarly shifted to a focus on household practices, religious studies embraced a focus on everyday religion and its practices, and anthropology explored the interconnections between globalization and local cultures. The ethnographic methodological approaches of Gillespie, Mankekar, Meyer, and colleagues at the University of Colorado were highlighted for the ways in which each of these scholars utilized "close-up" explorations of media and religion in everyday life to question existing media theories, introduce the importance of reflexivity in knowledge construction, and highlight the metaphor of "translation" in the process of constructing research narratives. Similarly, the cultural analyses of McDannell, Zito, Sullivan, and Hendershot were reviewed for their insights into how humanities scholars embraced feminist methodologies bringing complexity to narratives of history, religion, media, power, and gender. Each of the methodological developments represented in these and in similar works influenced the ways in which scholarship in media, religion, and gender unfolded in the 1990s and afterwards, and enabled feminist researchers to introduce methods foregrounding the study of power relations, the body, collaborative knowledge construction, and a critique of the role of the researcher into studies of media and religion. Participatory research methodologies such as those Ginsburg advocated grew out of these commitments to understanding power and shifting research narratives into the hands of research participants, but such approaches present new research challenges at a time when resources for research are dwindling.

We feel that part of the reason why women, gender, and queer thought has not been a focus within media and religion research is related to questions of legitimacy and methodology. On the one hand, there are studies that foreground the development of theories such as religion and visual culture or the mediatization of religion, which might consider focusing on gender to be too particular or limiting quantitatively, as methodologies embraced in theoretical studies tend to draw upon either traditional research paradigms or frameworks of logics and hermeneutics. Alternately, there are anthropological and textual analytical studies that foregrounded previously unexamined communities and religious practices. In such studies, the general category of gender must be considered with intersections such as socioeconomic status, age, ethnicity, geographic location, and a host of other issues such as trying to address gender without reinforcing the gender binaries framework. This difference in methodological commitments may partly explain why few studies in religion and media have focused exclusively on gender, and why studies foregrounding women seem to be less frequently cited than other studies. It also presents a challenge in generating dialogue between those interested in theoretical development and those, often more centrally influenced by feminism and queer theory, who are suspicious of the ways in which theories can collapse important distinctions and erase key questions of knowledge organization. In part, we believe that volumes like this set out to address this problem, in that we are able to collect and reflect upon the specific contributions of women and of feminism and queer theory within this area and to encourage budding scholars to see continuities and innovations upon which they can build.

This chapter has also offered some explanations as to why some methodological innovations of feminism are incorporated into research more than others. In particular, this chapter demonstrates that feminist, gender, and queer contributions require increased scholarly labor, particularly as such work becomes more focused on discourse and more participatory. In order to reach feminist, gender, and queer scholarship's complex goals of developing nuanced contextual analyses, including poly-vocality and examining the various intersections of religion and media, and as scholars also consider the historical landscape, the political economy of media, various audiences and discourses regarding gender, class, nation, and family, there is much work to be done. We need to think and work collaboratively to address the issues that confront our field, and in this sense feminist methodologies offer important insights. We hope this article recognizes how feminist approaches re-conceptualize the role of the researcher and participants illuminating oppression and power distinctions and points to new directions, as participatory, collaborative, and reflexive research, despite its many challenges, can offer benefits to multiple stakeholders and to the development of key research insights within media, religion, and culture. This participatory form of methodology is enabling and can bolster the inclusion of gender and of underrepresented voices into the world of media production, engendering and modeling the positive social change that so many who embrace feminist, gender, and queer methodologies hope to work toward. In addition, it expands the field of media, religion, and culture, shifting frames of reference and deepening our understanding of identity, social groups, and institutions. As scholars in media, religion, and culture continue to embrace the interpretivist and participatory methodologies of feminism, our research promises to become both more engaged and more engaging.

Bibliography

Abu-Lughod, L. (1991) "Writing Against Culture," in R.G. Fox (ed.) *Recapturing Anthropology Writing in the Present*, Santa Fe: School of American Research Press, pp. 137–162.

——(1993) *Writing Women's Worlds: Bedouin Stories*, Berkeley: University of California Press.

Alters, D. (2003) "We Hardly Watch that Rude, Crude Show: Class and Taste in The Simpsons," in C. Stabile and M. Harrison (eds) *Prime Time Animation: Television Animation and American Culture*, New York: Psychology Press, pp. 165–184.

——(2004) "At the Heart of the Culture: The Hartmans and the Roelofs," in S.M. Hoover, L.S. Clark, and D.F. Alters *Media, Home, and Family*, New York: Routledge, pp. 103–130.

Ammerman, N. (2007) *Everyday Religion: Observing Modern Religious Lives*, New York: Oxford University Press.

Anthony, J. (2011) *The Ten Year Game*, available: www.thearriving.com (accessed May 13, 2012).

Baker, S., Randle, Q., Carter, E., and Lunt, S. (2007) "Democratic Learning and The Sober Second Thought: The Effect of Reading John Stuart Mill's Essay 'On Liberty' on Tolerance for Free Speech Among Highly Religious, Politically Conservative Students," *Journal of Media and Religion*, 6(1): 41–61.

Bobkowski, P. (2009) "Adolescent Religiosity and Selective Exposure to Television," *Journal of Media and Religion*, 8(1): 55–70.

Bromley, D.G., and Shupe, A.D. (1984) *New Christian Politics*, Macon, Ga.: Mercer University Press.

Bruce, S. (1990) *Pray TV: Televangelism in America*, London: Routledge.

Buddenbaum, J.M. (1981) "Characteristics and Media-related Needs of the Audience for Religious TV," *Journalism Quarterly*, 58: 266–272.

——(1998) *Reporting News about Religion: An Introduction for Journalists*, Ames: Iowa State University Press.

Butler, J. (1999) *Gender Trouble: Feminism and the Subversion of Identity*, 10th anniversary edition, New York: Routledge.

——(2009) "Performativity, Precarity and Sexual Politics" [Speech], AIBR, *Revista de Antropología Iberoamericana*, 4(3): i–xiii.

Casmir, F. (1959) "A Telephone Survey of Religious Program Preferences among Listeners and Viewers in Los Angeles," *Central States Speech Journal*, 10(3): 1–8.

Champ, J. (2004) "'Couch Potatodom' Reconsidered: The Vogels and the Carsons," in S.M. Hoover, L.S. Clark, and D.F. Alters, *Media, Home, and Family*, New York: Routledge, pp. 145–170.

Cirksena, K., and Cuklanz, L. (1992) "Male is to Female as _is to _: A Guided Tour of Five Feminist Frameworks for Communication Studies," in L. Rakow (ed.) *Women Making Meaning: New Feminist Directions in Communication,* Norwood: Ablex, pp. 11–44.

Clark, L.S. (2003) *From Angels to Aliens: Teenagers, the Media, and the Supernatural*, New York: Oxford University Press.

——(2004) "Being Distinctive in a Mediated Environment: The Ahmeds and the Paytons," in S.M. Hoover, L.S. Clark, and D.F. Alters, *Media, Home, and Family*, New York: Routledge, pp. 79–102.

——(2007) "Religion, Twice Removed: Exploring the Role of Media in Religious Understandings among 'Secular' Young People," in N. Ammerman (ed.) *Everyday Religion: Observing Modern Religious Lives*, New York: Oxford University Press.

——(2012) *The Parent App: Understanding Families in the Digital Age*, New York: Oxford University Press.

Clark, L.S., and Dierberg, J. (2012) "Digital Storytelling and Collective Religious Identity in a Moderate to Progressive Religious Youth Group," in H. Campbell (ed.) *Digital Religion: Understanding Religious Practices in New Media Worlds*, New York/London: Routledge.

Dart, J., and Allen, J. (1993) *Bridging the Gap: Religion and the News Media*, Nashville, Tenn.: First Amendment Center.

Davis, A. and Weinshenker, D. (2012). "Digital Storytelling and Authoring Identity," in C.C. Ching and B. Foley (eds), *Constructing the Self in a Digital World*. Cambridge: Cambridge University Press.

DeVault, M. (1990) "Talking and Listening from Women's Standpoint: Feminist Strategies for Interviewing and Analysis," *Social Problems*, 37(1): 96–116.

Einstein, M. (2011) *Compassion, Inc. How Corporate America Blurs the Line between What We Buy, Who We Are, and Those We Help*, Berkeley, Calif.: University of California Press.

Emerich, M. (2011) *The Gospel of Sustainability: Media, Market, and LOHAS*, Urbana: University of Illinois Press.

Fine, M. (1992) *Disruptive Voices: The Possibilities of Feminist Research*, Ann Arbor: University of Michigan Press.

Frankl, R. (1987) *Televangelism: The Marketing of Popular Religion*, Carbondale: Southern Illinois University Press.

Gillespie, M. (1995) *Television, Ethnicity and Cultural Change*, London and New York: Routledge.

Ginsburg, F. (1995) "Production Values: Indigenous Media and the Rhetoric of Self-Determination," in D. Battaglia (ed.) *Rhetorics of Self-Making*, Berkeley: University of California Press.

Green, A. (2002) "Gay But Not Queer: Toward a Post-Queer Study of Sexuality," *Theory and Society*, 31(4): 521–545.

Grosz, E. (1994) *Volatile Bodies: Toward a Corporeal Feminism*, Bloomington: Indiana University Press.

Hadden, J.K., and Swann, C.E. (1981) *Prime Time Preachers: The Rising Power of Televangelism*, Reading, Mass.: Addison-Wesley Publishing.

Hadden, J.K., and Shupe, A.D. (1988) *Televangelism*, New York: Holt.

Hall, S. (1981) "Notes on Deconstructing 'the Popular,'" in R. Samuel (ed.) *People's History and Socialist Theory*, London: Routledge and Kegan Paul, pp. 227–240.

Harding, S. (1987) *Feminism and Methodology: Social Science Issues*, Bloomington: Indiana University Press.

Haskell, D. (2007) "News Media Influence on Nonevangelical Coders' Perceptions of Evangelical Christians: A Case Study," *Journal of Media and Religion*, 6(3): 153–179.

Hendershot, H. (2004) *Shaking the World for Jesus: Media and Conservative Evangelical Culture*, Chicago: University of Chicago Press.

Hess, M. (2010, November). "In the Flow: Learning Religion and Religiously Learning," Presidential Address to the Religious Education Association, Denver, Colo.

Hochschild, A. (1993) *The Managed Heart*, Berkeley: University of California Press.

Hoff Kraemer, C. (2008) "The Erotic Fringe: Sexual Minorities and Religion in Contemporary American Literature and Film." Dissertation in *Religious and Theological Studies*, Boston: Boston University Press.

Hoover, S. M. (1988) *Mass Media Religion: The Social Sources of the Electronic Church*, Beverly Hills: Sage.

——(1998) *Religion in the News: Faith and Journalism in the American Public Discourse*, Newbury Park, Calif.: Sage.

——(2006) *Religion in the Media Age*, Oxford, New York: Routledge.

Hoover, S. M., Clark, L.S., and Raine, L. (2004) "Faith Online: 64% of Wired Americans Have Used the Internet for Spiritual or Religious Information," in Pew Internet and American Life Project, available: http://pewinternet.org/Reports/2004/Faith-Online.aspx (accessed May 12, 2012).

Hoover, S. M. and Emerich, M. (2010) *Media Spiritualities and Social Change*, London: Continuum Publishing.

Hoover, S. M., and Park, J. (2005) "Digital Religion in the Media Age: Field Notes from the Household Setting," in E. Rothenbuhler and M. Coman (eds) *Media Anthropology*, London: Sage.

Hoover, S. M. and Park, J.K. (2004) "Religious Meaning in the Digital Age: Field Research on Internet/Web Religion," in P. Horsfield, M. Hess, and A.M. Medrano (eds), *Belief in Media: Cultural Perspectives on Media and Christianity*, Aldershot, UK: Ashgate, pp. 121–136.

Hoover, S. M., and Coats, C. (2011) "The Media and Male Identities: Audience Research in Media, Religion, and Masculinities," *Journal of Communication*, 61(5): 877–895.

Horsfield, P. (1984) *Religious Television: The American Experience*, New York: Longman.

Jenkins, K., and Munslow, A. (1991) *Re-Thinking History*, New York: Routledge.

Johnstone, R. (1971) "Who Listens to Religious Radio Broadcasts Anymore?", *Journal of Broadcasting*, 16: 90–102.

Kaare, B.H., and Lundby, K. (2008) "Mediatized Lives: Autobiography and Assumed Authenticity in Digital Storytelling," in K. Lundby (ed.) *Digital Storytelling, Mediatized Stories: Self-representations in New Media*, New York: Peter Lang, pp. 105–122.

Kintz, L., and Lesage, K. (1998) *Media, Culture, and the Religious Right*, Minneapolis: University of Minnesota Press.

Kramer, L. (1990) *Sociology of Gender*, New York: Oxford University Press.

Lazarsfeld, P., Berelson, B., and Gaudet, H. (1944) *The People's Choice: How the Voter Makes Up His Mind in a Presidential Campaign*, New York: Columbia University Press.

Lofton, K. (2011) *Oprah: The Gospel of an Icon*, Los Angeles: University of California Press.

Lövheim, M. (2005) "A Space Set Apart? Young People, Exploring the Sacred on the Internet," in J. Sumiala-Säppänen, K. Lundby, and R. Salokangas (eds) *Implications of the Sacred in (Post) Modern Media*, Gothenburg: Nordicom.

Mankekar, P. (1999) *Screening Culture, Viewing Politics: An Ethnography of Television, Womanhood, and Nation in Postcolonial India*, Durham, N.C.: Duke University Press.

McDannell, C. (1998) *Material Christianity: Religion and Popular Culture in America*, New Haven, Conn.: Yale University Press.

McRobbie, A., and Gerber, J. (1976) "Girls and Subcultures," in S. Hall and T. Jefferson (eds) *Resistance through Rituals: Youth Subcultures in Post-War Britain*, London: Harper Collins Academic: 209–222.

Merton, R.K. (1946) *Mass Persuasion: The Social Psychology of a War Bond Drive*, New York: Harper.

Meyer, B. (1999) *Translating the Devil: Religion and Modernity among the Ewe in Ghana*, Trenton, N.J.: Africa World Press.

Mullikin, P.L. (2006) "Religious and Spiritual Identity: The Impact of Gender, Family, Peers and Media Communication in Post-adolescence," *Journal of Communication and Religion*, 29(1): 178–203.

Oakley, A. (1998) "Gender, Methodology and People's Ways of Knowing: Some Problems with Feminism and The Paradigm Debate in Social Science," *Sociology*, 32(4): 707–732.

Olson, B., and Vincett, G. (2011) "Hanging Out and Hanging On: Researching Spirituality with and for Young People," unpublished manuscript.

Orsi, R. (2005) *Between Heaven and Earth: The Religious Worlds People Make and the Scholars Who Study Them*, Princeton: Princeton University Press.

Parker, E.C., Barry, D., and Smythe, D.W. (1955) *The Television-radio Audience and Religion*, New York: Harper and Brothers.

Peck, J. (1993) *The Gods of Televangelism*, Cresskill, N.J.: Hampton.

Pooley, J., and Katz, E. (2008) "Further Notes on Why American Sociology Abandoned Mass Communication Research," *Journal of Communication*, 58(4): 767–786.

Press, A. (1991) *Women Watching Television: Gender, Class, and Generation in the American Television Experience*, University of Pennsylvania Press.

Radway, J. (1984) *Reading the romance: women, patriarchy, and popular literature*, Philadelphia: University of North Carolina Press.

Rosenthal, M. (forthcoming) *Mediating Religion, Sanctifying Media: Exploring the Nexus of Media Practice and Contemporary Religious Revival in Israel*, De Gruyter.

Seiter, E. (1999) *Television and New Media Audiences*, Oxford: Oxford University Press.

Shupe, A., Bromley, D.G., and Oliver, D. (1984) *The Anti-Cult Movement in America: A Bibliography and Historical Survey*, New York: Garland Publishers.

Silk, M. (1998) *Unsecular Media: Making News of Religion in America*, Chicago: University of Illinois Press.

Southgate, B. (1996) *History, What and Why? Ancient, Modern, and Postmodern Perspectives*, New York: Routledge.

Spickard, J., Landres, S., and McGuire, M. (eds) (2002) *Personal Knowledge and Beyond: Reshaping the Ethnography of Religion*, New York: NYU Press.

Spivak, G. (1988) "Can the Subaltern Speak?", in C. Nelson and L. Grossberg (eds) *Marxism and the Interpretation of Culture*, Chicago: University of Illinois Press, pp. 271–313.

Stout, D.A., and Buddenbaum, J.M. (eds) (1996) *Religion and Mass Media: Audiences and Adaptations*, Thousand Oaks, Calif.: Sage.

Sullivan, R. (2005) *Visual Habits: Nuns, Feminism, and American Postwar Popular Culture*, Toronto: University of Toronto Press.

Terdiman, R. (1993) *Present Past: Modernity and the Memory Crisis*, Ithaca: Cornell University Press.

White, H. (1978) "The Historical Text as Literary Artifact," in *Tropics of Discourse: Essays in Cultural Criticism,* pp. 81–100 (first published 1974 in *Clio*, 3(3): 277–303).

White, H. (2001) "Historical Emplotment and the Problem of Truth," in G. Roberts (ed.) *The History and Narrative Reader*, New York: Psychology Press.

Winston, D. (2000) *Red-Hot and Righteous: The Urban Religion of The Salvation Army*, Cambridge, Mass.: Harvard University Press.

——(ed.) (2009) *Small Screen, Big Picture: Television and Lived Religion*, Waco, Tex.: Baylor University Press.

Zito, A. (2006) "Bound to be Represented: Theorizing/Fetishizing Footbinding," in L. Heinrich and F. Martin (eds) *Embodied Modernities: Refiguring Body Politics in China*, Honolulu: University of Hawaii Press.

——(2007) "Secularizing the Pain of Footbinding in China: Missionary and Medical Stagings of the Universal Body," *Journal of the American Academy of Religion*, 75(1): 1–14.

Zuga, K. (1999) "Addressing Women's Ways of Knowing to Improve the Technology Education Environment for All Students," *Journal of Technology Education* 10, N 2(-Spring 1999.

Chapter 4

Material witnesses

Women and the mediation of Christianity

Pamela E. Klassen and Kathryn Lofton

Christian identity is inextricable from gender identity. Throughout Christian history, determining how individuals incarnate divine authority has been critical to the communication and legitimation of Christian testimonies. What can the words emanating from a particular physical body signify for the broader social movements that have fuelled Christianity? Evaluating such testimony might even be understood as the original practice of Christianity, insofar as the witness of a single male, Jewish body provided its genesis as a sectarian movement, and insofar as disagreements over subsequent witnesses and their ecclesiastical legitimacy became the grounds for nearly every denominational discord, theological innovation and mystical experimentation within that diverse tradition. Whether it was Peter appraising Mary Magdalene, Hilarianus adjudicating Perpetua, or John Winthrop assessing Anne Hutchinson, refereeing a witness's testimony has been a primary task of (male) ecclesial authorities. Knowing whether (and how) you, as a particular embodied witness, have the right to speak about God (and what it means when you do) has encouraged the grand diversity of Christian expression.

Within this history, women have played a central, if controversial, role. Women were integral to Christianity at its origins even as their gendered bodies posed real problems to the ecclesiology that emerged to fix and canonize its earliest texts. According to the New Testament gospels, women were reported to have been the first witnesses to the resurrection, but even their testimonies were suspect in the eyes of some of the men among their community. Despite this suspicion, women came to take on prominent positions in the early Jesus movement. They hosted and led house churches shielded from the hostile gaze of Roman authorities and some held ecclesiastical offices in the early church (Osiek *et al.* 2006).[1] Paul, for example, greets a deacon named Phoebe (Romans 16: 1) and assumes that women are praying and prophesying during worship (I Corinthians 11). In their practice as prophets, women would not only have been authors of ecstatic communal speech, but also would have served as material witnesses to the faith by preaching, teaching, leading prayer and perhaps even performing the Eucharist meal. Women's leadership, however, did not go unchallenged. Every variety of ancient Christianity that advocated the legitimacy of women's ritual and theological authority was declared heretical by the fifth century (Torjesen 1995).

Scholars of religion working with the insights of feminist theory have argued that women developed a particular kinship to Christianity because of the possibility that incarnation offered a revaluing of embodiment *per se* (Bynum 1987). Christianity thus comprised both the fixity of gender and its undoing, offering descriptions of a heteronormative dyad of male and female while also offering a process of materialization that can and has been more variable and queer (Butler 2003). Excluded socially and politically from certain formal roles within church life on anatomical grounds, Christian women consistently found source material in the gospels and even Paul's letters to argue on behalf of themselves as still integral to their churches – as vital members of the body of Christ even as they possessed complicating bodies, virginal or maternal, cloistered or in the world (Herrin 2004; Cooper 1999; Burrus 2007).

Partly because of their reduced access to education and ecclesial authority, women have understood their own bodies as testimony to and connection with the experience of Jesus. Women's bodies, thus, become sites of confessional articulation that take particular mediated forms. A material witness articulated through a woman's body was not necessarily that of a "woman" *per se* – early Christian texts about the virtues of female virginity could be voiced as debates among women without necessarily being written by women.[2] But whether the *Vita* of a "saintly" medieval woman written by her male confessor or the letters, or poems and diaries written by a woman's own hand in the twelfth or the twentieth centuries, accounts by and about women in Christianity almost always feature some sort of bodily referent (Elliott 2004; Peters 2009; Orsi 1998). With commentarial and juridical authority denied them, women became leaders in and through their material witness, by using available forms of mediation to convey the gospel as an articulation of their Christian experience. They described their bodies as, in some sense, incarnations of scriptural text.

The history of the significance of embodiment for women's authority *and* exclusion in Christianity is well attended to in feminist research, and continues to be a site of creative theorization and important historical inquiry (e.g. Elliott 2011). In this chapter, we think about the particular ways that women's bodies have been inextricable from their witness – how their gender contributed to, and became, their particular missionary and spiritual emphasis – even as they made use of an increasing diversity of communication technologies. In other words, we want to think about how women's bodies were media for their religion, with a specific focus on women in twentieth- and twenty-first-century North America.

Living within "semiotic ideologies" that have largely valued textuality itself, and the biblical text in particular, as privileged modes of communication, Christians also live with a pressure to put their witness in the material form of a testimony (Keane 2007). With a materiality rooted in the written text of the

Bible, Christians in North America have also been pioneers in the development and deployment of new media formats, eagerly embracing the printed word, newspapers, photographs, radio, television and the Internet as vehicles of communication (Bendroth and Brereton 2002; Gutjahr 2001; Brown 2004; Morgan 1999). Christians' efforts to communicate the gospel cannot be understood apart from these technologies of conveyance that are themselves material witnesses of a sort, functioning as intermediaries in which the message is also the messenger. In the midst of these proliferating forms of mediation, we ask, how and why does the materiality of being a "woman" continue to affect the authority, or lack thereof, of Christian women's testimonies?

New forms of media have been especially innovative channels for women seeking to give their testimonies outside of the strictures on women's speech. Working within a textual cosmology that includes scriptural passages arguing, "women should be silent in the churches. For they are not permitted to speak, but should be subordinate, as the law also says" (1 Corinthians 14: 34), Christian women have been eager to find media of witness to extend their specific embodiment beyond themselves and thus to make a mission of their particular Christian experience. For these women, face-to-face witness in a church was sometimes more difficult to perform than a disembodied broadcast through paper or airwaves. Mediation might allow the listener or reader to forget, in part, that they were listening to or reading a *woman*. New media provided channels for a woman's voice to speak to ever-broader audiences, without entirely erasing the gendered specificity of her incarnated form. Yet, as Leigh Schmidt demonstrated in the context of eighteenth- and nineteenth-century North America, the voice of witness may travel through the air, but is rarely received without finely tuned attention to material conditions of its production (Schmidt 2000). Performing their messages via both virtual and fleshly witness, women evangelists have both depended on *and* transcended the matter of their bodies. They have borne witness by telling the stories of their lives with what Elaine J. Lawless has described as "narrative strategies that reinforce and validate the identity sought in the living 'script' " (Lawless 1993: 45). All living scripts – all Christian testifiers – are gendered interpellations. But women's testimonies, we suggest, have been especially marked by evidence drawn from the matter, and matters, of their lives.

In this chapter, we consider how women have utilized various media to channel and articulate their testimonies in twentieth- and twenty-first-century North American contexts, paying specific attention to the connection between mediation and materiality. We argue that there seems to be a particularly comfortable connection between the material witness of women and the intimate commodification of their living scripts. We use the word "commodification" here with intention, tying together the process by which self becomes object, and object becomes a market good. In our studies of women in Christian history, we have found that there seems to be no form of distributing technology that is too alienating relative to its potential missionary power, and it seems further that there is an especially unbound relationship between the individual self and her story as commodity (see Lofton 2008; Klassen 2001; Klassen 2006). To be sure, packaging one's story for mass consumption in the name of Christian mission is an act always haunted by the fear of tripping from faithful testimony to advertising self-aggrandizement, between offering service and being self-serving.

Witnessing women

When Mary Lena Street Lewis Tate (1871–1930) founded the first predominantly black Pentecostal splinter church, the Church of the Living God (for which she became the chief apostle, elder, president and first chief officer), she did so through a determined personal evangelism – traveling up and down the American eastern seaboard – but also through an elaborate print culture. Tate's ministry emerged through her own struggles to name what she perceived as a great silence in her local church communities. For her, the subject of "cleanness" was of utmost importance, yet it was "totally ignored by her rural Tennessee audience who were not only tobacco growers and processors, but also tobacco chewers, pipe and cigar smokers, profanity users, and constant brawlers quite given to fisticuffs." Tate's advocacy of cleanness required her own purity of person, something accomplished in part through her divorcing of her husband, whom she described later as a figure prohibitive not only of her pieties but also her gendered voice. "Opposition developed, criticism mounted, dissension grew, and finally, resolution demanded," a biographer would explain. "Not welcomed in the family church and resented by her husband, Mary Lena's marriage was destined to failure" (Lewis 1989: 6). Distancing herself from the sullying effects of older churches and unclean individuals, Tate developed and mediated a story about herself that might be used as a model for others to imagine their strength independent from bad traditions, encroaching men and unclean habits.

Much of what Tate believed and taught was summarized in the church's *Constitution, Government, and General Decree Book* (1924), written by her and edited by her son and published by the church's publishing house, The New and Living Way Publishing Company, established in 1923. The importance of print culture was not a sneaking commercialism; it was integral to the evangelistic message itself. Tate wrote in her introduction to the Decree Book that:

> As we believe all human beings should know that it is the will of God that all true people should have a rule to walk by in any matter of business, both spiritual and temporal; and they should have their rules written up in books.
> (Tate 2003)

Tate continued: "Knowing these things, we do ask ministers of the Lord as they go through the land, in the city, in the country, and in every place to deliver the Decree for the Saints to keep" (Tate 2003: 76). The book becomes a system of delivery and itself a deliverance, bringing a common reading to diverse audiences. The entire volume offers an assemblage of materials, narrating her new denomination as a scrapbook of scriptural passages, sectarian memoir and rules of governance. Rather than imagining some purified concept of scripture, procedure or personal history, Tate translates her self into a pastiche text that models right piety and prescribes right churchly process.

Here, Tate's material production is not altogether unusual. All leaders of new religious movements must provide more than revelatory scripture, but also create handbooks on how to enact those messages – they don't just give a magical story, but they tell you (over and over) how to practice the magic *in* the story. Think of Mary Baker Eddy (1821–1910), founder of the primarily white Christian Science Church, who also found it necessary to divorce her husband in the process of writing the textbook of her movement, *Science and Health with Key to the Scriptures*. Not only did she write *Science and Health* to explain to her followers how to understand the Bible, but she also founded the Christian Science Publishing Society (1898), which continues to publish a number of periodicals including *The Christian Science Monitor* (1908) to provide regular outlets for the message and its reiteration. Eddy's personal experience of bodily healing was (ironically) central to her authority as a prophetess of immateriality; her testimony to her body's ability to rise up and walk forms the origin story of the Christian Science theology of matter as error, circulated via the Mother Church's media empire (Gill 1999; Schoepflin 2003). It's not enough to tell people to climb to the mountaintop if you don't have a way for them to repeat that climb, for themselves, over and over. Circulating their living scripts, Eddy, Tate and other Christian women rooted their revelations in intimate autobiographical detail in which their bodies – maternal, healed, clothed and saved – were the ground of witness (Brekus 1998; Klassen 2004).

Two preaching peers to Tate, Evangeline Booth (1865–1950) and Aimee Semple McPherson (1890–1944) spread theories of holiness within narratives of a more sensational nature. If Tate and Eddy focused on ministries that emphasized healing and prayer, Booth and McPherson buried those particulars in larger stage spectacles and revivals which iterated their ministerial charisma as a critical conduit to their parishioners' individual revelations. The first woman to command the Salvation Army in the United States, Evangeline Booth got her start collecting tales of London slums, which she deployed as fundraising anecdotes on stage and in print. Importing stories from the streets, Booth embodied suffering that was not her own, transfiguring herself into the witness and the witnessed on "secular" stages in London, Toronto and New York. As Diane Winston has explained, one of Booth's most significant innovations was to "sanctify commonplaces," from large-scale demonstrations on urban streets to fundraising efforts outside of mercantile centers (Winston 2000). This self-described campaign to translate sanctification beyond the individual soul and onto the public square was described in the Salvation Army's weekly newspaper in this way:

> The genius of the Army has been from the first that it has secularized religion, or rather that it has religionized secular things ... On the one hand it has brought religion out of the clouds into everyday life, and has taught the world that we may and ought to be as religious about our eatings and drinkings and dressing as we are about our prayings. On the other hand it has taught that there is no religion in a place or in an attitude. A house or a store or factory can be just as holy a place as a church; hence we have commonly preferred to engage a secular place for our meetings ... our greatest triumphs have been witnessed in the theaters, music halls, rinks, breweries, saloons, stores, and similar place.
>
> (Winston 2002: 115)

But as Christian women such as Booth and Tate slowly extracted themselves from the relative anonymity of domestic or maternal labor and positioned themselves on more public stages, they reimagined church as more than a privileged pulpit, but also as anywhere the minor tasks of life ("eatings and drinkings and dressing") transpired. Women may not yet be equal before ecclesiastical authorities in most denominations, but they gained ground in the commercial revolution – their sartorial choices and home decorating here gained messianic urgency as these actions were increasingly narrated as holy labors.[3]

As a child in Canada, Aimee Semple McPherson attended Methodist church services as well as Salvation Army Sunday school meetings. This Wesleyan revivalism informed her founding of the International Church of the Foursquare Gospel. McPherson mastered church as spectacle, incorporating into her services dramatic healings, motorcycle riders and charismatic sermons that invited an audience seeking celebrity encounters as much as faithful conversions. Simmering at the edges of her success were rumors of her own biographical subplots, which suggested that beyond her markedly prim (yet glamorous) preacher's wardrobe there was a more salacious "Sister Aimee" (Sutton 2007). In her many memoirs recounting her revival tours, McPherson revealed her struggles, emotional and material, to carry the word of the gospel while mothering her children without a steady husband. Her stories were overflowing with her anxieties and worries, with her weeping and her fear. Yet these confessions of human vulnerability only elaborated her effect on listeners. Visitors claimed her voice was mesmerizing, bringing them to trance just by listening to it. This voice and her clarion sermonic ability propagated a multi-media empire, including a newspaper (*The Bridal Call*), a radio station (KFSG) and her own school (LIFE Bible College). McPherson advocated on behalf of women in the ministry, arguing that anyone with a calling should join the effort to cajole souls for Christ. With her savvy media creativity, her mysteriously complicated private life, and fame beyond the average denominational leader, McPherson found a way to be profoundly intimate and familiar while also being larger than life. Her very person seemed tied to the women of the Bible who tended Jesus; she was both a witness to, and evidence of, his divine authority.

With Booth and McPherson, preaching expanded beyond the church-based podium and into new structures and contexts, blending lines between religion and popular culture, believers and consumers. Not coincidentally, then, they cultivated missions and creeds, which might supersede sect and nab a broader (and somewhat racially diverse) contingency of Christian America. These were fiercely Christian women, yet this Christianity was not as much a series of codes as it was a differentiating disposition toward the world. New media developments allowed their message to be propagated to far vaster audiences than nineteenth-century denominations ever imagined and, in that expanse of potential converts, invocations of deities became more generic and theology became more inclusive. Other female preachers of the late-nineteenth and twentieth centuries, such as the aforementioned Mary Baker Eddy or Kathryn Kuhlman (1907–1976), televised faith healer, likewise balanced a distinguishing emphasis (like an unusual stance toward sickness or a Protestant preaching on miracles) with points of universal access to that message (Christian Science reading rooms on major urban thoroughfares, non-denominational revivals broadcast on television).[4] Their success lay in their ability to self-mediate in the process of spreading the gospel.

Multi-mediated women

The twentieth-century apotheosis in the realm of female preaching must be Oprah Winfrey – talk-show host, book-club maven, magazine publisher, professional celebrity friend, benevolent leader and arguably one of the contemporary world's most famous testifiers – who has made the act of witnessing into her life's work. Whether telling her own story or eliciting that of another, Oprah has made the material witness a mode of both self-help and entertainment. Oprah has made the "secular rite" of the makeover – multi-mediated by her television show, her magazine and her website – into a ritual with religious "affect" that is rooted in the struggles, confessions and the very body of Oprah herself. Turning her pain into largesse, Oprah also transforms disclosure into a gift that effects if not a miraculous healing, then at least a minor makeover. The gift Winfrey gives physical renewal, including in its various incarnations rehearsal and reward, confession and redemption, intimacy and spectacle. The makeover is not only material – including the dispersal of new cars, new clothes, new dryers, etc. – but also a translation of the material into the spiritual: a material witness to your spiritual capacities.[5]

Demanding exposure and confession, testimonies in the *Oprah* world (including her daily television show, monthly magazine and Internet community) were rewarded with a promise of new self-knowledge and, sometimes, a new car. But what we seek to emphasize here is how the body is the site of redressing – how Oprah Winfrey has made her suffering body a means to cajole your confession. Consider the fact that no aspect of Winfrey's particularity receives more press, or more of her own self-appraisal, than her body. The public discussion of her weight problem formed a constant opportunity for her own makeover and that of others.[6] Winfrey's dream of a body that matches her best self, a body that fits the best clothes and the best vision she has for herself, is not only for herself. It also connects her to other similarly suffering women.

On May 12, 2011, *The Oprah Winfrey Show* hosted its "Last Ever Makeover Extravaganza." To open the familiar process, she gave the back-story and the creedal cry. "Over the years, there have been nearly 1,000 mothers, girlfriends, sisters, and wives transformed," her voice over described. "And we still believe without a shadow of a doubt that a good bra and a pair of Spanx can change your world." As she speaks, we watch a woman go to Oprah's Bra Boutique and discover she is (*she screams*) a 34C. The camera finds Oprah now in the studio, where she nods at the 34C memory: "*So fun. It's* – we love that. The gospel around here – a good bra and a pair of Spanx is the holy grail of the makeover." This is a gospel conveyed by objects seeking to shape the body – the good bra and a pair of Spanx formatting that, which is supposedly not formed rightly, or not formed enough. The gospel of straps, snaps, Spandex and *smooth*.

Body talk was the coin of Winfrey's realm. Her body, and her inability to control its size, makes it possible for Winfrey to sustain quotidian authenticity even as she achieved otherworldly status in fame, in funds and in experience. Robin Givhan wrote in the *Washington Post*: "Winfrey inspires her fans in part because she makes extraordinary accomplishments look possible. But as her weight continues to yo-yo, she confirms what folks have always suspected: *Just being average can be quite a challenge, too*" (Givhan 2008). Oprah Winfrey was perhaps the first major star to humanize her weight struggle and ennoble it into a parable of redemption and self-discovery. But as Caroline Walker Bynum and Marie Griffith have explained, rituals of body maintenance determine much of Christian history, and into this history Oprah may be seen as a peculiar exemplar, simultaneously denouncing asceticism as a viable option while identifying the body as a central document in your spiritual estimation (Bynum 1987; Griffith 2004).

Social media and the material witness

This genealogy of preaching women – from Mary Lena Street Lewis Tate to Oprah Winfrey – reiterates certain themes, showing time and again how women connected their embodiments of womanhood by deploying available technologies to render universal and accessible their respectively personal experiences of holiness. As the presence of singular church authority dwindled, the success of a particular message was not its adherence to right theology as much as it was its usability for the listener: Does what you preach to me work for me, in my body, in my particular immediate now? While throughout Christian history the material witness of women was a critical component of their religious practice, in the twentieth century such testimony seemed to become the *only* expectation for their Christian identity. In an increasingly decentralized landscape in which technologies format social communities, articulating your embodiment is the way you make yourself palpable before the unseen mediated masses. Contemporary social media not only give the Christian greater control over the mediation of her witness, but also demand that she names it, since her witness is not seen or felt without mediation via both words and images. The unlimited witness of the virtual world does not resolve the question of women's viability as religious authority, nor does it assist her effort to navigate the uncertain line between reverent witness and shameless self-promoter. Rather, the centrifugal spin of social media propounds such problems, offering further opportunity for community scrutiny and adjudication.

Social media have become an increasingly popular mode of Christian testimony, providing a fertile platform for a genre of witness that is at once virtual and rooted in material bodies. Blogging, one of the earlier forms of social media still popular with many Christian women, is a form of mediation that operates with an "ethos of immediacy," in the words of anthropologist Adam Reed. The virtual diary of the blog prompts both a solidification and a scattering of the witnessing self, in which bloggers strive for a more lively and fluid witness in which the "blogging subject remains sovereign," yet is simultaneously a "work in progress" (Reed 2005). For North American evangelicals in particular, the fluid medium of blogging has heightened dilemmas of what counts as "authentic" Christian spirituality. As anthropologist James Bielo has argued, evangelicals hope to make use of the dynamic proliferation of the blog as a tool for witness, while still being able to enact "the spiritual discipline of discerning truth from error" (Bielo 2009). A regular, if not daily, witness networked to an anonymous public, social media are at once heralded by evangelical Christians in particular as powerful tools to share one's testimony with a potentially massive, global audience, while also suspected as the means for self-aggrandizement and even heresy.

Visiting evangelical Christian Ann Voskamp's blog, "A Holy Experience," we can see how even the virtual witness accounts – both willingly and with coercion – for the materiality of her piety and its production. Voskamp, a reformed Christian from Aimee Semple McPherson's part of southern Ontario, is one of the more established of home-schooling Christian mom bloggers, and has a very active multi-media presence. She has written for the evangelical magazine *Christianity Today*, appeared on television shows such as *100 Huntley Street* and published a devotional book with evangelical publishing house Zondervan. Defining herself primarily as a Christian wife to "the Farmer" and home-schooling mother of six children, beset by a never-ending pile of laundry while charmed by the beauty of nature and her offspring, Voskamp's blog curates a twenty-first-century aesthetic of the "simple life" through professional-quality photo diaries and spare but elegant pages (Voskamp 2011).

Her prose attempts to be at once downhome, intimate and mystical, as her cheery welcome conveys: "Hi! I like you already! Yeah … wondrous, amazing you, just looking around for Deep Peace and True Beauty. I get it. Me too – hunting for a corner of joy and grace and God … and stillness" (Voskamp 2011). At the same time, Voskamp makes clear that her blogged testimony is rooted in a theology of the singular "Word":

> **I believe** in the infallibility of the Bible, God's Word – a sure Word, a pure Word, the only secure Word. I believe the words on those pages are breathed from the very throne room of heaven, are the love letter penned from the heart of the Lover of our souls … . **I believe** there is *more* than believing. There is *living* what I believe. Thus this journal.
>
> (Voskamp 2011; emphasis in the original)

Despite the security of the Word, and her insistence that believing is vouchsafed by a detailed accounting of her daily life, Voskamp remains plagued by worries that her blog-as-witness may be too self-referential and not sufficiently kenotic. Her blogger's prayer – offered via a "Free Gift for You" pop-up window – aims to counter such worries, with supplications such as: "Let me not desire hits but holiness. Let me be a follower, instead of seeking followers. Let my blog be full of Thee, and let it be empty of me" (Voskamp 2011). Attempting to tame the anxiety of hubris with a blogged prayer crystallizes the dilemma of the material witness; beseeching God to be both author and audience in front of an online community accentuates the tension between self-promotion and sacrificial proselytization.

For Voskamp, her blog was a first step to an ever-wider self-mediation as a Christian home-schooling mom who has moved from trauma to triumph, while remaining "a mess" surrounded by God's grace (Voskamp, March 20, 2011). Not unlike the widespread criticisms of the ministries of Mary Baker Eddy or Aimee Semple McPherson, Voskamp's gift of material witness, rooted as it is in intimate meditations on her piety and her motherhood, has not always been received with gratitude. Some evangelical, Reformed critics charge her with a heretically and overly emotional incarnational mysticism, while other skeptical critics declare her to be a "stealth-fundie" who hides her conservative Christian message with pictures of her garden and flowery, perhaps overwrought, language (Jules 2011; Wintermute 2011). More sympathetic readers, such as a Catholic scientist and mother of five with her own blog, credited Voskamp with forcing her to deal with "hard truths" and testified to the embodied, emotional effects of reading Voskamp's book and blog (Jamie 2011). The virtual call and response of Christian blogging has made a new kind of space for theological reflection and debate that blends creedal commitments with the intimate details of personal lives and their embodied memories. At the same time, the webs of comments – both harsh and sympathetic – provoked by Voskamp's multiple mediations of her testimony also demonstrate how social media have facilitated a crossing of creedal lines, as Catholics, evangelicals, liberals and skeptics read and comment on each others' posts. The harsh words that remain online offer hyperlinked testimony to the fragile authority of a woman intent on melding motherhood, sensuality and piety in a material, yet virtual Christian witness.

Blogs and other social media enable the piling up of personal testimony in a site that is at once virtual but also traceable. When women turn to blogs as technologies of witness, they participate in what Mia Lövheim has called "ethical spaces," in which they craft and elicit testimonies via a threefold strategy of inviting the personal confessions of their audiences, encouraging strong declarations of one's views and eliciting narratives of personal experience (Lövheim 2011). The ethical spaces of women's blogging, however, are inherently unstable, both because the materiality (whether in terms of race, gender or body size) of the online self is always in doubt, and because the authority of a blogger – even one who draws on the most personal of evidences – is always open to question and critique. Virtual as they are, social media nevertheless remain haunted by the material witness at the site of their production.

Conclusion

For Christian women it does not go far enough to say merely that the medium is the message – the matter of her body always haunts her words, staining their clarity and whatever channel transports them. Making a commodity of one's testimony with the purported end of spreading God's word is not a new transformation of witness in the history of Christianity. Over and over, testifying women have found ways to extend their particular knowledge into the marketplace of spirit. Social media merely renew the anxieties and conflicts of testimonial transmission. The online commodification of the self in the name of Christian witness takes the paradox of Christian testimony to a new level of tension, in which the ends of testimony and commerce are entwined in such a way that the literal value of a material witness is put in question. While a self-publishing, socially mediated Christian woman might destabilize church hierarchies by turning her computer into her pulpit, she is still subject to the judgment of theological orthodoxies. Indeed, if social media produce anything for certain it is an expanded field of judgment, since anyone – regardless of clerical authority – may cry "heretic!"

Christian women have used specific media – newspapers, books, television shows and websites – as channels to offer their testimony and cultivate their authority as worthy of testimony. The clarion call of the Christian prophetess of redemption, gratitude or consumption may be mediated far and wide through an increasing diversity of channels, but her witness to the spirit remains embedded in both her materiality and in the Christian textual traditions that continue to provide fodder for debates about what such matter can or cannot say. The question for subsequent researchers is the particular status of *Christianity* in these gendered mediations. As individuals take to the various airwaves at their disposal, how will they represent the authority of their abstracted religious identity (Christian, Muslim, Jew) as they seek to instantiate their own particular voices as worthy of a hearing? Is the history of Christianity – so tied to the determination of divine embodiment – especially articulated via claims of materialization (see Peters 2001)? How do the categories of race and gender shape such materialized witnesses? Beyond a focus on Christianity, research in religion, gender and media can profitably make use of the notion of a material witness by situating any "religious" testimony in multiple contexts: the material, embodied, conditions of its production and its producer; the semiotic ideologies of the particular religious tradition or traditions within which the testimony is framed; and the unpredictable spirals of its reception and influence.

Talking about the Christian body has always been easier to do than talking about the gendered body in Christianity. As forms of mediation continue to expand the forums for such talk, it seems likely that opportunities for women to claim authority will increase, while any such claims will be ever more diffused and contested. Whether writing as mothers, lovers, prophets or celebrities, women's self-mediations never have entirely predictable effects. Making material the witnesses of their Christian experiences via a range of media that distance their words from their bodies, women both deploy and dissolve the very tropes of femininity that help to constitute them, in effect, as women.

Notes

1 See Apphia in Philemon 2; Prisca in I Corinthians 16:19.
2 Virginia Burrus, personal communication, May 8, 2012.
3 For a more tempered view of women's role in the Salvation Army, see Eason 2003.
4 This discussion of female preachers from the early twentieth century derives from Lofton 2011: 134–137.
5 This section relies on the arguments of Lofton in Lofton 2011.
6 For a full accounting of Winfrey's weight loss journey, see Howard 2007.

Bibliography

Bendroth, M.L. and Brereton, V.L. (2002) *Women and Twentieth-Century Protestantism*, Urbana: University of Illinois Press.
Bielo, J. (2009) "Why Blogs Matter Among Emerging Evangelicals," Paper presented at the American Anthropological Association Annual Meetings, November, Philadelphia.
Brekus, C.A. (1998) *Strangers and Pilgrims: Female Preaching in America, 1740–1845*, Chapel Hill: University of North Carolina Press.

Brown, C.G. (2004) *The Word in the World: Evangelical Writing, Publishing, and Reading in America, 1789–1880*, Chapel Hill: University of North Carolina Press.

Burrus, V. (2007) *The Sex Lives of Saints: An Erotics of Ancient Hagiography*, Philadelphia: University of Pennsylvania Press.

Butler, J. (2003) *Bodies That Matter: On the Discursive Limits of "Sex,"* New York: Routledge.

Bynum, C.W. (1987) *Holy Feast and Holy Fast: The Religious Significance of Food to Medieval Women*, Berkeley: University of California Press.

Cooper, K. (1999) *The Virgin and the Bride: Idealized Womanhood in Late Antiquity*, Cambridge: Harvard University Press.

Eason, A.M. (2003) *Women in God's Army: Gender and Equality in the Early Salvation Army*, Waterloo: Wilfrid Laurier University Press.

Elliott, D. (2004) *Proving Woman: Female Spirituality and Inquisitional Culture in the Later Middle Ages*, Princeton: Princeton University Press.

——(2011) *The Bride of Christ Goes to Hell: Metaphor and Embodiment in the Lives of Pious Women, 200–1500*, Philadelphia: University of Pennsylvania Press.

Gill, G. (1999) *Mary Baker Eddy*, Boston: Da Capo Press.

Givhan, R. (2008) "We Share Your Loss, And Your Gain," *The Washington Post*, Online, available at: www.washingtonpost.com/wp-dyn/content/article/2008/12/12/AR2008121200907_pf.html (accessed May 11, 2012).

Griffith, R.M. (2004) *Born Again Bodies: Flesh and Spirit in American Christianity*, Berkeley: University of California Press.

Gutjahr, P.C. (2001) "The State of the Discipline: Sacred Texts in the United States," *Book History*, 4(1), 335–370.

Herrin, J. (2004) *Women in Purple: Rulers of Medieval Byzantium*, Princeton: Princeton University Press.

Howard, E. (2007) "From Fasting toward Self-Acceptance: Oprah Winfrey and Weight Loss in American Culture," in *The Oprah Phenomenon*, Lexington: The University Press of Kentucky, 101–123.

Jamie (March 6, 2011) "Penetrated" *Light and Momentary*, available at: www.mostgladly.net/cj/2011/03/penetrated.html (accessed July 7, 2011).

Jules (2011) *Just Jules*, http://justjules.me/?p=3459 (accessed July 7, 2011; no longer available at this address).

Keane, W. (2007) *Christian Moderns: Freedom and Fetish in the Mission Encounter*, Berkeley: University of California Press.

Klassen, P.E. (2001) *Blessed Events: Religion and Home Birth in America*, Princeton: Princeton University Press.

——(2004) "The Robes of Womanhood: Dress and Authenticity among African American Methodist Women in the Nineteenth Century," *Religion and American Culture*, 14(1), 39–82.

——(2006) "Textual Healing: Mainstream Protestants and the Therapeutic Text, 1900–1925," *Church History: Studies in Christianity and Culture*, 75(04), 809–848.

Lawless, E.J. (1993) "Not so Different a Story After All: Pentecostal Women in the Pulpit," in C. Wessinger (ed.) *Women's Leadership in Marginal Religions: Explorations Outside the Mainstream*, Urbana: University of Illinois Press, 41–54.

Lewis, M.H. (1989) *Mary Lena Lewis Tate – A Street Called Straight: The Ten Most Dynamic and Productive Black Female Holiness Preachers of the Twentieth Century*, Tuskegee: New and Living Way Pub.

Lofton, K. (2008) "Public Confessions: Oprah Winfrey's American Religious History," *Women and Performance: A Journal of Feminist Theory*, 18(1), 51–69.

——(2011) *Oprah: The Gospel of an Icon*, Berkeley: University of California Press.

Lövheim, M. (2011) "Young Women's Blogs as Ethical Spaces," *Information, Communication and Society*, 14(3), 338–354.

Morgan, D. (1999) *Protestants and Pictures: Religion, Visual Culture and the Age of American Mass Production*, New York: Oxford University Press.

Orsi, R.A. (1998) *Thank You, St. Jude: Women's Devotion to the Patron Saint of Hopeless Causes*, New Haven: Yale University Press.

Osiek, C., MacDonald, M.Y. and Tulloch, J.H. (2006) *A Woman's Place: House Churches In Earliest Christianity*, Kitchener: Fortress Press.

Peters, C. (2009) *Patterns of Piety: Women, Gender and Religion in Late Medieval and Reformation England*, Cambridge: Cambridge University Press.

Peters, J.D. (2001) *Speaking Into the Air: A History of the Idea of Communication*, Chicago: University of Chicago Press.

Reed, A. (2005) "'My Blog is Me': Texts and Persons in UK Online Journal Culture (and Anthropology)," *Ethnos*, 70(2), 220–242.

Schmidt, L.E. (2000) *Hearing Things: Religion, Illusion, and the American Enlightenment*, Cambridge: Harvard University Press.

Schoepflin, R.B. (2003) *Christian Science on Trial: Religious Healing in America*, Baltimore: Johns Hopkins University Press.

Sutton, M.A. (2007) *Aimee Semple McPherson and the Resurrection of Christian America*, Cambridge: Harvard University Press.

Tate, M.M.L. (2003) *Mary Lena Lewis Tate: Collected Letters and Manuscripts*, Tuskegee: New and Living Way Publishing Company.

Torjesen, K.J. (1995) *When Women Were Priests: Women's Leadership in the Early Church and the Scandal of Their Subordination in the Rise of Christianity*, San Francisco: Harper San Francisco.

Voskamp A. (2011) *A Holy Experience*, available at: www.aholyexperience.com/ann-voskamp/ (accessed July 7, 2011).

——(March 20, 2011) "Having an Attitude of Gratitude,: Interview on *100 Huntley Street*, available at: www.100huntley.com/video.php?id=375qXCyh8Po (accessed July 7, 2011).

Winston, D. (2000) *Red-Hot and Righteous: The Urban Religion of The Salvation Army*, Cambridge: Harvard University Press.

——(2002) "All the World's a Stage: The Performed Religion of the Salvation Army, 1880–1920," in L.S. Clark and S.M. Hoover (eds) *Practicing Religion in the Age of the Media: Explorations in Media, Religion, and Culture*. New York: Columbia University Press, 113–137.

Wintermute (April 2011) on *Free Jinger: A Quiver Full of Snark*, available at: http://freejinger.yuku.com/topic/6663/Ann-Voskamp-stealth-fundie#.ThdAP-Ax2RY (accessed July 7, 2011).

Chapter 5

Occupying pews, missing in news

Women, religion and journalism

Joyce Smith

The tiered lecture room was packed with journalists at all points in the lifecycle: students, early professionals and those who had plied the trade for decades. All day long, classrooms at Ryerson University's journalism school had housed discussions of how to be a woman and a journalist. How to have both a career and a healthy personal life, how to strive for equality in the newsroom, and now, late in the afternoon, how to be a foreign correspondent.

Coming just over five weeks after the 11 February 2011 attack on CBS reporter Lara Logan in Tahrir Square, Cairo, it wasn't surprising that this panel was particularly well attended. Moderated by Gillian Findley (once the American Broadcasting Corporation's Middle East correspondent), the panel featured security reporter Michelle Shephard of *The Toronto Star*, foreign affairs reporter Sonia Verma of *The Globe and Mail* and Kathryn Blaze Carlson of *The National Post*.

Like most North American journalism schools, Ryerson's study body is at least 75 per cent female, so the "Women in the Field" conference was an inspiring event. But the assault on Logan had cast a pall on what is considered a glamorous assignment: covering conflict from overseas. Many of the panelists had found themselves in situations where they were at physical risk. But all agreed that most women are loath to discuss dicey experiences for fear that they will stop being assigned to such stories.

There was also a frank discussion of what it meant to be a mother in such situations, in response to a column by *The Toronto Sun*'s Peter Worthington, who on 18 February 2011 asked: "Should women journalists with small children at home, be covering violent stories or putting themselves at risk?" His answer: "It's a form of self-indulgence and abdication of a higher responsibility to family" (Worthington 2011). Single, childless women could go, he wrote, but not those with small children. "A double-standard, perhaps, with men, but that's the way it is. Or should be." Mothers or not, the panelists rejected this double standard.

What went unmentioned in Worthington's column, and among the panel, was the Islamic backdrop to the Arab Spring reporting prompting this debate. Following the attack on Logan, some suggested her appearance as a blonde woman contributed to her vulnerability in a crowd where many dark-haired Egyptian women were also covered, and indeed, a woman in chador rescued her from further attack.

This lack of discussion about religious elements was a contrast to the blunt comments provided by Carole Jerome (once a CBC reporter), during a speech given two decades earlier at the University of Western Ontario, home to another Canadian journalism school. She began by describing her feelings at having to veil while covering the 1979 Iranian revolution:

> being a woman created certain obvious problems for a reporter, being immediately on a lower footing (how could you be equal with someone when you are wearing a rag on your head) and literally, out of some of the action.
> (Jerome 1990: 105)

It's difficult to imagine her description of a veil as a rag going without critique today in a Canada where many citizens choose to cover their heads. Veiling was not a topic which surfaced at the 2011 panel discussion; there were a number of veiled heads in the audience, however, belonging to journalists.

Jerome had made a point of saying, "I have never felt threatened in these places *as a woman*. I have often *felt* threatened as a reporter, and I have *been* threatened as a reporter, but I do not think it was because I was a woman" (Jerome 1990: 108; her emphases). At the time of her speech in 1989, Jerome noted that no woman journalist had been attacked while working in an Islamic country. She may well have been right, but given the revelations by female reporters following the Logan attack, there's a real possibility that assaults were taking place.

Whether or not violence is present, the subjects of religion (particularly Islam), women and reporting get mashed together more often than one might imagine. In responding to Canadian immigration minister Jason Kenney's decision in December 2011 to withhold citizenship from anyone veiling their faces during citizenship ceremonies, *The Toronto Star*'s Thomas Walkom strung together the concepts of sexual equality in terms of religion, journalism and everyday life, arguing that "sexual equality is a hard-won, if not always practised, Canadian value," to which veiling stands as "a kind of insult – a reminder of the 1950s, when wives could not obtain bank loans without their husbands' signatures, when women were expected to stay at home and when those who did work outside the house were routinely paid less than men." Walkom went on to draw on his own experience in a newsroom, remembering that when he began his career, his female peers were "routinely relegated to what were then called the women's pages." In true, Canadian diplomatic style, he does write that he has met "articulate, accomplished – and tough-minded – women who choose to wear the niqab. Nor is Islam the only religion in which some (not all) practitioners argue that women should be subservient to men" (Walkom 2011).

This chapter will consider the way in which women, journalism and religion connect and collide, and what the results suggest about the relationships between them. First I will discuss some matters with respect to the representation of women in news reporting, followed by a consideration of women journalists. Finally, drawing on the history of beat reporting, I will propose some ways in which the representation of religion has changed before concluding with suggestions for continuing research.

At the outset, I acknowledge my concentration here on Canadian mainstream news outlets. In many ways, Canadian journalism occupies a middle ground between the English-language traditions of the United Kingdom and United States, so it serves as a good source of examples for discussion.

I note that there is a rich history with respect to women's magazines, which I will not include here. And as Jan Whitt points out in *Women in American Journalism*, many women have sought alternatives to mainstream news for their reporting (Whitt 2008). However, in order to concentrate on the way in which women both produce and are reflected in reporting about religion, I have decided not to pursue these alternatives.

Representations of women

Judith Buddenbaum and Debra Mason trace the beginnings of modern religion reporting in the United States to James Gordon Bennett, a former Catholic seminarian and Scottish immigrant who founded the *New York Herald* in 1835 (Buddenbaum and Mason 2000: 89). They point to his shift in moving reporting from "religious journalism" to "religion journalism," his newspaper's investigative reporting about religion as well as the creation of what would become the church page, a section set aside for news about religious communities.

At this beginning, a sensational story about a veiled woman was among Bennett's most popular articles. But in the early 1800s, it was Roman Catholics, not Muslims, who occupied the headgear limelight. Excerpts from *The Awful Disclosures by Maria Monk*, a book published in 1836 that recounted sexual abuse by priests in Montreal, were printed in the *Herald*. The author was a woman who claimed to have been a nun, but who, most historians now agree, was manipulated by ghostwriters into creating a book which would appeal to the worst anti-Catholic sentiments present in the United States of the time. Upon taking vows, Maria is told that among her duties will be the sexual servicing of local priests. And she discovers that any babies resulting from these activities will be baptized before being thrown into a lime-filled pit.

The Maria Monk stories illustrate the explosive mix of sex, faith and crime which fuels much sensational reporting on religion. And although historians have debunked the lurid tales of Monk, it is hard not to be reminded of more recent proven sexual abuse and crime. The current investigation into the trafficking of babies (*niños robados* or stolen children) in Spain between the 1950s and 1980s has included religious orders of women accused of facilitating the kidnappings (Junquera 2012). Post-delivery, mothers were told their babies had died, when in fact they were given to parents deemed more suitable. Sr. María Gómez Valbuena, at 87 and part of the community of the Sisters of Charity, was the first person to be indicted by Spanish courts for the thefts. In Canada, in addition to scandals over abuse of aboriginal children in religious residential schools, a recent investigation by *The National Post* has the United Church of Canada, Salvation Army and Presbyterian Church reviewing their records of maternity homes where forced adoptions may have taken place (Blaze Carlson 2012). Australian and Irish religious communities have undergone parallel scrutiny.

In this century, the physical outcomes of heterosexual sex – sometimes, but not always outside of wedlock – have lost much of their power to scandalize. Instead, the sensational, newsworthy aspects are courtesy of the religious institutions and people involved in covering up such "sins." In what he describes as the "age-old topos of fallen maidenhood," Mark Silk notes that "where once religion might have been proffered as the means for averting the tragedy" of teenage pregnancy, "now it is professional medical help" (Silk 1995: 51). Where once a combination of religion and sex would result in silence, today it is far more likely to produce publicity.

In the Spanish reporting, it is remarkable to see how far the journalistic pendulum has swung. Where once the mothers of the stolen children would have been condemned for behaviour ranging from prostitution, having sex outside of marriage, to being anti-Franco, they are now heroines. Their search for their children, adopted without proper identifying information, provides a source of compelling stories. The religious sisters who once would have been elevated not only for their personal chastity, but also for their commitment to ensuring the welfare of infants, are now depicted as antediluvian witches. What hasn't changed is the emphasis on the women in these situations; despite male doctors and priests being involved at the highest levels and men both losing and gaining children through illicit adoptions, the stories center on the women.

Forced adoption/baby trafficking stories provide an example of coverage where women, religion and reporting intersect on the front page. But what happens on an average news day?

It's a more difficult question to answer than might be immediately obvious. Because of the cyclic nature of much religion reporting, and its prevalence in international conflict reporting, it can be argued that there is no such thing as an "average" day. But the Global Media Monitoring Project most recently chose 10 November 2009 to track the presence of women in Canadian daily newspapers, television and radio newscasts, and online news sites. The monitors noted 279 stories and 695 people as subjects. Unfortunately, religion does not appear among the categories used, which were: crime and violence; politics and government; celebrity, arts and media, sports; economy; science and health; social and legal; and "other." In my research of the same news outlets in the late 1990s and again in the mid-2000s, religion often appears intertwined with these categories.

However, the GMMP findings suggest some baselines. The monitors found that men were three times more likely to be found in stories about politics and government or celebrity/arts/sports stories. When women did appear, they were most often (35–36 per cent of the time) offering some kind of personal opinion, as opposed to the 27–29 per cent of occasions where the story was about them or they served as expert sources. Females were more likely to be identified as homemakers/parents (58 per cent of all such subjects), children/young people (56 per cent) or "non-managerial office worker" (59 per cent). Religious leaders were noted twice on the monitoring day, and both were men (Global Media Monitoring Project 2010: 12).

The Project noted that women are under-represented in all media, but are most likely to appear on television, where they accounted for 38 per cent of all news subjects. The nature of coverage of women and of religion presents a double whammy. If, as many media analysts have found, women are disproportionately covered using visuals (Gill 2007: 115–116), and religion is for the most part a subject not easily given to visual journalism, then it comes as no surprise that there are fewer stories in which women appear. Or that when they do appear, it is often visually.

Much has been written about the use of photos of women wearing veils or burkas as little more than a visual shorthand for Islam (see Klaus and Kassel 2005). This is indeed a journalistic tool to cut quickly to the identification of a theme. But such shorthand can quickly devolve into stereotype.

But there are opportunities as well; consider the winning World Press Photo for 2012. While freelancing for *The New York Times*, Spanish photojournalist Samuel Aranda captured Fatima al-Qaws cradling her 18-year-old son as he suffered the after-effects of teargas following an October 2011 street protest in Sanaa, Yemen. The image is striking for the contrast between the woman, whose face is not seen as she wears a black chador and white gloves, and her son's pale flesh (his face is also obscured, as his head rests on his mother's shoulder, turned away from the photographer). But its composition also strikes a chord due to its similarity to Christian "pietàs" of Mary (also veiled) cradling Jesus after he has been taken down dead from the cross. In the description of the photograph on the World Press Photo site, we learn that "Ms Qaws – who was herself involved in resistance to the regime – found her son after a second visit to look for him, among the wounded at a mosque that was being used as a temporary field hospital. Zayed remained in a coma for two days after the incident" (World Press Photo 2012).

One possible result of this much-publicized, photographic pietà is the ability to imagine the suffering of a Muslim mother and son as analogous to the suffering of the key Christian mother and son dyad. In a 19 April 2012 interview, Aranda said:

> I think this photograph is a little bit different because it shows a really intimate moment with a mother taking care of her son. I think for people

here in our culture, in the Western countries, it is not easy for us to get connected with these kind[s] of feelings. It is [easier] to see a guy with a Kalashnikov in the desert, shooting.

(World Press Photo 2012)

A further challenge to the inclusion of women is their under-representation in the leadership structures of most organized religions. In any reporting, journalists seek the "official" point of view. This is relatively simple to do with mainline Christian and Jewish communities, where well-defined and publicized organizational structures exist. In most cases, these easily found leaders are also men. Ease of access to recognized officials is critical for reporters who may not have much knowledge of the issues in question, and who try to get a story right by including the "right" sources. This reliance on hierarchical sources falls short when at least one of two things happens: the religious organization is not set up along traditional hierarchical lines, and when the vast majority of the community – those in the pews or facing the bimah – go unheard.

Decisions about who to include in a story rest with individual reporters, editors, producers, photojournalists and videographers. At this point it makes sense to turn our attention to what we know about women who occupy these roles, and to examine if their journalism is in any way different from that of men.

Women as reporters

Before trying to understand the relationship between women and the journalism they produce, it is instructive to consider what we know of these women as a group. Here I turn to my own surveys of journalists and those conducted by my colleagues. Following, I will consider what we know about religion and reporting from individual women.

In their study of television news directors (journalists occupying decision-making levels), Marsha Barber and Ann Rauhala found that

> the average news director is a White male who is educated and comfortably middle class. He tends to be more secular in outlook than the average Canadian, more politically active, and more active in his community. His voting patterns mirror those found in the general population.
>
> (Barber and Rauhala 2005: 286)

While in the 2000s there were more women working in newsrooms than before, in the TV directors study, they were still the minority: only 20.9 per cent. Barber and Rauhala found that 38.8 per cent were Protestant, 20.9 per cent Catholic, and 23.9 per cent professed no religious affiliation (the rest named another tradition or didn't answer). Interestingly, only 38.5 per cent of women indicated they attended places of worship more than once a year, compared with 54.7 per cent of men (Barber and Rauhala 2005: 287). The General Social

Survey (GSS) of 2005 placed the number of Canadians who attended at least once a year at 67.2 per cent, down from 73.9 per cent in 2000 (Lindsay 2008).

The difference in female attendance is particularly noteworthy given research which has shown women to be more frequent attenders. David Eagle has found, using 2008 GSS data, that among those who indicate weekly attendance,

> women are more likely to attend religious services, as are those with post-secondary education, who are married, have children at home, and were born outside of Canada. For monthly attenders, the correlates are similar as for weekly attenders; for yearly attenders there is very little variation.
>
> (Eagle 2011: 198)

Following a year-long content analysis of Canadian news outlets, I sent out an invitation to 473 journalists who had at least one piece of reporting with a religious aspect appear during 2006–2007. It wasn't until later that I realized the gender inequities. Among those invited to participate in the survey, only 39 per cent were women. When it came to responding to the survey, even fewer women provided information: 26.4 per cent of respondents were women and 73.6 per cent were men.

Of those women who responded, 45.8 per cent identified themselves as broadcasters, 36 percent as newspaper reporters. Only 14 per cent were born outside of Canada, and the same percentage was under the age of 35. The majority was between 35 and 54 years of age, all had at least some post-secondary education, and all but 14 per cent were earning $100,000 or more a year.

Almost 29 per cent identified themselves as agnostic, with one respondent describing herself as an atheist. Protestants were present at 36 per cent, with Buddhist, Jew, Christian (other than Protestant), and Catholic each having 7 per cent representation. These figures (with the exception of the Catholics) are roughly in line with the Barber/Rauhala findings.

In addition to the quantifiable information, each participant was given the opportunity to respond to some open-ended questions. When asked about the way in which religion is covered, responses ranged from "much too respectfully" to "often with suspicion and misunderstanding."

> "the (...) media tends to stay away from the faith of our elected officials for the most part. This is our failing. (...) The Canadian public deserves to know exactly what our elected officials believe in and how it has influenced their decisions."
>
> "I find it very offensive when journalists write about religion as though everyone believed in it."

When asked to identify top-of-mind stories involving religion, the female participants mentioned coverage of the federal "Harper" Conservative party and gay marriage, as well as stories involving Islam, including the veiling of Canadian women. But international stories were in the majority: the Dalai Lama's visit to Canada, the Pope's visit to England, the prayerful thanksgiving following the rescue of Chilean miners, terrorism and war in the Middle East and an American preacher's threat to burn the Koran were mentioned.

My research has found that international sources dominate Canadian news about religion. This creates the potential for religion to be viewed as something which only (or primarily) exists "over there" rather than domestically. The presence of Muslims in Canada has certainly grown since 1989 when Jerome spoke about Islam as if it only existed outside of the country, but despite the jump from 0.9 per cent of the population self-identifying as Muslim in 1991 to 2 per cent in 2001, reporting tends to lean toward foreign affairs.

The Global Media Monitoring Project found in 2010 that in Canada women were slightly more likely to be quoted in stories that were national in scope (32 per cent) rather than local (29 per cent) or international (28 per cent) (Global Media Monitoring Project 2010: 10). As with the problems of women and religion being depicted visually, the fact of religion appearing mainly in foreign reporting, an area where women are less likely to feature, suggests another reason for under-representation.

The survey responses from women were not significantly dissimilar from their male colleagues, which is not surprising to those who push against the idea that gender differences alone result in reporting differences. In summarizing research, Rosalind Gill (2007: 126) notes only two qualities which seem to differ: women are more interested in the needs of their audiences, and female reporters tend to look for more female sources to include in their reporting.

These observations are supported by the Global Media Monitoring Project, which found that while only 8.8 per cent of all Canadian news stories had women as a central focus, those which "concerned" women were more likely (60 per cent of the time) to be covered by female reporters (Global Media Monitoring Project 2010: 5). The Project also found that reporting on the topics they considered dominant (crime and violence, and politics and government) was done predominantly by men.

In this context, do female reporters today consider religious issues to be of concern to women? This may be key to understanding future coverage decisions. Carole Jerome suggested that the sensibilities of female journalists may act as a bellwether:

> repression of women is usually the first indication of an Islamic fundamentalist movement – watch for it if you are a reporter. Being more sensitive to that, perhaps, I talked about the growing power of the Iranian-backed Hezballah in South Lebanon, and my male colleagues poo-pooed me as paranoid.
>
> (Jerome 1990: 108)

Historically, before women outnumbered men in journalism schools, religious institutions were important in the formation of women journalists. Whitt and other historians note this particularly with respect to African American women who approached journalism as a calling, prompted by a sense of religious mission (Whitt 2008). Anecdotally, in reviewing applications to the undergraduate program where I teach, I see similar expressions by young Muslim women.

A number of important women have straddled both worlds of journalism and religion: Mary Baker Eddy (founder of the *Christian Science Monitor* in 1908) and Dorothy Day (co-founder of the *Catholic Worker* in 1933) are but two examples (see Klassen and Lofton, this volume). Baker Eddy wanted to cut down on crime reporting and sensationalism in news reporting, and emphasize international events, an area of reporting for which the *Monitor* continues to be recognized (Whitt 2008: 18–19).

While in Canada there are few journalists of either sex specializing in religion reporting, internationally there are a number of high-profile female religion reporters in the English-language press. South of the Canadian border are Laurie Goodstein (now of *The New York Times*), Michelle Bearden in Tampa, Peggy Wehmeyer, who did a seven-year stint as religion reporter on ABC News, and Diane Winston, who between 1983 and 1995 covered religion at a number of top papers.

But for Canadian news outlets, there are few such names. This doesn't mean women are not including religion in their reporting: I did find 184 female bylines in a year of Canadian journalism. However, these women and their contributions aren't always found in traditional spaces.

To wit: *The Globe and Mail* added Zarqa Nawaz to their "Group Therapy" roster, where well-known Canadians offered advice alongside reader input. Nawaz is best known for creating *Little Mosque on the Prairie*, a sitcom that ran for six seasons on the CBC, and was syndicated in regions as diverse as Finland, France, Turkey and the West Bank. She weighed in on the most Canadian of topics ("Our new cottage neighbours drop in too much") and handled less than traditional relationship issues.[1] Her responses – appearing below a smiling headshot of her in her veil – have provided something other than the stereotypical repressed Muslim woman. In response to a letter from a twenty-something woman looking for a man who would "fight for her," Nawaz wrote that:

> finding a future spouse is not in the same category as ordering extra croutons on your salad. Here's what I tell my daughters: Strategize about finding a life partner the same way you'd strategize about finding the right career. Both are important to a woman's future happiness, so why be pro-active with one and lie around like a beached, romantically sick whale with the other? (…) My sister-in-law spied a handsome fellow counsellor while volunteering at Muslim camp. After getting to know him and learning that he had the qualities she valued – she proposed. She's now happily married with four kids. In the 21st century, self-respecting, modern women can make the first move. So get cracking. You don't want

to wake up one morning and wonder where all the good men have gone. Possible answer: They're married to women who were willing to fight for themselves.

(Nawaz 2012)

A high-profile Muslim serving in a role traditionally described as an "agony aunt" provides a good segue way for discussing the traditional and evolving place for news involving women and religion.

Religion and women's pages: beats or beaten?

So much of the discussion around the reporting of religion and the reporting of and by women revolves around the beat. "Beats" give specialized attention to certain kinds of news, and traditionally include crime, foreign reporting, health and science, business and sports reporting. When a journalist is assigned a beat, they are guaranteed time to build a level of expertise which outstrips that of a general assignment reporter.

Being a beat reporter (along with being posted to a bureau) is a mark of success but a pecking order exists. For many years – at least in Canada – being a religion reporter meant occupying a rung at the lower end of the ladder, almost on par with reporting for the women's pages. In newspapers, the church and women's pages were kept far from the front section, often appearing only in weekend editions. Physically and psychologically, journalists given these tasks had their work ghettoized and taken less seriously than the reporting of other beats.

Women's pages were meant to attract female readers, and female journalists were assigned to cover stories which would accomplish this. Today, this attention to the needs of the audience is one of the few aspects that Gill and others have suggested differentiates men from women in their reporting. However, the segregation of what would interest women to a few pages away from the rest of the news (which must, therefore, be for men) couldn't but be interpreted as a lesser form of journalism.

During World War II, women had stepped into reporting positions once held by male colleagues, but following the war, they were expected to return to their previous posts. Maureen Beasley and Sheila Gibbons include the text of a speech given by the dean of Columbia University's School of Journalism in 1949 to members of the Seminar on Women's Pages of the American Press Institute. Carl Ackerman compared the daily newspaper to a home:

> The front pages of newspapers are filled each day with stories of crises, disaster, tragedies (...) But the inside of a newspaper is like the inside of a home. There are tragedies, unhappiness and strife in many homes, but in the overwhelming majority of homes there is a wholesome quest for

improvement; there is more happiness than sorrow; more love than hate. The spiritual strength of a nation is safeguarded in the home. In writing about health, schools, the church, food, child care, home living and other similar subjects women as journalists contribute to the uplifting of our national life. There is as much wholesomeness in the inside of a newspaper as there is in the inside of a home. The newspapers are indebted to women as journalists for this development.

(Beasley and Gibbons 1993: 177–178)

He went on to note that women would have to take the lead in improving working relationships in the newsroom, since "as every wife knows, men are set in their ways." He concluded by saying the challenges ahead of these women surpassed their achievements.

As you improve the inside of the daily newspaper you also contribute to the improvement of the inside of the home which is more important to the progress of civilization than any other social institution. Strive, therefore, always to make the inside of the newspaper resemble the inside of our homes.

(Beasley and Gibbons 1993: 177–178)

It's worth noting that Ackerman put "the church" firmly inside the home.

This message provides a very good sense of why feminists like Betty Friedan and Gloria Steinem, no strangers to journalism, were unwilling to have their positions reported on the women's pages rather than on the front page (Whitt 2008: 43–45). Ironically, as women's pages folded, many experienced female journalists were demoted. Whitt suggests that even women historians have slighted those who produced women's pages, as they "are perceived to have reified the status quo by celebrating the woman as wife, mother, and homemaker" (Whitt 2008: 2).

Women's pages – at least in name – are today few and far between. But the link between beats and gender is not. A survey of female newspaper journalists in the United States conducted between 1993 and 1995 discovered that more than a quarter thought they had been "denied a desirable assignment at least once because they were women" (Walsh-Childers, Chance and Herzog 1996: 75). A number of women thought story and beat assignments were also based on gender: "hard news goes to men, light stuff to women" (Walsh-Childers, Chance and Herzog 1996: 81).

"Hard" and "soft" are used to denote types of content as well as styles of reporting. A hard news story would be written in a straightforward manner, often in the most economical of styles, and would concentrate on something immediate and/or having serious consequences. A simple example would be a short report describing a highway accident killing a family. Soft news is not as immediate, and may be written in a less formal style. To follow on the highway example, a soft story could be a profile of a paramedic who has had to attend to such gruesome accidents.

While some specialists continue to have stories appear on the front page (especially when the content combines religion with some traditionally hard news topic, like corruption), for years religion too was gathered in a separate section inside the soft and happy newspaper home. For many women wanting to advance through the traditional hierarchy, reporting on religion was not conducive to being taken seriously as a journalist.

But the beat has waxed and waned. During the late 1990s, following the first World Trade Center bombing and the Branch Davidian crisis in Waco, Texas, journalists capable of reporting religion received recognition. This was most clearly seen in American newspapers, although the trends Buddenbaum and Mason describe were mirrored to a degree in Canada:

> Armed with market research showing that religion was of special concern to women – a key demographic group newspapers sought to lure – some newspapers created "megasections" with four and six pages weekly packed with stories about religion. But these megasections carried broader content than their precursors, including stories about values, ethics and spirituality. (...) Finally, religion reporting, it seemed, had come into its own. History, however, suggests that this renewed interest might not last.
>
> (Buddenbaum and Mason 2000: 346)

They were right: with the exception of particular interest in Islam following the 9/11 attacks, the religion beat has faded considerably. Religion pages and reporters from *The Toronto Star* to the *Dallas Morning News* have disappeared.

But religious beliefs – including atheism and agnosticism – have done anything but vanish. And women are still very much present on the Earth. I would argue that what Whitt says about the demise of women's pages can apply to religion beats just as well: If news centring on women

> did not (and does not) appear on the front pages of American newspapers, will it appear elsewhere, and would terminating women's pages guarantee that news for women will make its way onto the front page? The answer to both questions is a resounding no.
>
> (Whitt 2008: 47)

Based on my research, religion reporting is no longer a given. It may make it to the front or any other spot in a newspaper or broadcast, but there are none of the guarantees that come with a reporter assigned to the religion beat.

If individual journalists are responsible for who is included in a story, what difference is made by having women at the top of the editorial pyramid? As researchers like Barber and Rauhala have found, women occupy few positions at the highest levels of journalism, where decisions about creating and eliminating beats are made. A recent study found that newspapers helmed by women saw a slight decrease in the amount of "hard news" as compared with a growth in features (Beam and Di Cicco 2010). But the changes were minimal and the researchers found that traditional news judgments continue, regardless of who is at the top. Unfortunately, the topics coded in this study didn't include religion *per se*. They may be found within such clusters as "social issues, minority issues, and personal relationships."

Some news organizations have experimented with restructuring beats to move away from a focus on institutions. In the American context, these examples are given:

> instead of covering organized religious denominations, they're covering religions and ethics. (...) An example in the early 90s of this approach to beats came from *the State* in Columbia, South Carolina. Reporters were grouped into teams, one of which included a "community roots team" which was comprised of beats on religion, the military, workplace issues and South Carolina trends.
>
> (Collins and Schmidt 1993)

Writing in 1993 on these modifications, Colleen Collins and Karen Schmidt noted that:

> change may be slow, but it's visible. Easter morning, the *New York Times* had a page one story about the decline of housecleaning. "When the *New York Times* has a front page story about housework," [Deborah] Howell [then Washington Bureau Chief for Newhouse News Service] says, "That's progress."
>
> (Collins and Schmidt 1993)

The front page of the Easter Sunday, 11 April 1993 *New York Times* featured eight stories. Two dealt with the conflict in the former Yugoslavia (both by men), another looked at Russian monetary policy (reported by a man), there was a story about satellites providing the Chinese with more information (reported by a man) and a report on the assassination of South African Chris Hani (reported by a man). On the domestic front, there was a note leading to a longer story inside about the Rodney King trial in Los Angeles (by a man), and the beginning of a feature story on a young man living in a tough part of Chicago (reported by a man). There are three photographs on the page, all of men. Finally, there is the show of progress: "Drop the mop, bless the mess: the decline of housekeeping" by Molly O'Neill. But if progress meant having one of nine stories on the front page written by a woman, what did it mean for religion to have the holiest day of the year (for what was then about 87 per cent of Americans) go unremarked?

Future reporting and research

Journalism itself is being tested in this century. Old business models are not working in a new digital age, and news outlets are scaling down operations. Citizen journalism, blogs and aggregators are challenging the role of the reporter. Women occupy more journalism jobs than ever before, but are still not equally represented in the higher levels of editorial decision-making.

I agree with Gill and others that there is at least an opportunity in this period of flux to consider how so-called "softer" news reporting may influence the way in which women and religion are covered. I would wager, for instance, that the advice given by Nawaz might do more to change preconceived notions of female Muslims than more earnest stories on veiling. And her engaging tone will certainly attract the attention of more readers of all genders and religious viewpoints. Surely this is an important addition to more traditional reporting.

Institutional religion has not been an unalloyed friend to women. It certainly does not recognize a balanced number of female leaders for reporters to quote as experts. With the declining allegiance in Europe and North America to such forms of spirituality, perhaps the waning of religion beats is not such a bad thing. If the beat as a reporting tool privileges institutional, hegemonic structures, this method of reporting may not serve the coverage of religion as lived today. This is not to say that news outlets should not employ journalists whose expertise is religion. But perhaps they can report best on religion in its current, fluid form outside of the beat system.

The number of women covering religion and occupying leadership positions should continue to grow. It would be worthwhile to qualitatively track the coverage of religion by women as compared with that by men as these trends continue.

Whitt points to the work of literary journalists, and feminist and lesbian publications as an important part of the history of women and reporting (Whitt 2008: 3). Digital journalism is already providing new avenues for women seeking alternatives to mainstream news outlets. Continuing scholarship into these alternatives as they exist and evolve online will be fruitful for those interested in journalism about religion.

Finally, changes brought about by the nature of transmediated journalism, free of the shackles of set times for evening broadcasts and the space allotted to a single front page, is perhaps both the biggest and most obvious opportunity for renewed reporting about women and religion. The concept of ghettoized news is exploded by digital delivery. The sections of a newspaper all but disappear with the use of search engines and aggregators, and the order of stories heard on a radio newscast is moot once the material is podcast. The distinction of news as foreign or domestic blurs when journalism is available simultaneously to a global cyber audience. Stories about and by women and religion will have a much better chance of being read, heard and watched than ever before. But only if the opportunity to produce them is seized.

Note

1 Nawaz, Z. (2012) "Our new cottage neighbours drop in too much," *The Globe and Mail*, April 26, 2012 (online at http://www.theglobeandmail.com/life/relationships/our-new-cottage-neighbours-drop-in-too-much/article4103457/).

Bibliography

Barber, M. and Rauhala, A. (2005) "The Canadian news directors study: demographics and political leanings of television decision-makers," *Canadian Journal of Communication*, 30 (2): 281–292.

Beam, R.A. and Di Cicco, D.T. (2010) "When women run the newsroom: management change, gender, and the news," *Journalism and Mass Communication Quarterly*, 87 (2): 393–411.

Beasley, M.H. and Gibbons, S.J. (1993) *Taking their place: a documentary history of women and journalism* (rev. and exp. edn), American University Press in cooperation with the Women's Institute for Freedom of the Press, distributed by arrangement with University Pub. Associates, Washington, D.C.; Lanham, MD.

Blaze Carlson, K. (2012) "Curtain lifts on decades of forced adoptions for unwed mothers in Canada," *The National Post*, online (last updated 9 March 2012), available: http://news.nationalpost.com/2012/03/09/curtain-lifts-on-decades-of-forced-adoptions-for-unwed-mothers-in-canada/ (accessed 13 May 2012).

Buddenbaum, J.M. and Mason, D.L. (eds) (2000) *Readings on religion as news* (first edn), Ames: Iowa State University Press.

Collins, C. and Schmidt, K. (1993) "Slow down at gender gap," *American Journalism Review*, online (last updated July/August 1993), available: http://www.ajr.org/article.asp?id=1555 (accessed 9 May 2012).

Eagle, D.E. (2011) "Changing patterns of attendance at religious services in Canada, 1986–2008," *Journal for the Scientific Study of Religion*, 50 (1): 187–200.

Gill, R. (2007) *Gender and the media*, Cambridge: Polity Press.

Global Media Monitoring Project (2010) *Who makes the news? Canada Global Media Monitoring Project 2010 national report*, online, available: www.whomakesthenews.org/images/stories/website/gmmp_reports/2010/national/Canada.pdf (accessed 14 May 2012), World Association for Christian Communication.

Jerome, C. (1990) "A Canadian woman journalist covers Islam" in P. Desbarats and P. Giroux (eds) *Encounter '89: journalism, religion and development*, London, Ont.: Graduate School of Journalism, the University of Western Ontario, 104–109.

Junquera, N. (2012) "Prosecutors charge Catholic nun in alleged stolen baby scheme at Madrid hospitals," *El País*, online (last updated 15 March 2012), available: http://elpais.com/elpais/2012/03/15/inenglish/1331840415_803134.html (accessed 9 May 2012).

Klaus, E. and Kassel, S. (2005) "The veil as a means of legitimization: an analysis of the interconnectedness of gender, media and war," *Journalism* 6 (3): 335–355.

Lindsay, C. (2008) "Canadians attend weekly religious services less than 20 years ago," Statistics Canada, online (last updated 21 November 2008), available: http://www.statcan.gc.ca/pub/89-630-x/2008001/article/10650-eng.htm (accessed 14 May 2012).

Nawaz, Z. (2012) "Group therapy: I want someone who will fight for me – is that wrong?", *The Globe and Mail*, online (last updated 16 February 2012), available:

www.theglobeandmail.com/life/relationships/relationship-advice/zarqa-nawaz/i-want-someone-who-will-fight-for-me—is-that-wrong/article2340970/ (accessed 10 May 2012).

Silk, M. (1995) *Unsecular media: making news of religion in America*, Urbana: University of Illinois Press.

Walkom, T. (2011) "Walkom: what's right about Jason Kenney's very wrong no-veil rule," *The Toronto Star*, online (last updated 13 December 2011), available: www.thestar.com/news/canada/politics/article/1101357–walkom-what-s-right-about-jason-kenney-s-very-wrong-no-veil-rule (accessed 12 May 2012).

Walsh-Childers, K., Chance, J. and Herzog, K. (1996) "Women journalists report discrimination in newsrooms," *Newspaper Research Journal*, 17 (3/4): 68–87.

Whitt, J. (2008) *Women in American journalism: a new history*, Urbana: University of Illinois Press.

World Press Photo (2012) "2012 World Press Photo of the Year," online (last updated 2012), available: www.worldpressphoto.org/photo/world-press-photo-year-2011-0 (accessed 13 May 2012).

Worthington, P. (2011) "Women with young kids shouldn't be in war zones," *The Toronto Sun*, online (last updated 18 February 2011), available: www.torontosun.com/news/columnists/peter_worthington/2011/02/18/17331046.html (accessed 10 May 2012).

Chapter 6

Danish female fans negotiating romance and spirituality in *The Twilight Saga*

Line Nybro Petersen

> The mass media suggests lifestyles, forms of self-presentation and ways to find happiness (which may or may not be illusory) [...] Our relationship with our bodies, our sexual partners and our own emotional needs, will all also be influenced by media representations, but (of course) in complex ways which will be swayed and modified by our social experiences and interactions.
>
> (Gauntlett 2008: 123)

Religion and gender roles in Scandinavian countries have undergone considerable changes throughout the past decades. Specifically, religious practice has declined or moved into new cultural spaces, and women's roles in relationships and families are changing. These changes are reflected in different ways in media's representations of gender roles, intimacy, beliefs and religious values in fictional narratives. In the popular book and movie series, *The Twilight Saga*, gender and religion are salient themes as seventeen-year-old protagonist Bella Swan falls in love with vampire Edward Cullen, who has been seventeen for the past 104 years. On the one hand, this is a classic romantic story seemingly promoting traditional gender roles. On the other hand, the story has added a supernatural twist, which suggests that the couple is predestined for a life of eternal love. This chapter discusses Danish female fans' reception as they use *The Twilight Saga* as a new space for negotiating gender values and norms through the series' transcendental and emotional qualities. Their interpretations reveal a cognitive dissonance between the socio-culturally informed views these Danish teens have toward gender roles in relationships and their emotionally charged fascination with the supernatural. This cognitive dissonance is supported by elements of the series that create a distance in the reception, while other aspects are familiar and easily identifiable for Danish teens. For example, some Danish fans object to the storyline in the fourth book *Breaking Dawn* (divided into two movies) as the teenage couple gets married and has a child. Still, Danish fans are eager to dive into the romance story in *Twilight* and the stories' invitation to imagine a destined eternal love. The analysis identifies four tendencies that capture the ambiguity of Danish fans' responses to *Twilight*: (1) The Danish teenage fans object to the traditional gender roles that characterize the romantic relationship between Bella and Edward, but (2) simultaneously find the destined all-encompassing love to be the most fascinating part of the stories. (⚹ The Danish teenage fans oppose 'religion' that they connect to institutional practice and beliefs, but (4) simultaneously they are fascinated with having a belief in something bigger than themselves, which the series promotes.

The analysis applies the theory of mediatization (Schulz 2004, Lundby 2009, Hjarvard 2008a, 2008b) in order to discuss how the responses found in the Danish fan culture might reflect media-induced transformations of romance and spirituality. Regarding processes of mediatization, Livingstone states that, '"mediatization" refers to the meta process by which everyday practices and social relations are historically shaped by mediating technologies and media organizations' (Livingstone 2009: x). The study in this chapter is not claiming to identify long-term processes of change through analysis of a single case, but rather to argue that analysis on a micro level may reveal ways in which mediatization processes take place. The application of mediatization theory in this analysis aims to discuss whether these transformations inform attitudes and values on romance and spirituality in Danish fans.

Mediatization, romance and spirituality

The theory of mediatization suggests that the media play a role in societal transformations. Hjarvard understands processes of mediatization as having a dual character:

> This process is characterized by a duality in that the media have become *integrated* into the operations of other social institutions, while they also have acquired the status of social institutions *in their own right*. As a consequence, social interaction – within the respective institutions, between institutions, and in society at large – take place via the media.
>
> (Hjarvard 2008c: 113)

A Danish quantitative study of media use by Tufte, Puggaard and Gretlund (2009) illustrates how media are integrated into the everyday life of Danish teenagers; it shows that the average Danish teenager spends 6.6 hours on media use every day. The Danish fans in this study are active media users *and* producers that engage in *Twilight* on several media platforms: They read books and watch movies both in theaters, on DVDs and online, they post ⚹ comments on Facebook and other social networking sites and some have a personal blog. Abercrombie and Longhurst (1998) propose a research paradigm labeled 'the spectacle/performance paradigm' to capture media's integration with other social spheres and they state: 'the media are actually constitutive of everyday life. The media and everyday life have become so closely interwoven that they are almost inseparable' (Abercrombie and Longhurst 1998: 69). With

is media bigger than self?

regard to the *Twilight* fandom, this paradigm underpins that audiences are not simply exposed to media messages that they may or may not adapt, but that media narratives can have the potential to change social interaction in a given societal context. Furthermore, this perspective serves to clarify how negotiations amongst peers may invoke transformed worldviews on these issues. Schulz identifies four processes of mediatization for analytical purposes: *extension, substitution, amalgamation* and *accommodation* (Schulz 2004). Schulz clarifies that these processes are not mutually exclusive. Rather mediatization, he argues, is a concept that 'both transcends and includes media effects' (Schulz 2004: 90). As the issue of gender roles becomes interwoven with issues of belief and religious imaginations, Danish teens may adjust attitudes toward either subject.

Weber and Dixon (2007) identify the relevance of considering gender when studying the use of new media technologies (see also Weber and Weber 2007, Bell 2007). As will be described further below, this study includes content analysis of a popular Danish Facebook fan site and personal blogs related to the *Twilight* fandom. New media technologies become a space for the formation, shaping and performance of self-identity and negotiations of values, beliefs and norms for young female users. It is through the *Twilight* fan culture that Danish teen girls become *cultural producers* on fan sites and blogs, therefore having the potential to influence the culture they are part of. Stern (2007) argues: 'Girls appear to benefit from access to "safe spaces" where they feel comfortable expressing both who they are and who they wish to become' (Stern 2007: 161). When keeping a diary becomes an online activity in the form of a personal blog, the form, function and content of the diary may transform to include, for example, an element of *performance* (Petersen 2012). Lövheim (2011) argues how these new media technologies can serve as ethical spaces that frame discussions and performances related to socio-cultural values and norms, in a study of young Swedish women's blogs.

Gauntlett underlines that gender is only one axis of 'an individual's sense of self' (2008: 15). Religious belief (or an atheist worldview) is another axis along with other socio-demographic factors that make up an individual's identity. Furthermore, Gauntlett argues that although media overall still promotes good looks in both male and female representations, 'media has a more complex view of gender and sexuality than ever before' (2008: 98). The TV series *Ugly Betty* (2006–2010) portrays an intelligent brace-wearing plain Jane who manages to survive in the superficial world of fashion, while *Sex and the City* (1998–2004) portrays overtly beautiful and sexual women that struggle with relationships and love. In a media landscape with immense diversity it is relevant to ask, what has caused these fans to dive into the universe and gender roles presented in *Twilight*? Gill (2007) discusses gender roles in relation to romance and argues that choice and entitlement for women are key themes in post-feminist media narratives, but 'women are endowed with choice so that they can then use their "feminist" freedom to choose to re-embrace traditional femininity – white weddings, hen nights, the adoption of male surname on marriage etc.' (Gill 2007: 243).

Her statement certainly seems to hold some truth when it comes to *Twilight* as Bella chooses to marry Edward and join him in an eternal life as a vampire rather than pursue an education and a career. As such, *The Twilight Saga* series balances between what Giddens (1992) labeled a (traditional) romantic love and (modern) confluent love. In the case of the Danish fan group, I argue that Danish teenagers' fascination with the traditional romantic aspects of the series is rather a fascination with engaging in the religious emotions (Riis and Woodhead 2010, Hills 2002) connected with destined love that the series promotes. → fate ? supernatural

Fans' negotiations of romance and spirituality

This chapter presents the results of a qualitative study of Danish *Twilight* fans. The study combines the data from a single case (a small group of fans), with data from one of the largest online forums for Danish *Twilight* fans: Twilight Denmark's Facebook page (which at the time of writing had more than 160,000 adherents). The case study includes a focus group with three respondents (Silverman 2006) and an in-depth interview with one respondent (Kvale 1997) as methodological tools, while selected threads from online fan forums are exposed to qualitative content analysis (Stroman and Jones 1998). As such, the overall methodological strategy can be considered a *methodological triangulation* (Denzin 1970, Bruhn Jensen 2002).

Objections to representations of traditional gender roles

Despite expressions of all-encompassing devotion by the fans in the focus group, there were also concerns about the series finale as Bella and Edward get married and have a child. I understand their objections to mirror societal norms in Denmark that discourage teen pregnancies; a norm that is quite clearly supported by public responses to the television docu-soap *The Young Mothers*, which, as the title suggests, follows the hardships of Danish teenage mothers. McRobbie (2007) argues that the consequences of post-feminism create a new 'sexual contract' for young women. This, for example, has consequences for how society views and judges young motherhood: 'Young motherhood, across the boundaries of class and ethnicity now carries a whole range of vilified meanings associated with failed femininity and with disregard for the wellbeing of the child' (McRobbie 2007: 732). As the following quote illustrates, the Danish fans adopt a critical approach similar to the views mentioned by McRobbie.

REBECCA   I wouldn't mind a different ending to *Breaking Dawn* [the fourth book] ... in fact I would have liked to see the series end with *Eclipse* [the third book], because I do not think that *Breaking Dawn* is one of the most fantastic books. I think it ends really badly and I don't like the way it's written.
[...]

TINE   It's the worst one [final part of *Breaking Dawn*], because that's when Bella becomes a vampire and she is oh so beautiful and it's oh so good … and their little nuclear family is just so happy. If it was up to me, I think I would have liked to see Edward let Bella stay a human and just have her die of old age or something.

[…]

TINE   Also this thing about her having a daughter, because I just can't see Bella as a mom and I can't really see Edward as a dad […].

REBECCA   They are also just seventeen and eighteen, right?

In this sense, the respondents in the focus group carry forward a notion of gender roles that promote productivity (e.g. in the workplace) over re-productivity. But more so they are eager to have an open ending to the story where they are free to imagine the future of the young couple.

Other aspects of the ambiguity the focus group's reception are connected to Edward as boyfriend material. They struggle with his heroic and self-sacrificing qualities as he suppresses his vampire urges and continuously saves Bella from dangerous situations, but Edward is also attempting to control and limit Bella's friendship with Jacob.

TINE   […] Edward kind of has God-like status, right? The only bad thing about him is that he is a vampire, who is actually a good vampire, so he's a little … he is pretty amazing Edward, right?

INTERVIEWER   Yes, Rebecca?

REBECCA   He also gets jealous very easily.

TINE   Yeah, yeah …

REBECCA   That's not a good thing.

In a blog, Rebecca reviews the third movie *Breaking Dawn* and sarcastically offers her thoughts on Edward as boyfriend material:

> The part might be when Edward and Carlisle investigate Bella, Carlisle walks out and Edward is mad at Bella and says something along the lines that he thought they were a couple and she has decided to leave him (because he knows that she dies if something doesn't happen soon) – and he hasn't decided this, which doesn't make it ok! But well, dear little Edward. You are a little selfish. Because it's completely okay, when you leave Bella in *New Moon*, but it's not okay at all that Bella leaves you in *Breaking Dawn* … tsk tsk …
>
> ('Rebecca' 2011)

The focus group participants distance themselves from elements of the story that they do not consider socially desirable. This does not mean that the teenage girls disregard the series as such. In fact, they are fascinated with other aspects of a traditional romantic love in the series.

Fascination with a pre-modern romantic love

Despite the objections that some fans have toward the traditional gender roles displayed in the series, the most significant attraction for the Danish fans is the notion of a *romantic love* (Giddens 1992). From a genre perspective, *The Twilight Saga* borrows heavily from the traditional romance movie. Gill sums up the plot formula:

> a young, inexperienced, poor woman needs a handsome, wealthy man, ten or fifteen years her senior. The hero is mocking, cynical, contemptuous, hostile and even brutal, and the heroine is confused. By the end he reveals his love for her and misunderstandings are cleared away.
>
> (Gill 2007: 219)

Furthermore, Gill (2007) points out how the obstacles that stand between the couple and happiness are often related to race, class or simply mutual loathing. In *Twilight*, Edward's status as non-human or super-human creates similar obstacles. Bella is young and inexperienced and she moves to a new school in the small town called Forks. In her initial encounter with Edward, he seemingly cannot stand to so much as look at her or be near her and in response she finds him arrogant. During the first movie, Bella discovers that Edward's apparent contempt really is caused by the lust Edward feels when he smells her blood. From this point their love for each other resembles what Giddens labels a 'sublime love,' which can be understood as part of a pre-modern romantic love. In Giddens' terms, a romantic love is often thought of as 'love at first sight' and it involves identifying the partner's character as 'special': 'The "first glance" is a communicative gesture, an intuitive grasp of qualities of the other. It is a process of attraction to someone who can make one's life, as it is said, "complete"' (Giddens 1992: 40). The Danish fans in the focus group have a strong fascination with these elements of the series:

TINE It [the story] gives something to this dream ... of course there are obstacles in their path, but they can always ... their love is always strong enough to conquer all problems, right?

KATJA Who doesn't want someone who fights [for you]? Someone who will sacrifice his own life and fight until death for you?

[...]

TINE I think so too ... This thing where you are willing to die for one another, I really think that is what makes these stories interesting; that you can love someone so much that you are willing to die for each other.

The romantic couple's obstacles serve as a narrative drive that is typical for the romantic genre as Gill (2007) has pointed out, but it also means that the relationship is portrayed with a clear imbalance of power. In a famous line from the first movie Edward refers to the couple's love as a love between lion and lamb. In the end Bella sacrifices education, career and her family in order to spend forever (literally) with Edward. The notion of *romantic* love stands in opposition to *confluent* love that is dominant in modern societies (Giddens 1992), and perhaps some of the fascination with a pre-modern romantic love can be seen as a reaction to our approach to relationships today. Giddens argues:

> Confluent love is active, contingent love, and therefore jars with the 'for-ever', 'one-and-only' qualities of the romantic love complex. The 'separating and divorcing society' of today here appears as an effect of the emergence of confluent love rather than its cause.
>
> (Giddens 1992: 60)

Two of the participants in the focus group have parents that are divorced and it seems that romantic love's promise of *forever* is central to their fascination. Furthermore, the Danish fans also find pleasure in identifying with a female character that is not portrayed in an overtly sexualized way, as is the case in many other contemporary narratives. Instead, it is the men in the story that are subject to a sexualized gaze as the film series has a number of scenes in which the main purpose seems to be to show either Edward or Jacob with their shirts off. The fans in the focus group interpret the story of Bella as a confirmation that women can be worthy of love with natural beauty and intelligence. On Twilight Denmark's Facebook page, fans also mention the portrayal of female protagonist Bella as a part of their fascination. One fan comments 'I really like how Bella is not some unapproachable beauty, who is just perfect and girly, no she is clumsy, shy and something of a tomboy you can identify with' (Facebook, accessed February 8, 2012). While it might seem reasonable that the fans aim for permanent relationships, Giddens points out that romantic love is skewed in terms of gender equality: 'For women dreams of romantic love have all too often led to grim domestic subjection. Confluent love presumes equality in emotional give and take' (Giddens 1992: 62). The fans' attraction to a pre-modern romantic love might be understood as a reaction to contemporary portrayals of women as overtly sexual and celebrity culture's promotion of stunning beauty and contemporary relationships as dispensable and provisional. However, I argue that the fascination with an eternal love can also be understood in terms of the supernatural and religious elements in the story.

Secular Danes engaging in religious emotions

As young Danish (or other Scandinavian) people's 'religious sensitivities' and beliefs are no longer directed toward religious institutions (Davie 2002, 2007, Norris and Inglehart 2004), we need to consider the role of media narratives as a space for exploring these interests. Davie (2002) points out that institutionalized

Christianity is no longer a keystone in European culture and that belief has found a new space:

> there are commentators (including myself) who consider belief a more independent variable. An evident fall in both religious practice and *strictly Christian* beliefs in the post-war period does not lead either to a parallel in loss in religious sensitivity (indeed the reverse is often true as individuals sense a greater freedom to experiment), or to the widespread adoption of secular alternatives
>
> (Davie 2002: 8)

Based on the results of a quantitative study in Denmark, Hjarvard (2008a) argues that fictional narratives such as *Harry Potter*, *Lord of the Rings* and *The Da Vinci Code* stimulate an interest in religious themes and concepts. The respondents here have a similar approach to institutional religion as in Lövheim's study (2007) of Swedish teenagers' use of the Internet for religious discussions. Religion is seen as outdated, infantile and even hypocritical by these teenagers. They do not express an understanding that the adherence to a church community would add value to their lives. The respondents in the fan group do not find institutional religion as a source of belonging and moral guidance.

INTERVIEWER   How much is religion a part of your everyday life?
REBECCA   Not very much, I think. I have been confirmed, but I don't believe in God ... not really, not really a believer. Of course, there is something up there, but I do not believe that Jesus could walk on water and stuff like that.

The absence or irrelevance of institutional religion in these teenagers' daily lives does not mean that they are uninterested in belief and spirituality. The difference is, of course, that being a fan is not a lifelong commitment, but something they can choose to be part of for a period of time (although some of the fans claim that their commitment is forever). Perhaps we can understand the *Twilight* series to be the preferred resource for these issues for a period of time? *Twilight* becomes a resource in negotiations of gender roles and religious imaginations through its invitation for emotional investment. Riis and Woodhead's (2010) term 'religious emotions' is useful to understand the meanings and reactions that arise and circulate within the Danish *Twilight* fan culture. Riis and Woodhead discuss religion in terms of *emotional regimes*. They argue:

> To join a religion is to experience a new way of feeling about self, others, society, and the world. Religious people learn to sound the emotional notes approved by the religions to which they belong, and to do so in ways that are authorized by their communities of belonging.
>
> (Riis and Woodhead 2010: 11)

These Danish fans are eager to invest emotionally in everything that relates to the series and to allow for this emotional regime to spill into other social spheres. Hills (2002) underpins that being a fan of a media narrative is not equal to being part of a religious community, but being a fan does involve emotional practices that are negotiated within a fan community, which we can understand as a 'community of belonging.' Furthermore, the emotions triggered within the Danish fan group have a quality of 'pervasiveness' that Riis and Woodhead (2010) refer to as central to a religious emotional regime. The emotions that the story triggers for these teenagers and that are triggered by the social activity of being a fan can 'spill over' into other parts of their social lives.

The *Twilight* series offers a new space for exploring an emotional regime connected to belief in the supernatural and a sense of belonging. Thus, engaging in religious emotions is transformed in terms of content and form while the function is similar. In Schulz's (2004) terms, we can perhaps identify a process where the media *substitute* what has traditionally been the social function of institutionalized religions. This happens as the media narrative changes audiences' social interaction as fans becomes producers, establish new relationships and invest in emotional regimes that might not be available to them elsewhere. In the fan group, Mercer points out that reading for girls has power as a social practice:

> Reading popular young adult fiction is not merely an individual activity for girls even though they may engage in it principally in private settings. Rather, reading is a social practice [...] of which sharing the 'book world' with others is an important dimension in situating the identities of readers.
>
> (Mercer 2010: 266)

Furthermore, social media become an *extension* (Schulz 2004) of this social practice for the Danish fans: on the Facebook page for Twilight Denmark they join in the birthday celebration of actors and fictional characters in the series, they post pictures of themselves dressing up as characters or of the *Twilight*-themed cakes they bake. They have on occasion arranged *Twilight*-gatherings and walks to protest that none of the major stars have visited Denmark so far. And finally, their personal blogs become an instrument in this practice (Lövheim 2011, Weber and Dixon 2007, Weber and Weber 2007). Considering both the concept of religious emotions and the fan culture as a specific social practice, I suggest that the series offers a space that ties ordinary life to a spirituality that is otherwise a rare experience in their secular surroundings. This happens both through the supernatural and spiritual elements in the narrative, and as a result of the emotional investment these Danish teenagers actively *perform* (Abercrombie and Longhurst 1998, Petersen 2012) for their peers on several social media platforms and in a physical space such as premieres: 'When members of an audience attend a performance, they concentrate their energies, emotions and thoughts on the performance and try to distil from that performance a meaning of one kind or another' (Abercrombie and Longhurst 1998: 43). Hills suggests that it is the social practice rather than the text itself that generates meaningfulness for these fans. He argues that we can understand fandom as a form of *neoreligiosity*: 'Fandom both *is* and *is not* like religion, existing between "cult" and "culture"' (Hills 2002: 118): He continues:

> Neoreligiosity implies that the proliferation of discourses of cult within media fandom cannot be read as the return of religion in a supposedly secularised culture, nor as the social relocation of religion, both of which would assume religion's essential stability.
>
> (Hills 2002: 119)

Instead, *neoreligiosity* in fan cultures derives from fan practices and discourses. I agree with Hills on this point and argue that part of what fan culture has in common with religious cultures is the intense and unquestioning emotional devotion it allows for. In the in-depth interviews, Rebecca elaborates on the place *Twilight* holds for her:

INTERVIEWER   How much time does *Twilight* take up in your everyday life? Just on a regular day?

REBECCA   Oh it takes up a lot ... a lot of my time I think ... Almost all of the time. I have never felt this way about a movie or a book before, but now this thing, it takes up a lot. I don't think there is a day without me checking *Twilight*-news or reading in one of the books or watching clips from the movies or talking to somebody about it ... constantly.

A Facebook user answers questions about the importance of *Twilight* and if she thinks anything will follow *Twilight* for her:

> They [the series] have had kind of a big influence on my life, because, well, who doesn't want a guy like Edward or Jacob? [...] So yes, something supernatural will certainly have a place in my life and if I can't wait for a new *Twilight* film then I can always just watch the movies again or reread the books:-p
>
> (Facebook February 7, 2012)

A central element in the *performance* of fandom lies in the continuous process of proving that you are worthy of being considered a true fan by reaffirming that the books and movies have a place in your everyday life. Another Facebook user comments that the series has meant a better social life:

> It [the series] has had great meaning for me. I have always been sort of different/outside in school and I was afraid that it would be like that with

Twilight. On the contrary, I have made close ties to people because of the movies and also the books, when I 'finally' found something in common with the other girls my age […] For that I'm grateful!

(Facebook accessed February 7, 2012)

Being a 'true twi-heart' or 'fanpire' involves *performing* this meaningfulness to their peers. Social media aid this performance. One blogger writes:

In 2 hours … I'll be sitting in a wonderfully dark theater with lovely Louise and watching *Eclipse*!. I REALLY REALLY REALLY REALLY LOOK FORWARD TO IT! :D … Now, where are all my *Twilight*- and Team Edward bracelets? Hmm …

('Pernille' 2010)

Along the same lines Rebecca even labels certain emotions as 'having the *Twilight*-fever' on her blog:

REBECCA   … had a minor attack of the *Twilight*-fever today. You know … it's when you can't sit still, are breathing way too fast, have a big smile plastered on your lips and talk raging fast. Yes – that's me.

('Rebecca' 2010)

Furthermore, the supernatural elements in the stories add meaning. The fact that the series includes the supernatural has consequences for the kind of emotions that being a fan involves (Riis and Woodhead 2010).

REBECCA   … I think fantasy and the supernatural have always caught my interest […] And then you just dive into another universe and imagine that you're there, and dive into another person's thoughts. That's what I think is cool about books.

In popular culture, beliefs in and imaginations about the supernatural are considered cool and exciting to dive into, but they also provide something to believe in in a society where this is not an obvious choice:

KATJA   Uhm, I think … you don't have any clear answer to what happens [when you die], so perhaps when you read different things and watch different movies, then it gives you something … Perhaps not a clear answer, but more like 'oh, it happens like this' and then you can choose to believe it. Because then you have *something* you can believe in and you can choose to believe that. And you can hold on to that …
REBECCA   But I also think that all people need something to believe in.
KATJA   Yeah, I think so too.

These teenagers are looking for something to believe in, something that has value and something they can lean on. In a Danish secular society, engaging in religion is not an obvious choice – partly because of the status and authority institutionalized religion has in these teenagers' lives. Popular narratives, such as *The Twilight Saga*, provide an opportunity for these teenagers to engage in the fascination they have with the supernatural and belief.

Conclusion

> *Twilight* isn't a book, it isn't a movie, it isn't a story. At least not to me. To me *Twilight* is a universe that I can let myself into, when I can't deal with everyday life. *Twilight* is hope and dreams and *Twilight* has saved me when I have felt like action, excitement, dreams, and love. *Twilight* is my very own universe – that's the greatest thing about *Twilight*.
>
> (Facebook, accessed February 8, 2012)

There is no doubt that the *Twilight* stories have great value for the Danish fans that follow the series. For that reason it is necessary to understand the processes of meaning-making in these teenagers' lives that the series becomes part of. These processes can be understood through the theory of mediatization since being members of an audience today means more than being exposed to media messages. Audiences, and perhaps especially devoted fans, are active participants in the narratives they engage in and, as such, media have the potential to change social dynamics and interactions in audiences. The mediatization perspective offers insight into how *Twilight* becomes meaningful for the Danish fans in mediatization processes as media take over functions traditionally tied to other societal institutions, while simultaneously changing the form and content through media technologies.

The Danish teenagers object to the elements of the relationship that they find inappropriate for the young couple's age. They also recognize Edward's controlling behavior and view it as unflattering. But the Danish fans' main fascination with the series is still the romantic relationship between Edward and Bella. In particular, they are caught by the relationship's qualities that are similar to Giddens' description of *romantic love* in traditional societies. If we analyze gender aspects of the reception of *The Twilight Saga* by Danish female fans we might understand the Danish teenagers' fascination with the love story in *The Twilight Saga* as a return of traditional values in relationships – values that according to Giddens are tied to gender inequality (Giddens 1992). However, core elements of a *romantic love* have qualities that draw on spirituality and religious concepts such as destined, eternal love that overcomes all obstacles. If we understand Danish fans' fascination with the love story in this light, we can identify it as connected to a fascination with engaging with religious emotions, spirituality and belief in the supernatural. I want to suggest that *The Twilight Saga* and the fan culture that followed have become a place for Danish fans to direct their fascination toward religious emotions. In other words, being a fan of *Twilight* allows them to be part of a community of shared emotional experience. This experience invites negotiations of gender values through the emotional transcendence that the conjunction of the series' supernatural content and the fan culture permits.

Bibliography

Abercrombie, N. and Longhurst, B. (1998) *Audiences: A Sociological Theory of Performance and Imagination*, London: Sage.

Bell, B. (2007) 'Private writing in public spaces: girls' blogs and shifting boundaries,' in Weber, S. and Dixon, S. (eds), *Growing Up Online – Young People and Digital Technologies*, revised edition. New York: Palgrave Macmillan, 97–113.

Bruhn Jensen, K. (2002) 'Media reception: qualitative traditions,' in Bruhn Jensen, K., *A Handbook of Media and Communication Research: Qualitative and Quantitative Methodologies*, London: Routledge, 156–170.

Davie, G. (2002) *Europe: The Exceptional Case: Parameters of Faith in the Modern World*, London: Darton, Longman and Todd.

Davie, G. (2007) *The Sociology of Religion*, London: Sage.

Denzin, N.K. (1970) *The Research Act: A Theoretical Introduction to Sociological Methods*, New Brunswick and London: Aldine Transaction.

Gauntlett, D. (2008) *Media, Gender and Identity: An Introduction*, second edition, London: Routledge.

Giddens, A. (1992) *The Transformation of Intimacy: Sexuality, Love and Eroticism in Modern Society*, Cambridge: Polity Press.

Gill, R. (2007) *Gender and the Media*, Cambridge: Polity Press.

Hills, M. (2002) *Fan Cultures*, London: Routledge.

Hjarvard, S. (2008a) *En Verden af Medier – Medialiseringen af Politik, Sprog og Leg* (A World of Media: Mediatization of Politics, Language, Religion and Play), Frederiksberg: Samfundslitteratur.

Hjarvard, S. (2008b) 'The mediatization of religion: a theory of the media as agents of religious change,' in Hjarvard, S. (ed.), *Northern Lights*, vol. 6, Bristol: Intellect Press Ltd., 9–26

Hjarvard, S. (2008c). 'The mediatization of society: a theory of the media as agents of social and cultural change,' *Nordicom Review*, 29 (2), 105–134.

Kvale, S. (1997) *InterView – En Introduktion til det Kvalitative Forskningsinterview* (InterView: An Introduction to the Qualitative Research Interview), Copenhagen: Hans Reitzels Forlag.

Livingstone, S. (2009) 'Foreword: coming to terms with "mediatization",' in Lundby, K. (ed.), *Mediatization: Concepts, Changes and Consequences*, New York: Peter Lang, ix–xi.

Lövheim, M. (2007) 'Virtually boundless? Youth negotiating tradition in cyberspace,' in Ammerman, N. (ed.), *Everyday Religion: Observing Modern Religious Lives*, Oxford: Oxford University Press, 83–100.

Lövheim, M. (2011) 'Young women's blogs as ethical spaces,' *Information, Communication and Society*, 14 (3), 338–354.

Lundby, K. (2009) 'Introduction: mediatization as key,' in Lundby, K. (ed.), *Mediatization: Concepts, Changes and Consequences*, New York: Peter Lang, 1–18.

McRobbie, A. (2007) 'Top girls? Young women and the post-feminist contract,' *Information, Communication and Society*, 21 (4), 718–737.

Mercer, J.A. (2010) 'Vampires, desire, girls and god: *Twilight* and the spiritualities of adolescent girls,' *Pastoral Psychology*, 60, 263–278.

Norris, P. and Inglehart, R. (2004) *Sacred and Secular: Religion and Politics Worldwide*, Cambridge: Cambridge University Press.

'Pernille' (2010) *Speechless and Redundant* [blog], accessed June 30, 2010 at: www. speechless-andredundant.wordpress.com

Petersen, L.N. (2012) 'Danish *Twilight* fandom: Transformative processes of religion,' in Hjarvard, S. and Lövheim, M. (eds), *Mediatization and Religion: Nordic Perspectives*, Gothenburg: Nordicom, 163–182.

'Rebecca' (2010) 'The Eclipse to Dah Trailer' [blog entry], accessed December 19, 2012 at: http://breakingfree.dk/2010/03/11/the-eclipse-to-dah-trailer/

'Rebecca' (2011) 'En Lille Blog om *Breaking Dawn* Part 1, Forever is Only the Beginning' [blog entry], accessed February 18, 2012 at: http://breakingfree.dk/2011/11/19/en-lille-blog-om-breaking-dawn-part-1-forever-is-only-the-beginning/

Riis, O. and Woodhead, L. (2010) *A Sociology of Religious Emotions*, Oxford: Oxford University Press.

Schulz, W. (2004) 'Reconstructing mediatization as an analytical concept,' *European Journal of Communication*, 19, 87–101.

Silverman, D. (2006) *Interpreting Qualitative Data*, third edition, London: Sage Publications Ltd.

Stern, S.R. (2007) 'Adolescent girls' expression on web home page: spirited, somber, and self-conscious sites,' in Weber, S. and Dixon, S. (eds), *Growing Up Online – Young People and Digital Technologies*, revised edition, New York: Palgrave Macmillan, 161–181.

Stroman, C.A. and Jones, K.E. (1998) 'The analysis of television content,' in Asamen, J.K. and Berry, G.L. (eds), *Research Paradigms, Television and Social Behavior*, California: Sage Publications, Inc, 271–285.

Tufte, B., Puggaard, B. and Gretlund, T. (eds) (2009) *Børns Opvækst Med Medier og Forbrug* (Children's Upbringing with Media and Consumption), Frederiksberg: Samfundslitteratur.

Twilight Denmark (2012) Facebook, accessed December 19, 2012 at: www.facebook. com/TwilightDenmark?ref=ts& fref = ts

Weber, S. and Dixon, S. (eds) (2007) *Growing Up Online: Young People and Digital Technologies*, revised edition, New York: Palgrave Macmillan.

Weber, S. and Weber, J. (2007) 'Girls adaption of new technologies', in Weber, S. and Dixon, S. (eds), *Growing Up Online: Young People and Digital Technologies*, revised edition, New York: Palgrave Macmillan, 51–68.

Chapter 7

Lwa like me

Gender, sexuality and Vodou online

Alexandra Boutros

Haitian Vodou—long a secret religious practice—has become increasingly visible in the flows of networked digital communications. Manifestations of online Vodou make visible other social relations, including cross-cultural mediations of gender, race and sexual difference. Rooted in a transnationalist feminist critique of the ways in which knowledge is produced and reproduced, this analysis traces online discussions about gender and sexuality through discussion forums, listservs and websites devoted to Vodou. It explores how both users and the technological affordances of networked, digital communication shape online forms of the religion.

Constructing gender and sexuality in transnational contexts

A transnational approach to feminism begins "from the premise that genders, sexualities, races, classes" and nationalities "exist not as hermetically sealed entities" (Shohat 2002: 68) but as intersecting, co-constituting identities, practices and performances. While this analysis explores how the cultural precepts of Haitian Vodou may shape gendered and sexual mores, it does not presume that there exists a single, unified approach to gender or sexuality within the Vodou tradition. Instead, I am interested primarily in how online manifestations of Vodou highlight certain cross-cultural collisions around the ways in which gender and sexuality signify within the religion. Once Vodou leaves Haiti, via the transnational mobility of its practitioners and the flows of media, it becomes a diasporic religion.[1] If we want to understand the knowledge produced by both transnational mobility and the complex social relationships engendered by new media, Ella Shohat suggests "we must place them in dialogical relation within, between, and among cultures, ethnicities, and nations" (Shohat 2002: 69). Transnational feminisms seek to explore how knowledge is produced in the context of a global mobility of people, images, signs and symbols.

   Part of a larger ethnographic study of online Vodou, this research is based on a combination of textual analysis and interviews with participants of one now defunct listserv. The Voodoo Group was hosted on Yahoo Groups from 2004 to 2007 and was moderated by a Haitian Vodou ritual specialist living in

Philadelphia, Mambo Marie Pierre.[2] Qualitative interviews were conducted largely via email with members of the forum who volunteered to be interviewed. Although interviews opened with a few standard questions about participation on the listserv, interviewees guided the shape of each interview. The list was an active one with up to 30 posts per day at its busiest period. Listserv participants frequently debated the veracity of the stories and practices of Vodou. Gender, sexuality and their relationship not only to Vodou, but also to conceptualizations of religious authenticity and cultural specificity were often flashpoints for discussion.

Scholarship that focuses primarily on Vodou in the Haitian diaspora illuminates not only how the religion has adapted to diasporic conditions, but also how connections back to Haiti are maintained and nurtured.[3] What often remains unexamined is the role of newcomers (or non-Haitians) in the constitution of diasporic Vodou communities. Such an exploration requires acknowledging the intersection of media and diaspora—in the formation of what Appadurai (1996) calls global ethnoscapes. In the context of this analysis it also requires an examination of the ways in which categories of gender and sexuality are produced in a diasporic context. Can sexuality or gender be understood as a mobile category in the same way that diaspora is understood as constituted by vectors of mobility? Do both disrupt assumptions about fixed identity positions in the context of contemporary globalization? And are both circumscribed by online media practices that are at once representational and participatory? If, as postmodern theorists maintain, gender and sexuality are constituted,[4] what does it mean when this constitution occurs "at the interstices of specific geopolitical territories?" (Patton and Sánchez-Eppler 2000: 2). In the context of colonialism gender and sexuality have been constructed around Western fears of miscegenation and have been implicated as signs of the primitive and exotic other. This inevitably forms the ground against which publically mediated forms of Vodou are projected. And yet, the specificity of gender and sexuality in the Haitian Vodou context also intersects with Western notions of gender and sexuality. This intersection is not simply oppositional (Haitian notions of sexuality versus Western notions of sexuality). Instead, cross-cultural forms of gender and sexuality can be understood as mutually co-constitutive. As Patton and Sánchez-Eppler explain, identity can be understood as:

> strategic, rather than essential, contingent on, reproduced, decaying, co-opted, in relation to material and discursive factors that, especially in the context of sexualities, are always a complex lamination of local onto global onto local. Sexuality is intimately and immediately felt, but publicly and internationally described and mediated.
>
> (Patton and Sánchez-Eppler 2000: 2)

Cross-cultural interaction plays out in the public inscriptions and mediations of translocal, transglobal sexuality and gender that take place in online discussions of Vodou. Practitioners and web surfers negotiate a historicity of Vodou that carries with it complex constructions of black, gendered, sexualized bodies: an embodied historicity that stands in sharp contradistinction to the bodiless realm celebrated in some early theories of cyberspace.[5]

Colonialist qualms about the reach of black culture have fuelled discourses that position Vodou as wild, primitive and dangerous. As Haiti gained independence from French colonial powers (during the Haitian Revolution) fears that black insurgency would spread to other colonies and nations, including the US, laid the foundation for both concrete attempts to control the new nation and a particular strain of misrepresentation that posited Vodou not only as primitive and backward, but also as sexually licentious. As Barbara Browning explains a "conflation of economic, spiritual, and sexual exchange" in the colonialist era engendered a characterization of Caribbean culture in general and Haitian Vodou in particular "as a chaotic or uncontrolled force" (Browning 1998: 7). The locus for both this "uncontrolled force" and efforts to control it has often been the black female body. Fears of miscegenation have historically been linked to colonial anxiety over the moral degeneration of Western society through intimate contact with the bodies of the other (Sheller 2003: 114). The inscriptions of such colonial anxieties onto the bodies of women have shaped representations of Vodou in circulation today, reproduced in popular culture where Vodou is frequently depicted as hypersexualized. From Hollywood productions such as *White Zombie* (1932) (Bishop 2008) to *London Voodoo* (2004),[6] Vodou (or its pop culture counterpart, Voodoo) is exotified, in part, through discursive eroticization. While it is easy to argue that pop culture representations of Voodoo have little to do with "actual" or "authentic" Vodou, these representations construct the ground against which Vodou—carrying with it a historicity of colonialism and racialized constructs of gender and sexuality—becomes visible.

From participation to compendium: how Vodou comes to be "known" online

Online practitioners contribute to the visibility of Vodou in the digital public sphere by creating and maintaining informational and educational websites, listservs, forums, chat rooms and e-commerce sites as well as by using social networking platforms (such as listservs and Facebook) to create Vodou-related content. Often much of this online content—even when focused around participatory practices—is devoted to providing rudimentary information or dispelling misinformation about the religion. This content contributes to an ever-changing compendium of information about Vodou on the world wide web, much of which is geared toward those unfamiliar with the religion. When websites, listservs and social media sites turn posts about Vodou into a searchable compendium, what becomes most visible is often that which aggregates the most online attention. This is because the systems through which online information flows highlight that which receives the most hits, the most re-posts or the most "likes." This is an example of what Alexander Galloway (2006) calls action-based media—or media in which action taken by users works in conjunction with machinic action—and is an instrumental part of how what we tend to call "the Internet" functions. Whether it is the algorithms of search engines that rank search results by bumping some web pages to the top of any search list,[7] or it is the latest meme that is shared via multiple social networking platforms, the most visible online content is that which attracts the most views. When it comes to online Vodou, the content that attracts the most attention tends to be that which is most controversial. Online discussions of gender and sexuality in Vodou become flashpoints for discussion, in part, because these issues seem to demand a particular form of cross-cultural negotiation.

Some of the most visible users producing content about Vodou online are those who could be termed newcomers to the religion—individuals who have no genealogical or geographic relationship to Haiti or Haitian Vodou. While, arguably, ethnic kinship with those connected to a genealogy of Haitian Vodou is not necessary for affiliation with the religion, Vodou is closely tied to the cultural and historical specificity of Haiti; rituals involving possession, one of the defining characteristics of Vodou, often evoke historical narratives and figures, rituals are often performed in Haitian Kreyòl, and kinship lines are an important aspect of religious praxis. Those in the process of becoming affiliated with Vodou, or those who have recently come to define themselves as practitioners, wrestle with how to identify with a religion so closely tied to the history and culture of Haiti. When this struggle takes place online it also becomes part of the compendium of online information about Vodou.

Newcomers frequently justify their interest in Vodou by claiming that the deities (the *lwa*) of Haitian Vodou mirror their own identities and experiences. The diversity of identities represented in the pantheon of Vodou is sometimes employed by newcomers to authorize their own position within the religion. Vodou gods, or *lwa*, who are portrayed as white, gay or lesbian, or women, are seen as reflecting and indeed making ontological room for non-Haitian newcomers. This can create tension in online contexts, particularly when newcomers to Vodou are seen to be emphasizing aspects of Haitian Vodou that some see as inauthentic. While claims of authenticity and authority in ritual practice may be of concern in offline Vodou communities, the stakes around authenticity and identity are different in the online context. Discussions about what counts or does not count as authentic Vodou become part of a searchable database of online information. Issues of access (who has it and who does not have it) are important considerations for feminist media scholars exploring online mediation of identity (see, e.g. Consalvo and Paasonen 2002). The affordances of digital media give weight not only to those who have the most access, but those who garner the greatest visibility in the online context, rather than to those who are necessarily the most authoritative.

From mother to *madivin*: identifying with Vodou online

Often, online contestations of Vodou are most visible in discussions around the rituals and stories associated with particular *lwa* (or deity). One such story is that of Ezili Danto. In the cosmology of Haitian Vodou, Ezili Danto, like many of the *lwa*, is closely tied to the cultural specificity of Haiti. She, in some ways, emblemizes experiences of poor women in the socio-economic worlds of rural Haiti, where motherhood is of paramount importance. However, Danto does not signify a timeless, universal image of divine motherhood so much as one clearly rooted in the history and culture of Haiti. Said to have fought in the Haitian Revolution (1791–1804), Danto is almost always identified as a dark-skinned *lwa*. The complexities of racial identity, as a legacy of colonialism and slavery, play out in the ways in which the *lwa* of Vodou are remembered both in story and in ritual. As Elizabeth McAlister explains, Danto can "be read as a psychic remembering of slavery, where dark-complexioned women suffered specific kinds of brutality centered on overwork, physical torture, and sexual abuse" (McAlister 2000: 134). The ways in which the *lwa* of Vodou signify both the historical and cultural specificity of Vodou is something that must be negotiated by newcomers to the religion. Arguably, the *lwa* of Haitian Vodou are implicated in cultural memory. When those with no direct memory of Haiti participate in the religion, issues of ontology are highlighted. Newcomers, in a process of becoming affiliated with Vodou, often seek out those aspects of the religion that allow them to feel as if they belong. Sometimes this desire to belong engenders a comparative approach as newcomers search for similarities between Vodou and other religious traditions with which they may be familiar.

Different groups with different investments may compare Vodou to different religions. Those engaged with the ideologies of Black Nationalism and Afrocentrism, for instance, may see Vodou as a religion that retains the cultural memory of a pre-colonial past and so may compare it to other religions that they recognize as similarly pre-colonial. Others, and particularly those newcomers whose voices surface in this analysis, tend to compare Vodou to spiritual traditions such as neo-paganism and Wicca, lighting upon the practice as part of a self-perceived spiritual journey. Often dissatisfied with institutional religions they consciously seek what they see as alternative religious or spiritual communities. Although these individuals may make similar comparisons (between, for example, Vodou and neo-pagan spirituality) within actual Vodou communities, online comparisons allow Vodou to become sometimes literally (hyper)linked with other religious and spiritual traditions. These links, as we shall see, shape the visibility of Vodou online.

Perhaps because of the propensity of newcomers—some of the most visible discussants of Vodou online—to seek out familiarity, online discussions of specific *lwa*, such as Ezili Danto, highlight not so much her relationship to the socio-cultural specificity of Haiti, slavery or colonialism, but her connection to universal notions of "motherhood." Online comparisons between Vodou and neo-paganism or Wicca often position Danto as a "fertility goddess." Positioning Danto as a divine mother allows newcomers to find reflections of themselves in the religion. As June, a member of the listserv, explained: "I see a lot of myself in Dantor. She is a fierce, protective mother who loves her children unconditionally." Another makes the comparative approach even more explicit: "To me, Dantor is the Haitian Gaia.[8] She is the divine mother who looks over us all. She is the mother that is in all women." Undoubtedly Danto is closely associated with motherhood, but she signifies particular aspects of that role. McAlister, discussing Danto's place in Vodou cosmology, explains:

> Motherhood is one of the few roles available to poor women and crucial in a culture where children provide one's support in old age. Everyone— whether single, disabled, or homosexual—all women and men are expected to have children. Ezili Danto is a divine representation of the Haitian wisdom that the mother–child bond is far more important than the bonds of romance and marriage.
>
> (McAlister 2000: 134)

This is a practical counterpart to the universal motherhood revered in fertility-based religions. Karen McCarthy Brown calls Danto "the-woman-who-bears-children," arguing that, in the context of ritual, Danto evokes "the many possibilities in the mother–child relationship ... from the mutually nourishing to the mutually destructive" (Brown 1989a: 232). Danto may be an example of a divine mother, but she signifies a conceptualization of motherhood that is, again, rooted in the specificity of Haitian culture and the praxis of Vodou.

Networked communication practices, mediated via digital platforms, are often conceptualized as inherently "disembedding"—a term Anthony Giddens uses to describe how Internet-based communication can detach individuals from the immediacy of social relationships and remove them from social consequences. This affects experience of what Giddens has called "time–space distantiation:" the stretching out of social relationships that were once defined by proximity and that are now defined by the pull between presence and absence (Giddens 1991: 64). The hierarchical authority found in many actual Vodou communities is often either missing in the online context, or lacks the social weight it is given in actual Vodou communities. Online practitioners may be part of "real" Vodou communities, but discussions of the religion online are removed from the communal practices that lend them context and specificity. Issues of ownership—of who gets to represent (or even what it means to represent) an orthopraxic religion that has neither central organizing religious text nor a central organizing religious institution to offer definitive interpretations of religious practice or narrative—are magnified in cyberspace where it is easy to lose track of who is speaking for what. Efforts to police the boundaries of online Vodou are not only fraught with concerns around defining what constitutes authentic Vodou or accurate interpretation of Vodou cosmology, but are also circumscribed by the conditions of online forums, which lift the stories of Vodou out of the intimate context in which they circulate in actual Vodou communities.

The ways in which Danto signifies online is complicated by the fact that she is also sometimes called a *madivin*. While this term translates from Kreyòl into English as "lesbian," the two terms are not necessarily commensurate. Newcomers, who seek out Vodou, sometimes due to intolerance in their inherited religious community, tend to valorize Vodou as a highly tolerant religion that accepts both women and queers as practicing members and "ordained" ritual specialists. Such individuals often justify their understanding of Vodou as tolerant by reading, for example, Ezili Danto as a clearly identified and identifiable lesbian. In the Voodoo Group forum a thread on "serving female *lwa*" became increasingly focused on Danto's identity. Participants started out discussing aspects of the service of this *lwa* (the types of foods to be set out at a ritual feast in her honor, the behaviors of those "mounted" by Danto in possession, and objects found on alters devoted to her), but quickly shifted to a discussion of Danto's sexuality. Many of the newcomers to Vodou on the forum not only defined Danto as a lesbian but also saw her lesbianism as evidence of openness and tolerance in the religion. Shuana, a listserv participant who identified herself as a lesbian, explained the reasons for her affiliation with Vodou:

> I was raised Christian. My parents thumped the bible so hard (when I came out), I walked away from it. I wanted to belong to a more tolerant spirituality. I can be myself here, I could be a *mambo* [priestess] if I wanted. And Dantor is a lesbian. What is more tolerant than a religion where a lesbian is a goddess?
>
> (Shuana, Voodoo Group, June 2006)

Some may argue that Vodou *is* a religion that is tolerant of queerness—lesbian, gay, bisexual and transsexual people are, arguably, initiated into all levels of the religion, including as priests and priestesses—but this tolerance does not necessarily negate the stigma associated with homosexuality in Haiti, where the political and cultural force of Catholicism has contributed to the demonization of the religion as sexually licentious, feeding into colonial representations of the black nation of Haiti as primitive, exotic and promiscuous. In the online forums I observed, Danto is almost always identified as a "lesbian," rather than as *madivin*. Language brings with it cultural specificity. Because the Voodoo Group was conducted primarily in English, it is perhaps unsurprising that participants translated Kreyòl words into English, but in so doing they both link the terms "lesbian" and "Vodou" in the algorithmic database that structures the visibility of Vodou online and erase the cultural specificity of constructs of sexuality rooted in the Haitian-ness of Haitian Vodou.

The specificity of a Haitian Vodou practitioner's understanding of sexuality, based in the language and culture of Haiti, is potentially lost in an online context where newcomers are often more numerous than Haitian practitioners.

Contested language: negotiating cultural and religious specificity online

And yet, despite the prevalence of newcomers and "spiritual seekers"(Roof 1993), Haitian Vodou practitioners are active in shaping the direction of online discussions. Jean, a Haitian in the Voodoo Group forum, expressed frustration with a preoccupation with sexuality that he saw as "not at all Haitian." Jean saw Vodou as an intrinsic part of Haitian culture and felt that discussions of Danto and lesbianism were impinging on a particularly Haitian way of understanding the religion:

> Vodou is a very tolerant religion. But this thread is stupid. There was not even such a thing [or such a word as lesbian] in Kreyòl for a long time. I am not saying that Vodou is intolerant. I just think that these are American ideas, not Haitian ones.
>
> (Jean, Voodoo Group, June 2006)

By evoking Kreyòl, Jean reminds the forum of the cultural specificity of Vodou. More than that, he evokes the specificity of Haitian culture and its difference from "American" culture in a bid for an "authentic" or accurate online definition of aspects of Vodou. Jean's concern was less with the potential for inauthentic Vodou practices or discourses perpetuated by newcomers to the religion, and more with the attention that issues of sexuality were receiving in relation to online discussions of Vodou. As he later explained, he felt that there were "more important" things to talk about in relation to Vodou, which he felt was not being given serious consideration as a "bona fide religion." When Jean calls for a focus on "more important" aspects of the religion which, for him, include the details of how a *lwa* like Ezili Danto should be served (the songs that should be sung to her, or the food that should be prepared for her), he is acknowledging that the forum is shaping how Vodou is being understood. Even as they are engaged in social and participatory practices, practitioners who police definitions of Vodou are aware of how online discourses about Vodou can reinforce stereotypical representations of the religion.

While Haitian practitioners are active in directing online discussion, non-Haitian practitioners also take up policing of online discussions of Vodou. In a blog post titled "Sex and Sexuality in Vodou" a non-Haitian *houngan* (priest) takes an individual to task for asking about the homosexuality of Vodou divinities. Houngan Matt, who argues that "[t]here are no gay lwa. Period," insists that issues of sexuality (or what he calls "sex") are inherently private and have no place in the communal practices of Vodou:

> Sex doesnt enter into Vodou; we just dont care, the spirits dont care, so the religion doesnt care. Sex doesnt serve the community, so it has no place in a community religion. Out of that, you find that neither being gay or straight matter ... the point of the religion is to serve the spirits ... and as long as you serve the spirits and do it well, they will love you and continue to serve you in turn (whether youre straight or gay.) If you're looking for a divine copy of you, or a source of divine inspiration that for you to be happy with it has to be gay, this is not the religion for you.
>
> (Houngan Matt 2011)[9]

Where Jean evokes the specificity of Haitian culture in his insistence that discussions of the sexuality of the *lwa* are less than germane to a "true" understanding of Vodou, Houngan Matt targets the tendency of newcomers to seek *lwa* whose identity and experience mirrors their own. Despite his insistence that the *lwa* are never "gay," Houngan Matt acknowledges that Danto is sometimes categorized as a lesbian, although he frames this identity in gendered rather than sexual terms:

> The reason why [she is thought to be a lesbian] is her social status, but not her sexuality ... she's seen as a peasant woman of a specific class, one where the women are frequently left utterly alone while the men in their lives migrate to the cities for work ... women in those places are known to comfort each other, so she too is seen as having certain lesbian characteristics even though she has no problems being with a man if it means she will bear a child.
>
> (Houngan Matt 2011)

Echoing the work of Elizabeth McAlister discussed earlier, Houngan Matt's reading of Danto positions her sexuality in the context of the cultural conditions of rural Haiti. But Houngan Matt's insistence that Danto's identity can be simply reduced to a (it should be noted, highly gendered) "social status" that has little to do with sexuality—offered as a corrective to a misreading of Danto—is itself a particularly inflected interpretation of Vodou. The *lwa* of Vodou signify possible selves. They are not so much a direct mirror of the lives and experiences (or social statuses) of their practitioners as they suggest a range of possibilities. Arguably, Houngan Matt's reading of Danto closes off some of those possibilities.

Both interpretations of Vodou by newcomers and "corrections" offered by those claiming religious authority become part of online Vodou, rendering textual what would traditionally be oral and ritual aspects of the religion. In this context, the signifiers of Haitian Vodou become unmoored from local specificity and enmeshed in what Jodi Dean calls the "reflexive networks" of new media. In *Blog Theory*, Dean suggests that forms of new media are characterized by a decline of "symbolic efficiency"—the power of the symbol to make meaning in multiple contexts. Participatory and performative forms of networked new media make it, according to Dean, virtually impossible for us to assess the plethora of information online (Dean 2010: 5). Dean's argument resonates when, despite constant contestation of meaning, a definitive, authoritative or politicized "reading" of Vodou never really emerges online. And yet, the open-endedness of forms of online Vodou reflects, however distortedly, the open-endedness of Vodou itself. Although ritual specialists may offer definitive interpretations of the stories of the *lwa* in actual Vodou communities, such oral stories are inevitably fluid, changing with time and the relocation of practitioners.

On the other side of the policing of online Vodou by those who feel the religion is being undermined by the curiosity of novice and arguably ill-informed newcomers who may not understand it (but who nonetheless voice strong opinions about it) are those searching for religious affiliation that makes them feel welcome as women or as queers. An exploration of the discourses and practices of these individuals is a necessary part of understanding the implications and iterations of transnational flows of religion, often mediated through forms of new media. There has been little sustained examination of sexuality in Vodou; in part because such explorations run the risk of either reifying cultural specificity as "other" or dissolving that specificity in an attempt to find cross-cultural commonalities (Conner 2005: 144). Both approaches fail to acknowledge how transnational constructions of gender and sexuality generate complex cultural interactions. As Cindy Patton and Benigno Sánchez-Eppler observe: "Western sexual and diasporal discourses are fundamentally, if anxiously, related" (Patton and Sánchez-Eppler 2000: 2). Gendered and sexual identity as understood within Haitian Vodou cannot be somehow held apart from other formations of gender and sexuality in other places and times.

As we have seen with the story of Ezili Danto, both gender and sexuality in the cosmology of Vodou are performed against histories of colonialism and slavery. They are also performed in relation to the life experiences of Vodou practitioners. As those experiences change throughout time and as the constitution of practitioners changes—not simply through the introduction of newcomers to the tradition, but also through the lateral motion of diasporic flow–both the ritual interaction between *lwa* and practitioner and the narratives of the *lwa* themselves will inevitably shift and change. Exploring transnational expressions of queer and gendered identities make visible new forms of identification—identifications constituted precisely in the negotiation with national and cultural boundaries and historicities. These new forms of identification are also constituted, in part, by the affordances of networked, digital media which, as we have seen, make the complex cross-cultural mediations of gender, race and sexual difference found in online discussions of Vodou visible in particular ways.

Axel Bruns argues that we are currently witnessing a "paradigm shift in our engagement with information" (Bruns 2010: 24). What Bruns calls "symmetrical media technologies," including networked, participatory social media, amplify existing cultural activities. For Bruns, the biggest change generated by new media is that "these activities no longer take place in isolation but can be aggregated ... Groups of participants can pool their resources, coordinate their efforts, and develop central platforms from which their outcomes can be disseminated to the wider world" (Bruns 2010: 25). This is what he calls "distributed creativity." It is this type of open source aggregation of data that takes place, for instance, on web forums and blog posts devoted to Vodou where stories about Ezili Danto are told and retold. And yet, the open source creation that is such a part of the affordances of networked digital media also risks decontextualizing the very information Bruns sees us having a new engagement with. Much of what can be found on the net is pastiche or collage, made from cutting and pasting (pinning and liking) bits and pieces from around the web, forming them into something that seems cohesive. The most ungenerous reading of the engagement of newcomers with Vodou would suggest that their approach to Vodou in itself mirrors the cut and paste practices of networked information flows online. The public inscription and mediation of transglobal sexuality and gender that take place in online discussions of Vodou are governed, in part, by the way networked communications work to bring together sometimes disparate signifiers and communities. But while the affordances make visible particular mediations of race, gender and sexual difference in Vodou online, cross-cultural intersections are hardly determined only by the structures of new media.

Although some online practitioners remain wary of the way in which "queerness" is configured across transnational space, fearing the interpolation of Haitian culture by what they see as North American values and ideals, Barbara Browning points out that the interest of newcomers in Vodou is not the only way in which North American queer communities figure in relation to Haitian identity and community. For example, Browning explains that "in the U.S., racist and xenophobic policies implicating Haitians for the spread of HIV have led to the creation of political coalitions between Haitian immigrants and gay and lesbian activists" (Browning 1998: 36). Such cultural crossroads are suffused with both danger and possibility (Browning 1998: 35). The dissolution of cultural specificity is always a risk of intercultural contact, particularly when that intercultural contact is embedded within unequal power relations. But it is important not to simply read the interactions of newcomers to Vodou with Haitian practitioners as somehow oppositional, with the former embracing queer identity, and the latter insisting upon (a "queerless") cultural specificity. While some online exchanges around gender and sexuality are clearly oppositional, others demonstrate a fluidity that merits attention.

As the discussion about Ezili Danto continued on the Voodoo Group forum, several voices emerged that identified Danto not only as a lesbian, but also as an example of female empowerment. Julie, a non-Haitian practitioner from Philadelphia who had recently undergone the first level of initiation in Vodou, described Danto as a powerful, "angry spirit who isn't under the spell of any man" (Julie, Voodoo Group, July 2006). Natalie, who identified herself as a Vodou practitioner and also a "high priestess of the Dianic Wiccan" tradition, echoed this provocative statement, explaining that:

> Ezili Danto is powerful and she empowers me when she descends. As a lesbian I identify with Danto deeply. She is a revolutionary woman and she can fight along men, as an equal to men. She doesn't buy into the ideals of femininity or heterosexuality.
>
> (Natalie, Voodoo Group, July 2006)

In some respects, it is true that Danto signifies a form of female independence. Elizabeth McAlister asserts that Danto "is not searching for romantic partnership" (McAlister 2000: 134) and it is true that she is seldom clearly romantically linked (as are some other *lwa*) to other male (or female) counterparts in the spirit world.[10] In addition, Danto is, as Natalie observes, closely associated with a revolutionary impulse, having fought and, it is said, been wounded during the Haitian Revolution (Brown 2001: 424). Danto is undeniably a strong, powerful, independent female *lwa*, but her strength is complicated by the multiple possibilities of womanhood that she represents. She is, perhaps, one of the most complex *lwa* of Vodou and so it is unsurprising that online practitioners wrestle with her identity and significance. While Julie and Natalie's portrayals of Danto are neither inaccurate nor inauthentic, they valorize certain aspects of her persona, leaving her narrative untempered by those parts of Danto's story that complicate her strength and power. As Joan Dayan explains:

> Recognized as the most powerful and arbitrary of gods in vodou, Ezili is also the most contradictory: … a woman who is the most beloved and yet feels herself the most betrayed. She can be generous and loving, or implacable and cruel.
>
> (Dayan 1995: 59)

Mambo Pierre, a Haitian priestess who moderated the Voodoo Group forum, used her position as moderator to both invoke the cultural specificity of Haiti and also open up the narratives of Vodou to allow room for the experiences of others in the forum to be voiced.

Mambo Pierre explained to the list that:

> Ezilie ge rouge,[11] who you call Danto, is a mother to all. She protects her children, but she also gets angry with them if they do not do what she wishes. She loves men and women … but she gets very angry if a man beats a woman or hurts his child.
>
> (Mambo Pierre, Voodoo Group, July 2006)

Mambo Pierre clearly identified Danto as a powerful *lwa*, but also went on to challenge the valorization of Danto as unconditionally empowered, stating that:

> Some people want to make her strong. She is very strong, a very powerful spirit, but ... sometimes she gets hurt ... She is angered by the sight of blood. That is why when we give a ceremony for her it is *mange sec*.[12] You can have no blood [sacrifice] in a ceremony for Danto. Blood reminds her of how she has been hurt.
>
> (Mambo Pierre, Voodoo Group, July 2006)

Mambo Pierre subtly corrects the re-visioning of Danto as a divinity that is inherently subversive and empowering, reminding discussants—by drawing the conversation back to the specifics of ritual practice—that Danto can be vulnerable as well as strong. The retelling of the narratives that lie behind the *lwa* who possess their practitioners is an important part of the Vodou religion. Although online practices turn these oral and ritual stories into texts, these texts are not reified but are collectively created, remaining open to revision.

Complex social interactions occur when diverse groups of people come together online for the purpose of discussing *their* religion. Participatory media ostensibly allows individuals to contribute to new forms of cultural production and to develop new social relationships around religious identity. It also undoes the hierarchies found in the real-life interactions of Haitian Vodou rituals and communities. What is potentially lost as Vodou crosses borders and becomes part of the digital public sphere is an understanding of the cultural specificity of the religion—the ways in which the narratives of Vodou signify for Haitians in a particularly Haitian context. And yet, it cannot be assumed that Haitians themselves have no ability to intervene in the digital representations of their religion ... or that those engaged in the labor of reimaging identity online inevitably dilute authentic religious traditions. Digital media shape the public visibility of Vodou, rendering it accessible in new ways to newcomers and spiritual seekers who have and make varying claims to the religion. The visibility of Vodou online also makes visible other social relations. Gender, sexuality and their relationship not only to Vodou, but also to notions of authenticity and cultural specificity are interwoven into online discussions of Vodou that produce, thanks to the particular affordances of new media, new ways of knowing the religion. Understandings of gender and sexuality cannot be simply mapped onto the ways that Vodou is known in the digital public sphere, but instead they have to be understood as intersecting, co-constituting identities engendered by cross cultural negotiations brought about by the mediated flows of people, images, signs and symbols.

Notes

1 For further discussion of what constitutes diasporic religion see Tomas Tweed's *Our Lady of the Exile* (1997) and Paul Christopher Johnson's *Diasporic Conversions* (2007).

2 In order to preserve the anonymity of participants, pseudonyms are used throughout. The Voodoo Group forum was last accessed in August 2007.

3 See, for example, Karen Brown (2001) and Karen Richman (2005).

4 For further discussion of gender as discursively constructed, and performed, see Judith Butler's agenda setting work in *Gender Trouble* (1999). See also, Gayatri Chakravorty Spivak's "Can the Subaltern Speak?" (1988) for a discussion of women in subaltern constructions.

5 For example, John Perry Barlow's famous "Declaration of the Independence of Cyberspace:" "Ours is a world that is both everywhere and nowhere, but it is not where bodies live. We are creating a world that all may enter without privilege or prejudice accorded by race, economic power, military force, or station of birth" (Barlow 1996).

6 I discuss the film *London Voodoo* (2004) in greater detail in "Gods on the Move: The Mediatization of Haitian Vodou" (Boutros 2011).

7 Google, for example, creates search results by using an algorithm that ranks web pages with a "relevancy score" that privileges content that meets the "relevancy" criteria. Relevance includes how frequently the search term appears in a web page, how long the page has existed, and how many other pages link back to the ranked web page.

8 Gaia, or more colloquially "mother earth," is seen in the context of some neo-pagan traditions as the primordial divine mother.

9 Original spelling and grammar is preserved throughout.

10 While McAlister insists that Danto is "not looking for romantic" relationships, Karen McCarthy Brown, in *Mama Lola: A Vodou Priestess in Brooklyn*, links Danto romantically to the *lwa* Ogun, but still understands Danto as an icon of female independence, acknowledging that "Ezili Danto will take this man into her bed, but she knows she cannot depend on him, and she would never dream of marrying him" (2001: 235).

11 *Ge rouge* or "red eyes" is an appellation signaling that a *lwa* belongs to a particular "nation" or category of *lwa*.

12 Dry or without blood sacrifice.

Bibliography

Appadurai, A. (1996) *Modernity at Large: Cultural Dimensions of Globalization*, Minneapolis, London: University of Minnesota Press.

Barlow, J.P. (1996) "A Declaration of the Independence of Cyberspace," http://homes.eff.org/~barlow/Declaration-Final.html (accessed, February 2012).

Bishop, K. (2008) "The Sub Subaltern Monster: Imperialistic Hegemony and the Cinematic Voodoo Zombie," *The Journal of American Culture*, 31:2, 141–151.

Boutros, A. (2011) "Gods on the Move: The Mediatization of Haitian Vodou," *Culture and Religion*, 12:2,185–201.

Brown, K.M. (1989a) "Women's Leadership in Haitian Vodou", in Plaskow, J. and Christ, C.P. (eds) *Weaving the Visions: New Patterns in Feminist Spirituality*, New York: HarperCollins, 226–234.

——(1989b) "Mama Lola and the Ezilis: Themes of Mothering and Loving in Haitian Vodou," in Faulk, N. and Gross, M. (eds) *Unspoken Worlds: Women's Religious Lives*, Belmont, CA: Wadsworth Publishing Co.

——(2001) *Mama Lola: A Vodou Priestess in Brooklyn*, 2nd edn, Berkeley: University of California Press.

Browning, B. (1998) *Infectious Rhythm: Metaphors of Contagion and the Spread of African Culture*, New York: Routledge.

Bruns, A. (2010) "Distributed Creativity: File Sharing and Produsage", in Sonvilla-Weiss, S. (ed.) *Mashup Cultures*, Vienna: Springer-Verlag, 24–37.

Butler, J. (1999) *Gender Trouble: Feminism and the Subversion of Identity*, London: Routledge.

Conner, R.P. (2005) "Rainbow's Children: Diversity of Gender and Sexuality in African-Diasporic Spiritual Traditions," in Bellegarde-Smith, P. (ed.) *Fragments of Bone: Neo-African Religions in a New World*, Chicago: University of Illinois Press, 143–166.

Consalvo, M. and Paasonen, S. (2002) *Women and Everyday Uses of the Internet: Agency and Identity*, New York: Peter Lang.

Dayan, J. (1995) *Haiti, History and the Gods*, Berkeley: University of California Press.

Dean, J. (2010) *Blog Theory: Feedback and Capture in the Circuits of Drive*, Malden, MA: Polity Press.

Galloway A.R. (2006) *Gaming: Essays on Algorithmic Culture*, Minneapolis: University of Minnesota Press.

Giddens, A. (1991) *Modernity and Self-Identity: Self and Society in the Late Modern Age*, Stanford, CA: Stanford University Press.

Houngan Matt (October 2011) "Sex and Sexuality in Vodou," *Houngan Matt's Vodou Blog: A City Houngan's Life Among the Lwa*, http://blog.vodouboston.com/2011/10/sex-and-sexuality-in-vodou/ (last accessed, March 2012).

Johnson, P.C. (2007) *Diasporic Conversions: Black Carib Religion and the Recovery of Africa*, Berkeley: University of California Press.

McAlister, E. (2000) "Love, Sex, and Gender Embodied: The Spirits of Haitian Vodou," in Runzo, J. and Martin N.M. (eds) *Love, Sex and Gender in the World Religions*, Oxford: Oxford University Press, 130–145.

Patton, C. and Sánchez-Eppler, B. (2000) "Introduction: With a Passport out of Eden" in Patton, C. and Sánchez-Eppler, B. (eds) *Queer Diasporas*, Durham, NC: Duke University Press, 1–14.

Richman, K. (2005) *Migration and Vodou*, Gainesville: University Press of Florida.

Roof, W.C. (1993) *A Generation of Seekers: The Spiritual Journeys of the Baby Boom Generation*, San Francisco, New York: HarperCollins.

Sheller, M. (2003) *Consuming the Caribbean: From Arawaks to Zombies*, New York: Routledge.

Shohat, E. (2002) "Area Studies, Gender Studies and the Cartographies of Knowledge," *Social Text* 72 (20:3), 67–78.

Spivak, G.S. (1998) "Can the Subaltern Speak?", in C. Nelson and L. Grossberg (eds) *Marxism and the Interpretation of Culture*, Urbana: University of Illinois Press, 271–313.

Tweed, T. (1997) *Our Lady of the Exile: Diasporic Religion at a Cuban Catholic Shrine in Miami*, New York: Oxford University Press.

Chapter 8

Infertility, blessings, and head coverings

Mediated practices of Jewish repentance

Michele Rosenthal

And God blessed them, and God said unto them, "Be fruitful, and multiply, and replenish the earth, and subdue it: and have dominion over the fish of the sea, and over the fowl of the air, and over every living thing that moveth upon the earth."

(Genesis 1: 28)

In the Israeli orthodox context, the commandment to be fruitful and multiply stands at the center of cultural and religious life. Drawing upon materials from a broader research project that focuses upon media and religious revival in Israel, this chapter describes and analyzes mediated rituals practiced by women who attend the lectures of a popular outreach rabbi, Amnon Yitzhak, in order to ask for a blessing to cure their infertility.[1] Yitzhak often responds to these requests with a request of his own, namely, that the woman cover her hair/head, thus tying the practice of modesty (*tzniut*) to the miracle of childbearing.[2] To legitimate his request, Yitzhak cites sources in the tradition that suggests that women should cover their heads when leaving the house (Numbers 5: 18, *Ketuboth* 72 a–b) as well as a *midrash* that tells of Kimhit, who attributes her blessing of seven sons who became high priests to her devout practice of covering her head, even inside the home (*Midrash Leviticus Rabba* 20: 11).

Yet, despite these gestures toward tradition, I will argue below that the head covering practices depicted in the film and the live lectures I attended are innovative, mediatized rituals. Through a close reading of a video produced by Yitzhak's organization Shofar in 1998, entitled "Sons in exchange for head coverings,"[3] I show how the film simultaneously performs a didactic and miraculous function, teaching future audiences how to behave, and acting as a witness or proof text for miracles in the contemporary context. From the movie, we learn not only about infertility, but also about the powerful ways in which gender and religion are mediated in the contemporary context for live and future audiences.

My approach is ethnographically informed and self-reflexive (Lotz 2000), and the interpretative frame is implicitly comparative, drawing upon my previous research on American Protestantism, particularly in its evangelical manifestations for inferences and insights (Rosenthal 2007). While orthodox women have been the focus of a number of excellent ethnographies (El-Or 1994, 2002, 2006, Fader 2009) and Israeli saints and healers have been the focus of anthropologist Yoram Bilu's fascinating case studies (2010), this case study concentrates on analyzing: 1) the mediation of a non-liberal form of Judaism to a non-observant audience (aka seekers) and 2) the ways in which gender is inscribed through audience praxis and rituals, with an emphasis upon infertility (Davidman 1991, Roof 1999, Hoover 2006).

Religious outreach and infertility

In the contemporary Israeli context, bearing children is the cultural norm. Overall, Jewish families average 2.97 children, but in the ultra-orthodox community (Haredi), large families of six to eight children are normative, with some families having more than 10 children (and according to one tradition, telling the exact number of descendants may bring bad luck – so the census is problematic in this regard). Pronatalism is conceived within religious tradition and civil religion alike as the key to the survival of the Jewish people, and, subsequently, fertility interventions of all kinds are promoted and supported by the Israeli government through subsidies in the health insurance services (Birenbaum-Carmeli 2009, Ivry 2010, Kahn 2000). Here, secular and religious values concerning the importance of family meet and there is little public discussion or dissent about spending such a large percentage of the health budget (relative to other western countries) on fertility treatments (each woman can receive unlimited treatments for up to two live births) rather than other medical treatments.

Problems with fertility are part of the public discourse, and women who find it difficult to conceive live under considerable social pressure and religious stigma. According to tradition, the religious obligation (or commandment – *mitzvah*) is fulfilled when a couple has one boy and one girl, but since it is considered positive to have as many children as possible, ultra-orthodox families that are small are rare, and it is usually assumed that health-related issues are the cause. Reflecting these difficulties, recent Israeli films that focus on ultra-orthodox life highlight themes of infertility and families with only children (Dar 2004, Sivan 2010, Volach 2007). While self-defined Haredi (ultra-orthodox) Jews constitute only 8 percent of the population in Israel, another 20–25 percent (depending upon the survey) would define themselves as religious traditionalists or traditionalists, who observe many of the commandments and who also may support orthodox political parties (Arian 2009, Central Bureau of Statistics Israel 2010, 2011, Yadgar and Liebman 2009). For these traditionalists, health issues or other problems might evoke a visit to a rabbi for a blessing or to the grave of a famous kabbalist or healer (see for example, Bilu 2010). Desperate for solutions, folk religion often is a first/last stop when western medicine fails. The desperation produced by infertility creates unexpected alliances, and dormant religiosity suddenly finds its expression.

Amnon Yitzhak and Shofar

Since 1986, Rabbi Amnon Yitzhak and his organization Shofar have been actively involved in "kiruv" or bringing Jews "closer" to observant Judaism (Haredi Judaism). Toward that end, Yitzhak travels around Israel lecturing and answering questions about Jewish beliefs and practices. In addition, Shofar operates a very active website (www.shofar.net) as well as television site (www. shofar-tv) where a surfer can access the archives of his films, as well as watch video streaming of the live (and re-run) performances. In these media, Yitzhak addresses practical, political, theological, and existential issues. Throughout his talks, he quotes and interprets a variety of religious and secular texts from diverse sources including newspapers, television, and popular self-help books. Secular texts of all sorts and particularly those that discuss or analyze his own enterprise are of great interest to Yitzhak, and he uses them to legitimate the importance of his work.

Prior to Yitzhak's arrival at a venue, Shofar workers place posters, round up audiences, and distribute media of previous lectures. Usually the lectures take place in wedding halls (*olamot*) or community centers – notably not in synagogues (which are found in almost every neighborhood in Israel). The physical location of the lectures is not incidental; the choice of a football stadium or of a theater is intentional and symbolic (Yehoshua 2003). The hybrid genre of lecture (revival), performance, movie theatre, television and Internet streaming that Yitzhak has developed is unique as is the spiritual economy that he promotes. On the one hand, the media products that Shofar distributes are directed at a general (non-gender-specific) audience and cover topics such as: questions about the existence of God, the credibility of evolution, and the nature of miracles. On the other hand, several of the videos produced feature women prominently (i.e., "I, Gila Dorfman" or "Sons in exchange for head coverings") and seem to be directed specifically at women. Clearly, the non-liberal type of Judaism that Yitzhak is promoting is anything but egalitarian, yet the audience members seem largely to accept that as a given in the context of Israeli Haredi culture (El-Or 1994, 2006, Stadler 2008). I have witnessed audience members clash with Yitzhak about Zionism, army service, the belief in God and creation, but feminism or equal rights for women do not seem to be a central concern either for Shofar or for audience members.

In practice: "Sons in exchange for Head Covering"

In one of the lectures I attended in a mid-sized Israeli town in 2007, I followed my research assistants to the women's section (pushed off to the side of the stage, but in close contact with the men's section – necessitating that you pass through a crowd of men before being seated. There were only a few women without head coverings – myself included). The lecture began with the usual *Dvar Torah* (the interpretation of the weekly Biblical portion), but the audience was restless. Some listened, but many others were clearly waiting for the second part of the evening (the question and answer session). Almost an hour and a half after our arrival, Yitzhak opened the floor to questions, but not before he made a request himself – questions first, blessings at the end. Partially this seemed to be a tactical decision, which was tied to his desire to link blessings to donations and his knowledge that requests for blessings would dominate the meeting if he allowed it to. Those that ask for blessings are in some important way already one stage further along in their commitment to an ultra-orthodox lifestyle than the intended audience (the truly uncommitted or visibly non-observant), as they already believe enough to ask for a rabbinical intervention with God on their behalf. Since non-believers are usually a very small percentage of the actual audience members, there is quite a bit of jockeying and competition among those seeking blessings to receive the microphone.

Those audience members that evening that requested blessings who might be identified as non-observant (by their dress, manner, etc.) were usually asked if they would be willing to receive a skullcap (*kippah*) and prayer shawl (*tallit katan*) or, in the case of married women, to cover their head with a scarf.[4] For that purpose, the Rabbi carries skullcaps, prayer shawls, and pieces of cloth for head scarves to distribute to audience members. The individual that agrees to this new practice (and most do) is requested to come up to the stage (or is filmed at her place with her image broadcast on the two screens on the stage) to receive the head covering, while the blessing for a new occasion (*shehecheyanu*) is recited enthusiastically by the audience. Ironically, the act of covering the body, a symbolic representation of a commitment to modesty and religious observance, is documented by the cameras for future audiences to view. The once anonymous audience member exposes herself not only to those physically and temporally present but also to members of the audience viewing the lecture through live video streaming on the website, as well as to potential future viewers who choose to listen or view the lecture at a later date through the website (www.shofar.net).

Having viewed these events on film, or having attended these lectures in the past, women arrive knowing that the request for a blessing may result in the Rabbi asking them whether they are willing to commit to covering their head, dress modestly, or, if they already do so, whether they will read or study a particular text daily. On that evening, there was a woman who told Yitzhak, that despite her spiritual and practical efforts, she was unable to become pregnant. He asked a few questions regarding her medical care, and then he asked her if she would be willing to cover her head. She hesitated, and did not immediately agree – and at that moment, he called out to the technician to show the movie clip: "Sons in exchange for head coverings."

Viewing the clips: reflections on the text and the live audience

The movie clip "Sons in exchange for Head Covering" comprises three vignettes of different women who agreed to cover their heads and all experienced significant change in their lives as a result. That evening the first two of the vignettes which focus on infertility (the third features a woman who stops fainting as a result of covering her head) were presented. The lights dimmed – we quietly watched the film on one of the two big screens on stage: It begins with a visit to a yeshiva in Brooklyn, where Yitzhak is lecturing (in Hebrew). In the women's section of the audience, a young woman asks the Rabbi to bless her sister who doesn't have any children. The Rabbi asks the sister if she would be willing to wear a head covering – and after initial hesitation she agrees. The clip fast-forwards to 11 months after the gathering. The woman is interviewed and she confesses that after returning home, her husband was shocked and angry by her act. Although they had been slowly becoming more observant, he viewed the act of covering her head as an accelerant in the process and it was too quick for him. The woman claims there were a few very difficult days in the house – when he wouldn't even speak to her, but by the time the interviewer turns to ask the husband about his wife's decision, he can only praise his wife for her insightful act that solved their chronic problems of fertility, and employment. The vignette ends with a circumcision ceremony, with emotional music playing in the background, and the participants filmed crying with joy.

In the second vignette, we meet an angry woman from Jaffa who asks how it is that her Jewish neighbors married to Arabs are blessed with so many children and beautiful apartments and she who lives according to the Law of Moses is barren? The Rabbi answers: "I have one simple but difficult request. If you are willing with God's blessing, to cover your head with this kerchief I give you, I will pray that God will grant you children. God-willing, I hope that you will bear more children than all the Arabs" (Shofar Organization N.D.e). We see the young woman, dejected that she is unable to become pregnant, yet reluctant to cover her head. Finally, after Yitzhak tells her the story of a woman who agreed to cover her head and the miracles that occurred as a result, she reluctantly covers her head with the white cloth provided. In the next image, she appears wearing a black scarf/hat covering all of her hair like most Haredi women and a long-sleeved blouse buttoned up to the neck, and we witness the circumcision ceremony of her son, with Yitzhak as the Godfather holding the baby during the ceremony. The accompanying music makes the melodrama clear – and by the end of the movie, I'm almost crying (despite myself) with joy for the childless woman now holding a baby in her arms. The emotional register is effective and from the whispers in the audience, I'm not the only one to be moved by the joyous conclusion.

At the end of the clip the auditorium lights are turned on and Yitzhak resumes his interaction with the woman in the live audience again, asking her, if after seeing the movie (and the results), she doesn't want to cover her head, and now (miraculously?), she agrees. Against the background of canned music, Yitzhak throws a white cloth down to another (already observant) woman in the audience who helps her to tie it on her head and to recite the Shehecheyanu, with the audience enthusiastically responding with amen.

Mediated miracles: movies as proof texts

Here, the movie, rather than the words of the Rabbi, is what serves as a proof text of the miracles that can happen when a woman submits to God and observes the laws of modesty. While Yitzhak could have simply retold this story to the live audience on the evening that I attended, he chose to "show the film," so that we watched while we were being filmed (and streamed on his website) suggesting that the medium's emotional register had a persuasive power beyond live speech.

Yitzhak understands the rhetorical power of the film, and provides plenty of opportunities for audiences to view it (on cassette, CD, streaming video on the Shofar website, on YouTube, on the flash disk he distributes full of movies and lectures). In other moments, Yitzhak mentions the laws of family purity as another requirement, noting that he has not heard of women with infertility problems who did not solve them by covering their heads and keeping family purity laws. But, family purity laws, which require husbands and wives not to touch during the menstrual period and for seven clean days afterward until bathing in the *Mikvah* (the ritual bath), are not an easy sell to the less-observant crowd, nor are they a topic that can be visually illustrated (i.e., it would not be considered appropriate to film a woman leaving a *Mikvah*). In either case, adoption of the practice rather than belief is the important element. The innovative ritual (covering the head in public with a blessing), thus, becomes a visual meme for miraculous fertility – diffused in a variety of media and official and unofficial channels (Shifman 2012). If the individual's blessing request is later fulfilled, a next generation film might be produced of the process as well, showing how viewing the movie of the woman who agreed to cover her head inspired the next woman to adopt the practice of covering one's head, and thus is indirectly responsible for the miracle of fertility that ensued as a result. The pastiche of video clips is common practice in Shofar, and the same footage might appear in a variety of different films and contexts, especially if it is a clip that is shown at live lectures (the live lecture is filmed, and thus the clip is re-embedded and remembered by the audience at a different moment).

Through the ritual (covering one's head publically), gender and religion are invoked and mediated in different ways: 1) female piety is defined in terms of modesty in general, and as the covering of hair more specifically; 2) fertility is claimed as a central sign of womanhood and as a gift from God; 3) Jewish womanhood is publically performed and mediatized, that is, choosing to cover one's head becomes a visual meme for socializing future female audiences (Shifman 2012). Viewing the video not only teaches the women in the audience what to expect when they attend a meeting, but also reinforces the gender script that is normative in Haredi Judaism. While Yitzhak does quote the relevant Jewish texts that underly his request, he does not discuss them or their possible diverse interpretations.[5]

On the gendered audience

Once the favored object of communication research, the construct of the "audience" is almost a relic of the mass communications past, representing an era when researchers focused upon effects of media and when scholars interested in the relationships religion, media, and culture looked at the efficacy rates of televangelists, asking how many viewers converted as a result of seeing specific programs (Frankl 1987, Hadden and Shupe 1988). In the contemporary context of media ubiquity and technological convergence, scholars are far more interested in understanding how the process of mediatization informs religious practice in everyday life (Hoover 2006). Accordingly, I approached the subject of the "audience" at Rabbi Amnon Yitzhak's lectures cautiously. I was far less interested in their demographic characteristics (Goodman 2004, Leon 2003),[6] and far more interested in understanding the discourse, practices, and rituals that emerge in the context of the lecture, and the ways in which they are mediated to future audiences. Still, despite the criticism directed at the concept as well as the problem, the "audience" remains an evocative term, implying both an actual and imagined community of sorts – a connection between the live audience, and the mediated or virtual audience, especially since many of his recent lectures are broadcast live through his website (www.shofar.net). While enthusiastically incorporating certain popular texts, Yitzhak is critical of most secular media, calling it the lying media (*tishkoret*),[7] yet he is still desperately seeking an audience – and a mass audience at that (Ang 1991).[8]

The live audience at the lecture serves the imagined mass (anonymous) audience of the films – socializing them for future attendance, showing them what to expect and how to behave in the lectures. Most that participate in the live audience are aware of the cameras around them, and the role they play. In fact, it is a drawing point – at moments in the lecture the camera is not only directed upon the audience (and not just the talking head of the Rabbi), but also pans across the audience and reflects their image back to them on screens on either side of the stage. They are active partners in his enterprise, and their appearance on film reassures them of that. By attending the lecture they support Shofar's efforts. At the lectures I attended, most of the members of the live audience appeared to have attended similar events in the past as they were fully aware of the scripts that define their role. While there are women (and men) who do not agree to Yitzhak's specific request (i.e., to cover their head, wear skirts, put on a prayer shawl, etc.), they still fill a particular role for the video, as the questioning and stubborn inquirer (see, e.g., Shofar Organization N.D.a).

The audience members may or may not during a particular evening lecture decide to commit to regular donations (forms are provided so that they can fill out their personal and financial details for monthly donations and a blessing request), but by simply being present and filmable they sense that they are furthering the cause. Like the televangelist audience of 1980s America, they identify with Shofar's aim of outreach, and view their participation in the lecture as a contribution toward that end (Hoover 1988).

During most of the meeting, the cameras focus on the men's area of seating and microphones are pointed in their direction. In the past, there may have been more film footage of the women's section, which was edited out before being produced as a video or posted on the web. Currently, the lectures are streamed live, and the potential audience could be exposed to a "strange" woman or to a woman who is not dressed modestly. As the restrictions on women in the public sphere have become more stringent in recent years, as has the concept of "mixed audiences," women seem to be appearing less often on the screen. Still, when a woman asks a specific question the cameras do quickly scan the female audience.

The audience at the lectures varies from location to location, but the arena is always divided into two sections, with the women's section often being on the balcony (often the case with synagogues as well) overlooking the main floor, or behind the men's section. Occasionally, the men's and women's sections are split down the middle aisle – men to the left and women to the right. These seating arrangements are commonplace in the ultra-orthodox world, but for the merely interested or not-already observant, entrance to the lecture is already an act of socialization.

In a small-sized town in the center of Israel in 2007, I learned how the live audience was constructed by and for the camera, and how gender segregation might be flexible when necessary. I arrived on the late side – 21:30 – and the Rabbi still had not arrived. I climbed the stairs to the balcony where the women were sitting. Earlier that day, the Rabbi's son had been implicated in a media scandal – the facts of which were still not clear (see Grossman 2007). Would Yitzhak show up at all? Soon we saw his organizers looking at the audience, worried that the rows were not full enough, especially on such a trying evening. The men were asked to move down to the front rows, and the women were coaxed to come down the stairs and join the male audience downstairs in the back rows. The cameraman looked around, pleased with the results. After a few rounds of phone calls between the various organizers, the canned music accompanying the Rabbi's arrival began and he entered the auditorium and climbed onto the stage, sitting at a table with large video screens on either side of him that act as video mirrors reflecting the audience looking at the Rabbi. Separate seating was fine when the audience was big enough to warrant it, but here the priority was to fill the camera lens – making the appearance of a sold-out event. We had a role to play – we were the audience – the bodies that filled up the seats (35 in a row, 8 rows to the back) and the screens of the people watching at home.

The gendered body as the object of the blessing and the site of repentance

Gender socialization as it is expressed on and through the body is a central aspect of repentance as constructed by Yitzhak; if you treat your body as if you were observant, then you will eventually become more observant. From this perspective, the potentially repentant (aka secular) Jewish body sitting in the audience is not the same as the Haredi body that Gideon Aran refers to; it has not been "disciplined" in the same way (Aran 2003). The public (and mediated) act of covering the potentially repentant Jewish body has deep spiritual implications. Indeed, as Goodman has suggested, the religion that emerges out of ultra-orthodox efforts to convert secular Jews indicates a new kind of practice – that is neither Haredi nor *masorti* (traditional) by definition. The public and mediated rituals of repentance (*teshuva*) produced by Yitzhak are innovative. While women are asked to cover their heads, men are asked to put on a *kippah* and *tallit katan* (Goodman 2004). On stage in front of the audience, the repentant audience members are asked to recite the *shehecheyanu* prayer, for "arriving at this moment" after which members of the audience may sing and dance enthusiastically. Unlike other moments of repentance in the Jewish liturgical cycle (e.g., *Yom Kippur*), the ritual of repentance celebrated on stage is both public and individual (and not communal). The rituals are dynamic and they change focus and structure depending on current social and cultural fashions. Nonetheless, they share an emphasis upon gender distinction and the symbolic importance of reshaping conceptions and markers of gender identity (i.e., how womanhood is defined, and how it is expressed through clothing, etc.).

Not just women

Perhaps one of the most unusual practices of gendering entailed cutting young men's pony tails on stage, a practice that dominated many of Yitzhak's meetings when long hair was in style in the late 1990s among secular Israelis. In the movies, the young men are seen to struggle with the decision to part from their hair, and the act is framed as a rebirth or new beginning, the transformation of the body preceding the transformation of the soul. Echoing other pre-existing ritual moments – such as the *Halekeh* custom of cutting three-year-old boys' hair on the holiday of *Lag B'omer* in order to grow *peyot* (ritual sideburns) or the practice of tonsure in other religious traditions, the pony tail ritual symbolizes the individual's commitment to a change in lifestyle and belief. One Shofar movie traces such a transformation of an American Israeli (Hebrew speaking but residing in America), who arrives at a lecture with a question for the Rabbi regarding dating and marriage (Shofar Organization N.D.d). Yitzhak responds by suggesting that if he wants to find a woman then he needs to look like a man and suggests that he cut his hair. With the audience cheering him, and taped music accompanying him, the young man walks up onto the stage where Yitzhak cuts his pony tail off with a pair of scissors, and blesses him for a fruitful future. The movie cuts to a scene from a celebration a year later at a yeshiva in Williamsburg where the same short-haired young man is now seen dressed in a black suit and white shirt, donning a black hat, thanking Yitzhak for his intervention. Embracing Haredi Judaism, then, is also a process of masculinization, a return to the patriarchal tradition, and the possibility of a traditional marriage (usually through matchmaking).

As the indirect subject of every film available on the website, these rituals occur over and over again in the lectures and in their mediated versions – socializing viewers, and potential audience members to the rules: to heal the body, one must ask for a blessing, and change bodily practice. The body is the first site for repentance, bearing witness to the individual's beliefs; and in its newly gendered version, it is the site for not only physical healing but also for the far more important value of spiritual healing.

Toward a conclusion

In these outreach meetings, the repentant female and male Jewish body is produced and displayed (in contrast to the already religious body or the secular body) not only for the immediate participants but also for a mediated audience behind the camera, suggesting that the body mediates religion on more than one level. The body could arguably be understood to be at the heart of Jewish ritual, but the rituals that have developed in this context are notably camera ready and photogenic, highlighting the innovative aspects of this religiosity. The visual media play a central role in this spiritual economy, socializing the live and future audiences of men and women, teaching them to emphasize the place and the role of the gendered body in Jewish practice. By promoting a belief in supernatural intervention that is directly connected to the adoption of a devout lifestyle and practice, the movies (and their media off-shoots) directly challenge westernized conceptions of healing and medicine, particularly the modern, rationalist body, and promote a reified vision of male and female according to the current criterion in the Haredi world.

In her book, *Mitzvah Girls*, Ayalah Fader describes how girls who are raised Hasidic in Brooklyn are taught to discipline their bodies and their attire from a young age. She suggests that the practice of *tznies* (modesty) is one of the ways in which the community constructs an alternative religious modernity (2009: 147). Dress acts as a symbolic means for identifying an individual's level of religiosity – from very Hasidic to more modern. Head coverings are part of that code, with particular communities preferring wigs, while others deem wigs to be immodest in contrast to scarves. Some Hasidic communities require women to shave their heads when they marry, but most do not. For the girls born into these communities, covering their heads is a rite of passage which is part of marriage, and just one aspect of the way in which they practice modesty (others include the length of skirts, colors of clothes, kinds of stockings).

For Yitzhak, convincing women to cover their heads is one of the most important steps toward adopting a new lifestyle; the new apparel has semiotic significance both for the participant and for those who see her in the public sphere. As Gila Dorfman, one of Shofar's favored "converts" to observance notes: "Head covering is a very difficult thing – especially for people with a big ego. I have a big ego, and I have lots of hair (you don't see it here). It is a means of giving up my ego" (Shofar Organization N.D.c). While these appeals to tradition or to spiritual ideals to wear a head covering are consistent across orthodox Jewry, viewing the head covering as a causal factor in blessings (i.e., if you keep the mitzvoth, you will be healed, or you will become pregnant, etc.) is rare.

How should we understand these efforts by Shofar and the innovative rituals and blessings that Yitzhak has promoted in his lectures and films? During her research among *Gur* ultra-orthodox women in Israel, El-Or noted that lectures or lessons on modesty are extremely popular, especially "in the midst of a delicate social situation like mourning for a loved one or a child, following a disaster like a terrorist attack or a train wreck, during the spread of a dreaded disease, or in the middle of a war" (1993: 592). The women attending the Shofar events and asking for blessings to cure their infertility (or other diseases) are in a similarly vulnerable state, yet they have not been socialized to expect "modesty" to provide the answer. Rather, these non-ultra-orthodox women exercise their agency by choosing to don head coverings (Duits and van Zoonen 2006), and to adopt a patriarchal ideology of modesty (El-Or 1993). For the women depicted in the film clip "Sons in exchange for head coverings," giving up secular liberal constructions of self, individuality, and freedom for the choice to live according to the interpretative strictures of (male) rabbinic authority is evidently a small price to pay for the end result of a "son" (and not a daughter?). Wooed by images of miraculous cures for illnesses and infertility, the women in Shofar's films and lectures who participate and embrace this spiritual economy provide viewers at home with an endless flow of miracles. As proof texts that question the secular-rational worldview and its correlative conceptions of gender and religion, the "head covering" movies offer an opportunity to witness the formation of non-liberal, patriarchal religion in all of its mediated glory.

Notes

1 The chapter draws upon materials from a broader research project: *Mediating Religion, Sanctifying Media: Exploring the Nexus of Media Practice and Contemporary Religious Revival in Israel* (De Gruyter, forthcoming). It is based on participant observations in live and streamed performances during 2004–2007 and 2008–2010 as well as textual analysis of the website, video materials, and printed materials. The research was funded by the Israel Foundation Trustees and the Memorial Foundation for Jewish Culture. I am grateful to my research assistants Calanit Tsalach and Neta Kligler Vilenchik for their assistance and contributions to this project. Thanks also to Jonathan Cohen for reading some of the relevant texts with me.

2 Chabad has its own suggestions for religious piety when seeking to become pregnant. See for example, Citron N.D.

3 A shortened version of the film with subtitles in English: "Rabbi Amnon Yitzchak – A Miracle – Importance of Covering One's Hair – English." Available at: www. youtube.com/watch?v=Y4yuQ2Nb2JM&feature=related (accessed 20 June 2012).

4 Notably, not a wig, which Yitzhak claims may be acceptable for Ashkenazi women living in particular communities, but not generally speaking for all Jewish women.
5 For example, the story of Kimhit is explicitly discussed by the Rabbis and it is noted that there is *no* causal relationship between the head covering and having seven sons as high priests (*Midrash Leviticus Rabba* 20: 11).
6 Leon (2003) and Goodman (2004) both describe the audience as mostly middle to lower middle class Sephardic Jews that come from traditional (*masorti*) backgrounds. However, to my knowledge there has been no empirical study of the audience to confirm the impression of these researchers.
7 He calls it the *tishkoret*, a word play on *tikshoret* (communication) and *sheker* (lie).
8 On this pun, see Ang (1991).

Bibliography

Ang, I. (1991) *Desperately Seeking the Audience*, London: Routledge.
Aran, G. (2003) "The *Haredi* Body: Chapters from an Ethnography in Preparation," in E. Sivan and K. Caplan (eds) *Israeli Haredim: Integration without Assimilation*, Tel Aviv: Hakibbutz Hameuchad and Van Leer Institute, 99–133. (In Hebrew.)
Arian, A. (2009) "A Portrait of Israeli Jews Beliefs, Observance, and Values of Israeli Jews," Jeruslam: Guttman Center for Surveys of the Israel Democracy Institute for The AVI CHAI–Israel Foundation. Available at: http://en.idi.org.il/media/1351622/GuttmanAviChaiReport2012_EngFinal.pdf (accessed 20 June 2012).
Bilu, Y. (2010) The Saints' Impresarios: Dreamers, Healers, and Holy Men in Israel's Urban Periphery, Brighton, MA: Academic Studies Press.
Birenbaum-Carmeli, D. (2009) "The Politics of 'The Natural Family' in Israel: State Policy and Kinship Ideologies," *Social Science and Medicine* 69 (7): 1018–1024.
Birenbaum-Carmeli, D. and Carmeli, Y. (eds) (2010) *Kin, Gene, Community: Reproductive Technologies Among Jewish Israelis*, Oxford: Berghahn Books.
Central Bureau of Statistics Israel (2010) "Live Births." Available at: www.cbs.gov.il/reader/cw_usr_view_SHTML?ID=630 (accessed 20 June 2012).
——(2011) "Population, By Religion." Available at: http://www1.cbs.gov.il/reader/shnaton/templ_shnaton_e.html?num_tab=st02_02&CYear=2012 (accessed on 20 June 2012).
Citron, A. (N.D.) "Be Fruitful and Multiply Parshat Bereishit." Available at: www.chabad.org/library/article_cdo/aid/1005203/jewish/Be-Fruitful-and-Multiply.htm (accessed 20 June 2012).
Dar, G. (2004) *Ushpizin*, New Line Cinema (film).
Davidman, L. (1991) *Tradition in a Rootless World: Women Turn to Orthodox Judaism*, Berkeley: University of California Press.
Duits, L. and van Zoonen, L. (2006) "Headscarves and Porno-Chic: Disciplining Girls' Bodies in the European Multicultural Society," *European Journal of Women's Studies* 13 (2): 103–117.
El-Or, T. (1993) "The Length of the Slits and the Spread of Luxury: Reconstructing the Subordination of Ultra-orthodox Jewish Women through the Patriarchy of Men Scholars," *Sex Roles* 29 (9/10): 585–598.
——(1994) *Educated and Ignorant: Ultraorthodox Jewish Women and their World*, Boulder, CO: Lynne Rienner Pub.
——(2002) *Next Year I Will Know More: Identity and Literacy Among Young Orthodox Women in Israel*, Detroit: Wayne State University Press.

——(2006) *Reserved Seats: Gender Ethnicity and Religion in Contemporary Israel*, Tel Aviv: Am Oved. (In Hebrew.)

Fader, A. (2009) *Mitzvah Girls: Bringing up the Next Generation of Hasidic Jews in Brooklyn*, Princeton, NJ: Princeton University Press.

Frankl, R. (1987) *Televangelism*, Carbondale: Southern Illinois University Press.

Goodman, Y. (2004). "Hazra Beteshuva and New Religious Identities in Israel at the Beginning of the 21st Century," in Aviad Kleinberg, (ed.) *Hard to Believe: Rethinking Religion and Secularism in Israel*, Tel Aviv: Tel Aviv University Press and Keter, 98–177. (In Hebrew.)

Grossman, G. (2007). "Indictment: The Son of a Rabbi Blackmailed a Rabbi." Available at: www.nrg.co.il/online/1/ART1/629/231.html (accessed 20 June 2012). (In Hebrew.)

Hadden, J. and Shupe, A. (1988) *Televangelism* New York: Holt.

Hoover, S. (1988) *Mass Media Religion: The Social Sources of the Electronic Church*, Beverly Hills, CA: Sage.

——(2006) *Religion in the Media Age*, London: Routledge.

Ivry, T. (2010) "Kosher Medicine and Medicalized Halacha: An Exploration of Triadic Relations among Israeli Rabbis, Doctors, and Infertility Patients," *American Ethnologist* 37 (4): 662–680.

Kahn, S. (2000) *Reproducing Jews: A Cultural Account of Assisted Conception in Israel*, Durham, NC: Duke University Press.

Lehmann, D. and Siebzehner, B. (2006) *Remaking Israeli Judaism: The challenge of Shas*, London, New York: Oxford.

Leon, N. (2003) "Mass Repentance Rally among Mizrahi Haredim," in E. Sivan and K. Caplan (eds) *Israeli Haredim: Integration without Assimilation*, Tel Aviv: Hakibbutz Hameuchad and Van Leer Institute, 82–98. (In Hebrew.)

Lotz, A. (2000) "Assessing Qualitative Television Audience Research: Incorporating Feminist and Anthropological Theoretical Innovation," *Communication Theory* 10 (4): 447–467.

Muchnik, M. (2005) "Discourse Strategies of Maxzirim Bitshuva: The Case of a Repentance Preacher in Israel," *Text* 25 (3): 373–398.

Neuman, Y., Lurie, Y., and Rosenthal, M. (2001) "A Watermelon Without Seeds: A Case Study in Rhetorical Rationality," *Text* 21 (4): 543–565.

Peck, J. (1993) *The Gods of Televangelism*, Cresskill, NJ: Hampton.

Roof, W.C. (1999) Spiritual Marketplace: Baby Boomers and the Remaking of American Religion, Princeton: Princeton University Press, 1999.

Rosenthal, M. (2003) "Rabbi Amnon Yitzhak and the 'Tishkoret' (The Lying Media)," *Religion in the News* 6 (2): 22–23.

——(2007) *American Protestants and TV in the 1950s: Responses to a New Medium*, New York: Palgrave Macmillan.

——(2011) " 'Are You Willing to Cover Your Head?' Notes on the Spiritual Economy of Blessings at Rabbi Amnon Yitzhak's Lectures," *Les Cahiers du Judaisme* 31: 48–56. (In French.)

——(forthcoming), *Mediating Religion, Sanctifying Media: Exploring the Nexus of Media Practice and Contemporary Religious Revival in Israel*, Berlin: De Gruyter.

Sharavi, Y. (20 October 2004) "What is the Secret of Amnon Yitzhak's Success." Available at: www.nrg.co.il/online/11/ART/802/062.html (accessed 20 June 2012).

Shifman, L. (2012) "An Anatomy of a YouTube Meme," *New Media and Society* 14: 187–203.

Shofar Organization (N.D.a) "Rabbi Amnon Yitzhak – Headcovering for a Woman – Explosive [literally – cannon], Funny, Strong Clip." Available at: www.youtube.com/watch?v=aPQ8muDmZqA (accessed 20 June 2012).

——(N.D.b) "Rabbi Amnon Yitzchak – A Miracle – Importance of Covering One's Hair – English." Available at: www.youtube.com/watch?v=Y4yuQ2Nb2JM&feature=related (accessed 20 June 2012).

——(N.D.c) "The Struggle Against the Ego." Available at: www.youtube.com/watch?v=ikdWIXxQXzA&feature=fvsr (accessed 20 June 2012).

——(N.D.d) "Rabbi Amnon Yitzhak Cuts Hair: One Pony Tail Brings Another Pony Tail! Moving and Tearful." Available at: www.youtube.com/watch?v=l1XFM7ALUY4 (accessed 20 June 2012).

——(N.D.e) "Sons in Exchange for Head Coverings." Available at: www.youtube.com/watch?v=RjI4omFf7Cg (accessed 20 June 2012).

Sivan, A. (2010) *The Wanderer*. The Mouth Agape (film).

Stadler, N. (2008) *Yeshiva Fundamentalism: Piety, Gender, and Resistance in the Ultra-Orthodox World*, New York: New York University Press.

Volach, D. (2007) *My Father My Lord*. Sophie Dulac (film).

Yadgar, Y. and Liebman, C. (2009) "Beyond the Religious–Secular Dichotomy: Masortiim in Israel," in Gitelman, Z. (ed.) *Religion or Ethnicity? Jewish Identities in Evolution*, New Brunswick, NJ: Rutgers University Press.

Yehoshua, Y. (2003). "Suddenly You Encounter an Announcement: 'Tonight in the Cameri: A Hazara Beteshuva Meeting'," *Haaretz* (newspaper, in Hebrew). Available at: www.haaretz.co.il/misc/1.867254 (accessed 20 June 2012).

Chapter 9

Claiming religious authority

Muslim women and new media

Anna Piela

This chapter addresses issues arising from the juxtaposition of gender, Islam, and new media in the context of women-only, English-speaking Muslim newsgroups. These online forums serve as a platform for Muslim women who are interested in developing their interpretative skills, which helps them in applying Islamic teachings to real-life questions. This study bridges a gap in existing research because to date neither studies on Islam and the Internet (e.g., Bunt 2009, Eickelman and Anderson 2003), nor studies exploring gender-based interpretations of Islamic sources have discussed the potential of the new media to facilitate Muslim women's engagement with the Qur'an, *Sunnah* (traditions of the Prophet Muhammad), and *Fiqh* (Islamic jurisprudence) (Piela 2011). As some ordinary, 'grassroots' Muslim women attempt to highlight the importance of gender and gender justice, absent from many mainstream interpretations of Islam, other women prefer to preserve the primacy of classical Islamic interpretations produced by male scholars. This chapter explores competing understandings of gender roles and responsibilities in Islam, and tensions that arise from the enactment of these understandings. It also addresses identities that are shaped and reproduced by these understandings as well as discourses defining 'the position of women in Islam' (Ahmed 1993).

In 2008, Al-Azhar University in Cairo approved an interpretation of the Qur'an produced by a woman, for the first time in its history. This event was widely reported globally (see BBC News 2008), but several female Muslim bloggers criticized the way it was presented by the mass media. For example, Muslimah Media Watch, a collective of online writers acting as an informal watchdog monitoring news stories about Islam and Muslims, pointed out that the BBC News article suggested incorrectly that the approved interpretation was the first ever, and that it falsely implied that the interpretation critiqued patriarchal understandings of the Qur'an. In fact, in Egypt all publications dealing with the Qur'an or Islamic traditions have to be recognized by Al-Azhar scholars, and Kariman Hamza, the woman in question, had to apply for their approval before she could publish her *tafsir* (interpretation of the Qur'an) aimed at young people.

This haphazard reporting in the BBC News article illustrates aptly the continuing confusion about the relationship between women, gender, Islam, and the media. The acceptance of Hamza's tafsir by Al-Azhar, a prestigious and 'mainstream' Islamic academic institution, was undoubtedly a breakthrough, as the right of women to read out and interpret Islamic sources to mixed-gender audiences has often been hotly contested (van Zoonen, Vis and Mihelj 2010). Those women who challenge the position denying women that right include the now famous names of Amina Wadud (1999 and 2006), Asma Barlas (2002), Fatima Mernissi (1987), and Nimat Hafez Barazangi (2004). All of these and many other authors have engaged with Islamic sources not only to demonstrate that women are equally capable to interpret them, but also to identify and challenge what they saw as patriarchal prejudice in Islamic tafsir and practice to date. All of them have argued that Islam is a religion which ultimately promotes gender equality, and that this original message has been distorted by a culture shaped by patriarchy. Through these objectives, and despite the fact that some of these authors may not define themselves as being feminists, they can be associated with Third Wave feminism in challenging the conceptualization of feminism and women's rights as white, middle class, and West-specific. Third Wave allows for plurality and flexibility, and by rejecting the rigid paradigm of Anglo-American feminist project, it enables other frameworks to serve as points of reference in the struggle for women's rights and empowerment (Saadallah 2004, Afshar 1993). Importantly, it removes the conflictual framework dividing the world between 'us' and 'them,' and allows for shifting, tentative identities and alliances (Rowe 2008). For Muslim women, work such as that discussed above has opened new possibilities of conceptualizing gender roles as being endorsed by Islam, and of joining the interpretative project on their own terms, and across ethnic, class, and political boundaries (Haddad, Smith, and Moore 2006).

All these authors also have another thing in common: all of them have either been educated or lived and worked in American (or, in Mernissi's case, French) academia. Even those who earned qualifications as Islamic study scholars have often been dismissed as 'apologist,' or pandering to the West. Some *ulama* (religious scholars) have even branded them as heretics who threaten the Islamic civilizational heritage and the Arabic language (see al-Shafii 2011). These criticisms aside, the impact of female advocates for women's right to interpret Islamic sources is probably strongest in the West. It is quite possible that Kariman Hamza obtained Al-Azhar's approval because she did not attempt to re-interpret the Qur'an from a perspective in any way related to gender (or any other) equality, feminism, or critiques of the *status quo*. Her aim was to facilitate young people's engagement with the Islamic scripture. And this is where the author of the BBC News article commits the main error – the fact that Hamza is a woman does not mean that her tafsir is feminist-oriented. What she has in common with the female interpreters of Islamic sources from the West, discussed here, is that she enjoys privilege, being a daughter of a professor of the Cairo University, and having worked in prestigious occupations such as media and public affairs consultant for banking and media institutions (Saleh 2008). This privilege means that she most likely has access to financial and institutional resources crucial to somebody wishing to circulate their writings. At the same time, Hamza cannot be defined as a typical interpreter of Islam – she is a woman, and she is neither an academic nor an Islamic scholar. Is it then possible that there are more women, feminist or not, who engage with Islamic sources outside of ulama or Western academic sources; and if there are such women, where does one find them and their writings?

Methodological concerns

This was one of the first questions I asked when I started my Ph.D. project in 2005. I was interested specifically in grassroots Muslim women's interpretations of Islamic sources and traditions. The epistemology I adopted in my research was interpretivist (Blaikie 2009); ontologically, I approached women's discussions on the application and meaning of Islamic sources as specific constructions, existing in particular context and produced by people occupying particular social positions (see Ramazanoğlu and Holland 2002). Therefore, my interaction with data involved de-coding participants' interpretations of both the Islamic sources (at the theological level) and their social realities (at the sociological level). In turn, my analysis involved my own interpretations of these arguments; thus, the investigator (I) and the object of investigation (the online conversations) were interactively linked and the analysis was created as my research proceeded (Guba and Lincoln 1994). The social and theological constructions were interpreted using conventional hermeneutic approaches to data (Kinsella 2006).

This analytical approach was particularly appropriate considering my position as a feminist researcher who recognizes the fact that knowledges are created by people who are socially situated, partiality of vision (the fact that we are limited by our situatedness), the difference between strong and weak objectivity (as opposed to positivist, disinterested objectivity), and who views 'established truths' with a critical mind (Haraway 1988, Harding 1991). Furthermore, I did not seek to explain or assess the understandings of Islam that the contributors presented; rather, I hoped to gain an insight into ways in which women conversed using Islamic argument and justified their right to do so. Having previously scoured the Internet looking for websites produced by and for Muslim women, I noticed that such websites were quite static and did not facilitate dialogue between women. Thus, I began browsing Muslim women's online forums. After a few months I managed to identify several forums of interest to me – they were women-only and welcomed all Muslim women (as well as interested non-Muslim women) to enter conversations about understandings of Islam that took place online. All of these forums required registration, and this comprised a short statement regarding why the applicant wished to join the forum. Keen to build a positive relationship of trust with my participants I introduced myself, provided as much verified information about myself as I could (this included links to my profile on the departmental university website), and submitted a rationale for my research in order to demonstrate my views on the question of women in Islam, after all, a very politically charged topic. Eventually I was granted access by moderators of all forums, which meant that I could read all archival content – in some cases that included conversations, which took place in 2001. I also introduced myself in order to inform forum members that I was going to conduct research using the data generated by some of them; mindful that these were 'private spaces' I also stated that I would personally contact every member whose postings I would like to use to ask her for informed consent, in line with ethical guidelines published by the Association of Internet Researchers (Ess 2002). All participant and group/site names have been anonymized in order to protect their identities and prevent identification through 'Googling' of the quotes; all quotes, unless stated otherwise, are used in their original, unchanged versions.

The data that I generated for the purposes of my study – transcripts of online archival discussions in which contributors offered various understandings of Islamic sources (both the Qur'an and the *Hadith*) also lent itself to interpretivist analysis, as it did not constitute organized or internally coherent entities. On the contrary, it was incredibly messy and convoluted; in that sense, my analytic experience was very similar to that of Markham (2004). Threads (the online conversations) branched out into multiple other topics, and suddenly went back to the original question, or they came to a stop in the middle of a vivid exchange only to re-start two years later, and sometimes initial postings contained intriguing statements but did not attract a single reply. There was no consistency in length; threads varied from one posting to those with hundreds of replies. Finally, most inconveniently, the demographic data about the contributors were usually completely absent. The snippets of information available to me were usually distributed across tens of postings produced by a contributor who went by a pseudonym. Some of them were quite open about their geographic location, age, ethnicity, or social background, but others did not wish to disclose personal information. Due to this anonymity, I could not even be 100 percent certain that every single contributor was female and Muslim.

The research involved the analysis of a variety of topics such as marital relations, employment, and sisterhood. Due to the limited scope of this chapter, in this section I will focus on the ways in which the contributors conceptualized their own engagement with Islamic sources. These discussions on women's own methodologies of interpretation are key to understanding the importance of a systematic process, guiding this 'grassroots tafsir.' Very often contributors explained that they had joined the newsgroups in order to increase their Islamic knowledge, and they stated that this was only possible through engagement with the sources. However, they all prized very much the opportunity to discuss specific problems and the applications of Islamic knowledge in their solutions, and collectively create their own bank of answers. It is very significant that these women chose to seek these answers themselves – after all they could refer to existing fatwa websites, available on the Internet, or send a query to scholars who run such services online. This suggests that the fragmentation of traditional religious authority, noted by Anderson (2003), who described the Internet as populated by 'new interpreters' of Islam, gradually grows and affects the lives of more and more individuals. Taking into account this and other research on Islam online (e.g., Bunt 2009, Sisler 2011, Larsson 2011), I addressed the multiple, complex ways in which technology, which I see as a social construct, has shaped identities and social realities in the Muslim world; however, my focus has been mainly on the interplay between gender, technology, and religion, and real and perceived relationships between these elements. My research on Muslim women's interpretative engagement investigates an area previously unexplored by theorists of Islam and the Internet; however, my strategy is not based on adding gender to this mix, but rather constructing an analytic framework where gender is a constitutive and constituted element of the social world where religion and technology also exist. Below I demonstrate the multifaceted ways in which all these elements interact and shape the participants' identities, which they in turn perform in various ways in the online newsgroups (Nakamura 2002).

The analysis

Regardless of their methodological and political differences, all contributors agree that Islamic education is the main prerequisite of Islamic piety. It is prioritized above other kinds of knowledge because it is considered the only knowledge that leads to righteousness. Secular knowledge is also considered important, but it is always secondary to continuous, active Islamic education:

> Anyone can be a graduate, a phd holder, a super-woman, but when it comes to their religion, what is it that they possess compared to the sahabiyaat[1](...)? I know many women, some of my friends even, they are extremely successful, but extremely ignorant in their religion.
>
> (Zohra)

Zohra's musings illustrate the existence of competing knowledge, religious and secular. In particular she mentions the terms 'graduate' and 'phd' to conceptualize the secular in the form of formal, institutional education. She also recognizes that there are Muslims who abandon religious frameworks, but does not consider their successes to be meaningful in the absence of Islamic consciousness. She refers to female companions of Prophet Muhammad, and contrasts them with modern-day 'super women' (presumably women who successfully juggle professional and domestic commitments). At the same time, she emphasizes the importance of Islamic education for the wellbeing of Muslim women and the potential significance of the newsgroups for those women who wish to develop their Islamic knowledge.

The contributors feel that it is imperative to obtain Islamic education in order to ensure that their life choices and conduct will be firmly grounded in Islam; for example, this may be relevant in selecting a profession that is appropriate for a Muslim woman. However, it is not sufficient just to decide to study Islam using any materials; the knowledge has to come from an appropriate source. This is a reference to the fact that there are competing authorities and knowledges within Islam (Sisler 2011, Zaman 2008), and that one has the responsibility to make the right choices in this respect. Following is an interesting posting as Samira talks about 'correct' Islamic knowledge in contrast to 'illegitimate' knowledge marked by *bida* (innovation) and *shirk* (idolatry):

> its our first most duty to get the CORRECT religious Knowledge. We come across many confusing things in our life and if you don't have knowledge, anyone can get you astray. So to anyone whos seeking Knowledge, first Deen[2] and then other things. When one completes religious education then he/she can go for something else they are interested in. but always first religion so that any thing that you are doing wrong (unknowingly) like Bid'ah/shirk etc, which mostly people do unknowingly (despite of calling themselves Muslims), can be eliminated.
>
> (Samira)

The last sentence of this excerpt suggests that Samira may be a member of the Salafi movement, which rejects innovation, that is, any changes to beliefs, lifestyle, and social conventions contemporary to the Prophet Muhammad and his companions (Katz 2008: 468). Salafis are unpopular amongst Muslim communities in the US and Europe as they are perceived as rigid, confrontational, and with too many links to the Saudi state (Ramakrishna 2009). In spite of various criticisms, the Salafi movement gained much popularity amongst US converts of both genders, and Salafi women had a pronounced presence in the newsgroups. However, the above excerpt can also be understood as an appeal for careful examination of what is described as 'Islamic,' because erroneous knowledge must not be incorporated into one's system of values. This preoccupation with finding proper knowledge is no doubt related to the pluralization of Islamic authority online (Zaman 2008, Anderson 2003), likely to be perceived by some Muslims as problematic. In particular, Sisler (2009) pointed out that the Internet, paradoxically, simultaneously undermines and reinforces traditionally understood religious authority.

All newsgroup members, regardless of their political views, expect high scholarly standards in the interpretative debates. The first and foremost requirement in the discussions is to include Islamic references – either from the

Qur'an or the Hadith – in the postings with opinions about 'proper' Islamic conduct or responses to preceding contributions. Postings without such grounding are considered to be personal opinions, given less attention and result in fewer responses. Whilst this is in contrast to the general view that the Internet encourages a variety of personal perspectives (Witschge 2004), this is not a regular discussion; the stakes here are much higher, as outcomes of these debates seem to regulate women's Islamic conduct offline. Therefore even converts, who are new to the religion and are often unsure about competing versions of the Islamic narrative, insist on grounding of personal responses in Islamic sources. One of the converts, Leila, asks about the right of Muslim women to drive cars, and requests advice based clearly on Islamic teachings, demonstrating that she is aware of the weight that a reference to Islamic sources carries:

> Can someone help me understand and give me some information from a Surah, etc. as to why it is haram for women to drive? I'm not trying to be disrespectfull to ask this question, but I am a convert and am still learning about Islam and what I should be doing/not doing. I like the articles that get posted with specific references on subjects and just wondered, mashallah, if anyone could do the same for this subject.
>
> (Leila)

Leila constructs her posting in a non-conflictual way making it clear that she is not attempting to challenge anyone in the group; she is almost apologetic. By stressing her novice status, she indicates that her priority is to acquire source-based Islamic knowledge. Subsequently, other participants recognized this request and provided references with interpretations. Interestingly, although she is a new convert, she has already acquired some Arabic/Islamic phrases, such as 'mashallah' (whatever God wills), which in her case may be serving as an indicator of the shared Islamic identity. Such phrases can be further identified across many quoted excerpts.

In the newsgroups there are also competing methodologies of interpretation, and all contributors are working very hard in the narrative sense to advocate their points of view. In the next three sections, I will identify three different modes of interpretation, and the ways in which they are championed.

Individual engagement

There is a group of women who argue that every Muslim must individually engage with the Islamic scriptural sources, as the Qur'an never nominated a single religious authority or institution, similar to the Pope or the Church, that would mediate between believers and God. These women are particularly keen to reject the stereotype of an uneducated Muslim woman, and any attempts to prevent them from achieving education. Amira writes:

It is mandatory for Muslim women to study and learn the Deen for themselves, not waiting around for men to tell them. Knowledge of the religion is not a masculine thing – it's a Muslim thing <smile>.

(Amira)

Women advocating individual engagement with the Islamic sources invoke the example of Aisha (a wife of the Prophet Muhammad) who had the reputation of one of the best-educated Muslims of her time, and who was consulted on religious matters. Many contributors believe that Muslim women should follow the example of Aisha and other educated female companions of the Prophet, and develop Islamic knowledge in order to guard their Islamic rights and fulfill their Islamic responsibilities. Yasmin states:

Aisha, radiallahu 'anha,[3] was not only knowledgeable about the Prophet, peace be upon him, but was a judge. The Sahabah,[4] may Allah be please with them, used to come to her and ask her many questions years after the passing of the Prophet. There have been many other outstanding women in Islam with great knowledge who in turn, educated other women. Not long ago there was an article on this list about the elderly Egyptian woman who was not only haafitha of Qur'an,[5] but taught others as well and had been doing it since she was a young woman.

(Yasmin)

Samia expresses her consensus: 'I agree with you, according to the Quran, men & women have equality & also women are encouraged to seek for a better education.' Samia sees equality and education as two complementary, inseparable concepts. Her declaration indicates that she believes that women should have access to education precisely due to the concept of gender equality introduced by the Qur'an, but also because Islamic education protects and facilitates this equality. It is central for these women because it is integral to effective challenging of patriarchal or misogynist interpretations of Islamic sources, which emerged and gained influence after the death of the Prophet. Furthermore, knowledge of Arabic is considered as key to uncovering the polyvalence of Arabic words in the original version of the Qur'an (translated versions are considered only *interpretations* of the meaning of the Qur'an). Such ability allows for the understanding that a particular translation is, in fact, a choice between many possible words dictated by one's social position and belief in what the Qur'an represents. For example, the infamous translation of verse 4:34 which allegedly permits wife beating, is fiercely debated on linguistic grounds:

Words in Arabic are based primarily on three letter root words and derivations are changed somewhat by adding letters to them. (...) daraba ('drb') means to beat and the word in the Qur'an which people have translated as 'beat' is actually adriba ('adrb'). According to the dictionaries where I have been able to find the word adriba the meaning is to abandon, forsake, leave alone – not beat.

(Nisa)

Here, Nisa demonstrates that the choice of some interpreters to translate *daraba* as 'to beat' is contestable; she argues that such a translation constitutes abuse of the Qur'an, as the overarching message of the Qur'an, according to her, is that of gender equality and love and respect between spouses. As a result, there is wide consent in the newsgroups that thorough knowledge of Arabic is an invaluable tool in deconstructing interpretations of the Qur'an that they do not agree with. Thus, the contributors strive very hard to achieve their fluency in Arabic, even if they do not have easy access to Arabic classes or native Arabic speakers. They are able to exchange website addresses of Arabic courses online and practice together by use of simple Arabic phrases with explanations of their meanings.

Moreover, Nisa explains that it is essential to speak Arabic to understand the Arab culture, which is important because Prophet Muhammad was an Arab. She writes: 'The understanding of these things is expressed in the language. The true understanding of culture is expressed in the language. The language is the heart of the people. If we have not learned the language, we need to find a teacher.' In a similar vein, Bakarat emphasizes the strong links between the Arab identity and the Arabic language (1993: 33). Participants' appreciation of these links demonstrates their motivation to develop their comprehension of the Islamic sources, in particular the linguistic nuances.

Employing a mixed methodology

This methodology emphasizes the importance of Islamic education and individual engagement with the sources of Islam, but also accepts interpretations from a range of Islamic scholars, some of whom are considered legitimate authorities in regard to Islamic knowledge. The women are careful in selecting scholars they follow, and do not tend to take scholars' reasoning at face value. Such a critical approach ensures that other interpreters' potential incorrect understanding does not affect the reader's proper Islamic conduct. One of the contributors, Khadija, responding to her opponent in a discussion about the merits of following scholars, expressed a view that Islamic knowledge at the theological level is attainable to both lay people and scholars:

Please don't conclude that I mean to say scholars are not correct. True Scholars are correct. But my point here is that people who are not scholars, or not passed out from great colleges also may be correct. In fact, Allah swt[6] made Qur'an for us all.

(Khadija)

The last sentence in this extract is indicative of a deep-seated conviction that Islam is a religion accessible to anyone, regardless of his or her gender, formal education, or social status. Khadija defends the right of 'grassroots' Muslims to develop an intimate relationship with their religion, in spite of their lack of formal religious training. Women representing this strategy also carefully read the Hadith, always referring to the Qur'an in case of apparent contradictions. They appreciate the role and importance of the Sunnah, but they believe the Qur'an remains the ultimate word of God, complete and perfect, thus, remaining central to Islam.

In a heated discussion on the methodologies of reading the Qur'an and Hadith, one of the women explains her view. She states that the Qur'an tells Muslims what to do, whereas the Hadith specifies how to do it, and as an example she gives *salat* (the daily prayer). However, she writes that a 'blind' adherence to a Hadith is wrong; one should always cross-check the Hadith by referring to the Qur'an, which has priority over all human-made sources. Newsgroup members agree that there are weak Hadith in certain collections (for example, in Bukhari), but this is not a reason to neglect the entirety of Hadith collections. For example, Ameera expressed her view in relation to perceived contradictions present in Bukhari:

> And besides, what's so wrong in declaring it to be Saheeh,[7] when it's only an interpretation of the Qur'aan itself. It's not an entirely separate book; it's very much related to the Qur'aan, in that it explains the Qur'aan. It does not go against the Qur'aan in any way. The doubts that you have about contradictions present in Saheeh Bukhaaree, please clear them up with a REAL scholar.
>
> (Ameera)

Again, the last sentence in this excerpt suggests that Ameera believes that classically trained scholars are best equipped to solve problems such as contradictions within Hadith collections or differences between the Qur'an and Hadith. However, she does not advise against individual engagement with Islamic sources, in fact, her statement demonstrates that she herself has reflected on the above issues. The fact that both participants consider not only the hierarchy of the Islamic texts but also a methodology of reading them indicates their deep level of intellectual engagement with Islamic sources. In this discussion, the women did not agree on the extent of authority that the Hadith had. Whilst one of them claimed that because it was human-made, it had 'human' authority, the other cited verse (4:59) from the Qur'an, which, in her view, gave the Hadith divine authority. However, they both agree that sects that reject the Hadith altogether are misguided, which indicates a partial consensus between these two women.

Endorsing classically trained Islamic scholars

The third strategy of engagement with Islamic sources is more indirect, as it promotes engagement with readings of established Islamic scholars who explain the meaning of the Qur'an and Hadith. Proponents of this view warn that individual, 'unprofessional' interpretation may lead to an erroneous understanding of Islam, thus, 'asserting conformity and compliance with established religious authorities' (Sisler 2011: 1136). They argue that this is a safer strategy, because responsibility for a poor interpretation lies with the author, not the person who takes it on board.

> **stick to lectures of scholars and their students,** like one of our noble sister – admin of one sister group said, '**Insha Allah [we] will strive to only share information from those whom we have been** *instructed to take our religion from*' and she won't approve msg other than that source either. i was so happy to see it. may allah make us firm like her. ameen.
>
> (Zahara)

Zahara may be referring to verse 4:59 in the Qur'an which reads: 'O you who believe! Obey Allaah and obey the Messenger, and those of you who are in authority.' However, this group is a minority in the newsgroups; most women prefer not to rule out direct interpretations of Islamic sources completely. Such reliance on scholars is strongly criticized by women who prefer individual engagement. In response to Zahara, Amira wrote: 'It only adds "insult" to "injury" when we hear some women parroting what they have been taught by men about what the roles and rights of women are, instead of quoting what is actually correct.' Whilst this may seem like quite an unfriendly response, it has to be noted that responses are sometimes quite sharp on both sides. Dialogue between women representing different points of view, as in this case, is obviously more difficult, and sharp exchanges tend to briefly polarize these small online communities. However, moderators are very careful not to allow bullying, which in any case is a very rare occurrence compared to an average internet forum (Erdur-Baker 2010, Subrahmanyam and Šmahel 2011) and many participants take it upon themselves to keep peace and encourage 'Islamic sisterhood' in the newsgroups.

Conclusions

Quotes cited above indicate that there are both commonalities and differences between participants with regard to various aspects of Islamic education and reading of the sources. They discuss methodologies of reading and hierarchies of the Islamic texts, the question of independent engagement, using existing interpretations, and, finally, the implications of obtaining both correct and incorrect knowledge or not obtaining it at all. The right to Islamic education, also expressed as a responsibility, is unquestioned. As demonstrated above, there are three epistemologically different positions that emerge from the women's discussions: one group argues for personal, individual engagement with Islamic sources on the basis that all Muslims are required by God to study their religion; another group advocates reliance on scholars' rulings and interpretations, as they regard scholars to be the best equipped in the process of interpretation, having received classical Islamic education; and a final group oscillates between the former two, encouraging others to read human-produced Islamic texts, but with a critical focus, bearing in mind that the Qur'an is central to all other texts.

Many women who could be defined as ordinary, 'grassroots' Muslims feel that in order to apply Islamic laws to their lives in a correct way, they have to be able to understand the hermeneutic principles that guide the process of religious interpretation. Some of these women go online where they hone their interpretative skills in women-only newsgroups. Such newsgroups offer them the opportunity to not only engage with Islamic sources, but also to participate in a collaborative (albeit very messy and fragmented) project of creating a bank of Islamic solutions to problems that can be too personal to share in mixed-gender groups. They are also able to participate on their own terms, without being challenged by men, as in the case of similar, but mixed-gender groups studied by Bhimji (2005) and Brouwer (2006). The women-only online groups, however, are very eclectic both in terms of their members and purpose, and women who join them represent a whole spectrum of political and religious views. It would be incorrect to describe all group members as reformators attempting to undermine patriarchal aspects of Islam. Whereas there are women there who argue for reclaiming their rights within the Islamic framework, and women who openly sympathize with feminism, there are also women who reject it outright as a Western construct, or those who do not discuss it at all. This links back to the growing understanding, first started by the Third Wave movement, wherein not all women are interested in overthrowing patriarchy; indeed, some women are finding empowerment through specific 'bargains' with it (Kandiyoti 1988, Franks 2001). Therefore, my research question, originally focused exclusively on Muslim feminists (as well as my own budding feminist consciousness) had to be broadened to include non-feminist women, and my attention moved from Muslim feminist online communities to communities that attempt to build tentative, sometimes temporary and provisional bridges between women believing in gender equality and women who prefer to focus on their personal understandings of piety (Mahmood 2005), rather than gender issues. These tentative bridges and moments of rapport have emerged as one of the key findings as such cross-ideological connections are very rare (Badran 2001).

One characteristic that these women share is that they define themselves as active Muslims, regardless of the variety of Islam that they embrace. They rarely define this affiliation, preferring to outline their views, which helps them avoid being labeled with a fixed and not so useful tag of a 'reformist,' 'progressive,' 'moderate,' 'liberal,' 'conservative,' 'radical,' or 'revivalist.' People's views and positions often shift; depending on the context, they may almost simultaneously express views that, in traditional attitude research, would be classified diametrically differently. This lived reality of female believers, as reflected by their online communication and affinities, often reflects the contradictory nature of human identity, which may be linked to contrasting, rather than consistent views and identities. The novel feature of these groups is the potential to bring together women representing very varied religious and political attitudes in the ambitious project of learning about Islam and, often, learning to interpret Islam; the outcome of these debates may be equally a consensus or disagreement, but Islam-based arguments produced by the women to support their points of view are creative and constructive, thus, meeting the objective of engaging in Islamic education. At the discursive level, women are no longer merely an object of the 'Woman in Islam' discourse, but its authors, thus, contributing to a shift in power in the Islamic context of gender relations.

Perceptions of what is 'personal' and 'authentic' form one of the key challenges related to this women's online quest for a better understanding of Islamic teachings. Those participants who chose to engage directly with the Qur'an and Hadith as opposed to established interpretations, risk being branded as inauthentic, or, worse, as abusing Islam for their own political ends. This dilemma of legitimization has been aptly described by Campbell (2007). As new forms of interactivity emerge on the Internet, Muslim women are becoming more visible by participating in social networks, writing blogs, posting videos online, and setting up online businesses. There have been several small studies of Muslim women's online activities (Bastani 2001, Brouwer 2006, Bhimji 2005, Imtoual and Hussein 2009). These studies did not focus specifically on the creation of collaborative interpretations of Islam, instead exploring the social aspect of online interactions, but, collectively, this activity has a lot of significance, as it enables the simultaneous contradiction of several negative stereotypes about Muslim women, existing in both non-Muslim and Muslim communities worldwide. On the one hand, they challenge neo-Orientalist notions of a submissive, silent Muslim woman unable to voice her agenda (Said 1979, Spivak 1988, Khan 2002), and, on the other, they often openly critique misogynist prejudices in some traditional understandings of their religion (Othman 2006). All of these studies show how Muslim women actively negotiate their social realities using narrative strategies in online spaces; however, they are most likely to be able to transform or preserve these realities if these narrative strategies are underpinned by thorough knowledge and skillful use of Islam-based arguments; moreover, this chapter has illustrated how the Internet may facilitate the development of such strategies and knowledge. First, by giving access to the wealth of Islamic material, including fatwas, interpretations, and Islamic texts themselves, for example, digitized Hadith collections and various translations of the Qur'an; second, by providing a common site (the newsgroups) for such geographically dispersed, global communities of learning; third, by encouraging collaborative construction of shared meanings as well as intellectual addressing of tensions between meanings; and, finally, by providing opportunities for cross-ideological encounters.

Notes

1 *Sahabiyaat* means 'Female companions of Prophet Muhammad.'
2 *Deen* means faith.
3 *Radiallahu 'anha* means 'Allah's blessings be on her.'
4 The *Sahabah* means the 'Male companions of the Prophet.'
5 *Haafitha* of Qur'an means 'somebody who memorized the Qur'an.'
6 Swt is an acronym for the Arabic phrase: *subhanahu wa ta'ala,* which means 'the most glorified, the highest.'
7 *Saheeh* means reliable, authentic.

Bibliography

Afshar, H. (1993) 'Development Studies and Women in the Middle East: The Dilemmas of Research and Development,' in H. Afshar (ed.) *Women in the Middle East: Perceptions, Realities and Struggles for Liberation,* Basingstoke: Macmillan., pp. 3–17.

Ahmed, L. (1993) *Women and Gender in the Middle East: Historical Roots of a Modern Debate,* Yale: Yale University Press.

al-Shafii, H.M. (2011) 'The Movement for Feminist Interpretation of the Qur'an and Religion and its Threat to the Arabic Language and Tradition.' Online. Available: http://dialogicws.files.wordpress.com/2011/06/feminist-hermeneutics_shafii.pdf (accessed August 28, 2012).

Anderson, J.W. (2003) 'The Internet and Islam's new interpreters,' in D.F. Eickelman and J.W. Anderson (eds) *New Media in the Muslim World: The Emerging Public Sphere,* 2nd edn, Bloomington: Indiana University Press, pp. 45–60.

Badran, M. (2001) 'Locating Feminisms: The Collapse of Secular and Religious Discourses in the Mashriq,' *Agenda,* 50: 41–57.

Bakarat, H. (1993) *The Arab World: Society, Culture, and State,* Berkeley: University of California Press.

Barazangi, N.H. (2004) *Woman's Identity and the Qur'an: A New Reading,* Gainesville: University of Florida Press.

Barlas, Asma (2002) *Believing Women in Islam: Unreading Patriarchal Interpretations of the Qur'ān,* Austin: University of Texas Press.

Bastani, S. (2001) 'Muslim Women Online.' Online. Available: http://homes.chass.utoronto.ca/~wellman/publications/muslimwomen/MWN1.htm (accessed August 28, 2012).

BBC News (2008) 'Egypt Clerics Back Woman's Koran,' December 23. Online. Available: http://news.bbc.co.uk/1/hi/world/middle_east/7797921.stm (accessed August 28, 2012).

Bhimji, F. (2005) ' "Assalam u alaikum. Brother I Have a Right to My Opinion on This": British Islamic women Assert their Positions in Virtual Space,' in A. Jule (ed.) *Gender and Language Use in Religious Identity,* London: Palgrave Macmillan, pp. 203–220.

Blaikie, N.W.H. (2009) *Designing Social Research: The Logic of Anticipation,* Cambridge: Polity.

Brouwer, L. (2006) 'Giving Voice to Dutch Moroccan Girls on the Internet,' *Global Media Journal,* 5 (9). Online. Available: http://lass.purduecal.edu/cca/gmj/fa06/gmj_fa06_brouwer.htm (accessed August 28, 2012).

Bunt, G. (2009) *iMuslims: Rewiring the House of Islam,* Chapel Hill, NC: University of North Carolina Press.

Campbell, H. (2007) 'Who's Got the Power? Religious Authority and the Internet' *Journal of Computer-Mediated Communication*, 12 (3). Online. Available: http://jcmc.indiana.edu/vol12/issue3/campbell.html (accessed August 28, 2012).

Eickelman, D.F. and Anderson, J.W. (2003) 'Redefining Muslim Publics,' in D.F. Eickelman and J.W. Anderson (eds) *New Media in the Muslim World: The Emerging Public Sphere*, 2nd edn, Bloomington: Indiana University Press, pp. 1–18.

Erdur-Baker, Ö. (2010) 'Cyberbullying and its Correlation to Traditional Bullying, Gender and Frequent and Risky Usage of Internet-mediated Communication Tools,' *New Media and Society*, 12 (1): 109–125.

Ess, C. (2002) 'Ethical Decision-making and Internet Research: Recommendations from the AOIR Ethics Working Committee.' Association of Internet Researchers. Online. Available: http://aoir.org/reports/ethics.pdf (accessed January 5, 2013).

Franks, M. (2001) *Women and Revivalism in the West: Choosing 'Fundamentalism' in a Liberal Democracy*, Basingstoke: Palgrave.

Guba, E. and Lincoln, Y. (1994) 'Competing Paradigms in Qualitative Research,' in N. Denzin and Y. Lincoln (eds) *Handbook of Qualitative Research*, London: Sage, pp. 105–117.

Haddad, Y.Y., Smith, J.I., and Moore, K.M. (2006) *Muslim Women in America: The Challenge of Islamic Identity today*, New York: Oxford University Press.

Haraway, D. (1988) 'Situated Knowledges: The Science Question in Feminism and the Privilege of Partial Perspective,' *Feminist Studies*, 14 (3): 575–599.

Harding, S. (1991) *Whose Science? Whose Knowledge?* New York: Cornell University Press.

Hooks, B. (1989) *Talking Back: Thinking Feminist, Thinking Black*, Boston, MA: South End Press.

Imtoual, A. and Hussein, S. (2009) 'Challenging the Myth of the Happy Celibate: Muslim Women Negotiating Contemporary Relationships,' *Contemporary Islam*, 3 (1): 25–39.

Kandiyoti, D. (1988) 'Bargaining with Patriarchy,' *Gender and Society*, 2(3): 274–290.

Karmani, S. (2003) 'Islam, English and 9/11: An Interview with Alastair Pennycook,' *TESOL Islamia*. Online. Available: www.tesolislamia.org/articles/interview_ap.pdf (accessed March 2, 2009).

Katz, M.H. (2008) 'Women's Mawlid Performances in Sanaa and the Construction of "Popular Islam",' *International Journal of Middle Eastern Studies*, 40 (3): 467–484.

Khan, S. (2002) *Aversion and Desire: Negotiating Muslim Female Identity in the Diaspora*, Toronto: Women's Press.

Kinsella, E. (2006) 'Hermeneutics and Critical Hermeneutics: Exploring Possibilities within the Art of Interpretation,' *Forum Qualitative Sozialforschung / Forum: Qualitative Social Research*, 7. Online. Available: www.qualitative-research.net/index.php/fqs/article/view/145/319 (accessed August 28, 2012).

Larsson, G. (2011) *Muslims and the New Media: Historical and Contemporary Debates*, Farnham: Ashgate.

Mahmood, S. (2005) *Politics of Piety: The Islamic Revival and the Feminist Subject*, Princeton: Princeton University Press.

Markham, A. (2004) 'Representation in Online Ethnographies: A Matter of Context Sensitivity,' in M.D. Johns, S. Chen, and G. Hall (eds) *Online Social Research: Methods, Issues, and Ethics*, New York: Peter Lang, pp. 131–145.

Mernissi, F. (1987) *Beyond the Veil: Male–Female Dynamics in Modern Muslim Society*, Bloomington: Indiana University Press.

Nakamura, L. (2002) *Cybertypes: Race, Ethnicity, and Identity on the Internet*, New York: Routledge.

Othman, N. (2006) 'Muslim Women and the Challenge of Islamic Fundamentalism/ Extremism: An Overview of Southeast Asian Muslim Women's Struggle for Human Rights and Gender Equality,' *Women's Studies International Forum*, 29 (4): 339–353.

Piela, A. (2011) *Muslim Women Online: Faith and Identity in Virtual World*, Abingdon, Oxon: Routledge.

Ramakrishna, K. (2009) *Radical Pathways: Understanding Muslim Radicalization in Indonesia*, Westport, CT: Praeger Security International.

Ramazanoğlu, C. and Holland, J. (2002) *Feminist Methodology: Challenges and Choices*, London: Sage.

Rowe, A.C. (2008) *Power Lines: On the Subject of Feminist Alliances*, Durham, NC: Duke University Press.

Saadallah, S. (2004) 'Muslim Feminism in the Third Wave: A Reflective Inquiry,' in S. Gillis, G. Howie, and R. Munford (eds) *Third Wave Feminism: A Critical Exploration*, Houndmills: Palgrave Macmillan, pp. 216–226.

Said, E. (1979) *Orientalism*, New York: Vintage Books.

Saleh, Y. (2008) 'Kariman Hamzah: Egypt's First Female Quran Interpreter,' *Daily News Egypt*, December 21. Online. Available: www.masress.com/en/dailynews/ 116591 (accessed January 5, 2013).

Sisler, V. (2009) 'European Courts' Authority Contested? The Case of Marriage and Divorce Fatwas On-line,' *Masaryk University Journal of Law and Technology*, 3 (1): 51–78.

Sisler, V. (2011) 'Cyber Counsellors: Online Fatwas, Arbitration Tribunals and the Construction of Muslim Identity in the UK,' *Information, Communication and Society*, 14 (8): 1136–1159.

Spivak, G. (1988) 'Can the Subaltern Speak?' in C. Nelson and L. Grossberg (eds) Marxism and the Interpretation of Culture, Urbana: University of Illinois Press, pp. 271–316.

Subrahmanyam, K. and Šmahel, D. (2011) *Digital Youth: The Role of Media in Development*, New York, London: Springer.

van Zoonen, L., Vis, F., and Minhelj, S. (2010) 'Performing Citizenship on YouTube: Activism, Satire and Online Debate around the Anti-Islam Video Fitna,' *Critical Discourse Studies*, 7 (4): 249–262.

Visser, T. (2002) 'Islam, Gender, and Reconciliation: Making Room for New Gender Perspectives,' in J.D. Gort et al. (eds) *Religion, Conflict, and Reconciliation*, Amsterdam: Rodopi, pp. 186–194.

Wadud, A. (1999) *Qur'an and Woman: Rereading the Sacred Text from a Woman's Perspective*, New York: Oxford University Press.

Wadud, A. (2006) *Inside the Gender Jihad: Women's Reform in Islam*, Oxford: Oneworld Publications.

Witschge, T. (2004) 'Online Deliberation: Possibilities of the Internet for Deliberative Democracy,' in P.M. Shane (ed.) *Democracy Online: The Prospects for Political Renewal Through the Internet*, Abingdon: Psychology Press, pp. 109–122.

Zaman, S. (2008) 'From Imam to Cyber-mufti: Consuming Identity in Muslim America,' *The Muslim World*, 98 (4): 465–474.

Chapter 10

Meanings and masculinities

Curtis D. Coats and Stewart M. Hoover

Of all the rocks upon which we build our lives, we are reminded today that family is the most important. And we are called to recognize and honor how critical every father is to that foundation ...

... we've got to set high expectations for ourselves ... It's a wonderful thing if you are married and living in a home with your children, but don't just sit in the house and watch "SportsCenter" all weekend long. That's why so many children are growing up in front of the television. As fathers and parents, we've got to spend more time with them, and help them with their homework, and replace the video game or the remote control with a book once in a while. That's how we build that foundation.

(Obama 2008)

Here, we find the man as he was meant to be, mirroring the true character of God. Here we find the paternal male who generates, not destroys life—the benevolent provider and defender, not the aggressor or predator. Here we discover the man who finds his strength and purpose as a father and friend, a protector and provider, and mentor and a moral example ...

(Eberly 1999: 31)

... many of the most corrupting viruses [in society] are now being borne along not by sinister politicians but by an entertainment and information media culture, and that this omnipresent culture is displacing the core social institutions that once shaped and molded the democratic citizen.

(Eberly 1999: 9)

This chapter begins with these quotes to show the dominant discourse about masculinity in American life. The first excerpt is from a speech delivered by the American President, Barack Obama, at the Apostolic Church of God in Chicago in 2008. The other excerpts are from Don Eberly, a key player in George W. Bush's Office of Faith-based Initiatives, and founder of The Civil Society Project, a think-tank devoted to the development of a neoconservative discourse on civil society and civic engagement.

This masculinist discourse is one that transcends political boundaries. It is a discourse that draws on a symbolic inventory of "essential masculinity," an inventory that connects "manhood" to fatherhood, to the primacy of the heterosexual family in the "good society," to leadership (both public and private), to affective presence in the home, to character and to responsibility. In short, this discourse connects masculinity to provision, protection, and purpose.

These quotes also offer insights into how this dominant American discourse connects masculinity to religion. The conservative critic, Eberly, boldly expresses language of "God" and "truth" in a way that echoes the dominant Evangelical Christian discourse about righteous "Tender Warriors" (Weber 2006). This is a discourse of "headship," which creates a chain of being from God to men to their families. Obama's comments take a less explicitly religious turn, drawing instead on a moral character of "goodness" and "responsibility," which echoes mainline American Protestants' expressions of masculinity in a framework sometimes called "Golden Rule liberalism" (Wilcox 2004: 25). His is also a discourse that certainly situates men *inside* the home in an essential way but which does not use the same explicit coded language of headship or religion. This is not to say that mainline Protestant men do not play similar roles in their everyday lives as conservative, American Evangelical men (Wilcox 2004; Gallagher 2003; Bartkowski 2007); rather, it is only to say that these men, like President Obama, *express* this role in less explicitly religious and authoritarian language.

Finally, these quotes note an insidious role for media in the constitution of masculinity (and, by extension, the family and the "good society"). Media are a threat, whether in terms of the time media take away from more important domestic roles or in terms of a moral disease that is damaging the fabric of society. Again, there are clear differences in tone and content in these quotes, but the dominant American discourse of masculinity positions positive, essential masculinity against "the media."

This chapter seeks to explore the US cultural discourse about media, masculinity, and religion in greater detail by comparing self-described Evangelical and mainline Protestant men. We suggest that media, masculinity, and religion work together in more complicated ways than those expressed in the dominant discourse.

There are developed literatures on media and gender, media and religion, and religion and gender, but, as the general argument of this book suggests, there is a significant gap in the literature that explores the interconnections among media, religion, and gender. Similarly, there is a growing literature on religion and masculinity and media and masculinity, but both of these literatures ignore one another by either making religion invisible on the one hand or by positing reductionist notions of "the media" on the other.

Our task is to propose a way forward that might help bridge this gap. We propose an approach that is grounded in the "culturalist turn" in media studies, which points to the need to understand how men "in the pews" understand their religious, masculine "Selves" in the media age. We argue that religious men are reflexive in their media use and that they engage what they might consider "positive" and "negative" media in constructive ways. In short, rather than being the nuisance or viruses expressed above, media provide the symbolic resources that allow men to situate themselves in religious space.

Literature review

Compared with the prodigious literature focused on women and media, men and masculinity have received relatively little attention in media studies literatures. While most voices have accepted the contributions of feminist theory to understanding of the masculine, some have lamented this situation. Prominent streams of thought have assumed that there is something "essentially" masculine that has been overlooked or denied under the regime of feminist analysis. Mansfield (2006) and Farrell (2001), for example, look for evidence of this essential character in the context of lived experience. Within this school of thought, however, there appears to be little agreement on whether masculinity is primarily of *biological* or *cultural* origin. For many such voices, this seems not to matter, while it is of primary concern to media scholars. Macnamara (2006) and Nathanson and Young (2001), for example, concentrate on sources in the cultural—particularly the media—realm.

An important assumption remains in the background of all of this work—the extent to which masculinity must be understood in relation to heteronormative patriarchy in the context of public and private gender relations. Most voices agree this is the central issue, though with a range of expressions from "hypermasculine" to more egalitarian valences. The question of male prerogative remains central for most. Critical men's studies, as advocated by Connell (2003), problematizes this question, treating such affordances of masculinity as symbolic resources to meaning and action, through which men make "situationally specific choices from a cultural repertoire of masculine behavior" (see Wetherell and Edley 1999: 251). As noted by Hanke, though, such prerogatives are products both of gender and of class, with "white, middle-class, heterosexual, professional-managerial men" particularly able to exercise them (1998: 186).

But in much of this, media and masculinity remain as a kind of incommensurate pairing, with the natural world of "the gendered" existing in an assumed object relation to the media and processes of mediation. The culturalist turn in media studies has introduced the idea that gender is something constructed out of symbols, values, and other resources in the culture (e.g., Butler 1990). A role for the media is, of course, implied in this (Gauntlett 2002; Wetherell and Edley 1999). As Consalvo succinctly put it, the question is how media "construct masculinity in a particular time and place, and how these outlets differentiate between various forms of the masculine" (2003: 29).

This culturalist discourse exists against the backdrop of approaches that both focused on representations (within the powerful framework of hegemony) and, within that, were concerned primarily with negative or anti-social representations. Craig noted that sex roles, male violence, and pornography were the most common topics (Craig 1992: 4). Today, most agree that this pathological approach to masculinity in media ignores the fact of cultural construction, that "masculinity is what a culture expects of its men" (Craig 1992: 3; see also Hanke 1998).

Many studies have reinforced the earlier paradigm of representation by finding largely "traditional" images of masculinity and manhood (Consalvo 2003; Faludi 2000), but there is evidence that media representations of masculinity are in transition toward "softer" and "reconstructed" male characters (Craig 1993; Macnamara 2006). Macnamara points out, though, that while these transitional representations might be on the rise, traditional ones are still very much in evidence, with men still being portrayed as "violent and aggressive thieves, murderers, wife and girlfriend beaters, sexual abusers, molesters, perverts, irresponsible, deadbeat dads and philanderers" (2006: 166).

While the concerns of culturalist and constructivist approaches stand apart from earlier paradigms' implications that stereotypes were somehow influential of behavior, there remains a concern with whether media representations might also *constitute* masculinity in important ways. Subjectivities, Saco notes (1992: 25), are rooted in particular, located discourses. Much current work on media and masculinity assumes that the media are a central locus of discourse. She argues that in interactions between media and subjectivities, media do in fact construct gender. Consalvo also sees media representation in ideological terms. Mediated masculinities, she posits, are "made to seem natural and inevitable, therefore becoming ideological and seeming 'trans-historical'" (Consalvo 2003: 30).

Hanke (1992, 1998) has addressed this question of mere "representation" versus the more generative idea that gender mediation is actually constructive. He differs from received approaches by suggesting that there is not one, unitary view of masculinity even present in the media. Consalvo agrees that "as with representations of women, there are multiple representations of men, and therefore multiple masculinities" (2003: 29, see also Beynon 2002; Connell 2000). However, Hanke argues that any analysis of male gender must necessarily retain at its core an appreciation of the persistence of hegemonic masculinity. For Hanke, issues of domination must be appreciated in any analysis. Modern masculinity may have become modulated, and even "soft," but the traditional view persists (Hanke 1992, 1998).

The ways in which male gender is thought about in relation to media, then, is a complex challenge. On the one hand, the traditional view that media somehow affect or cause gender roles through their representations have given way to the idea that media constitute gender through a complex interaction with culture, experience, and practice. Representations themselves seem to be changing, with contemporary images of masculinity increasingly attuned to broader social goals of equality and balanced gender roles and expectations. At the same time, though, there persists the notion that there are some essential things that define and explain "the masculine." We have moved away from the view that the masculine exists in media as the obverse of, or the antagonist of, "the feminine," but there is a strong argument that something of the uniquely masculine needs to be retained in our analyses.

Gauntlett (2002) has more directly addressed the way mediated representations might be involved in constructing male identities. He dismisses the orientation of much prior work (including much of that detailed above) toward a paradigm of "media effects." Instead, he points to the increasingly influential notion that audiences must be understood as active in constructing meanings, and that it is their practices of consumption that bring about the mediation of gender. He draws on the work of Anthony Giddens (1991), who has suggested that contemporary social practice must be understood as a reflexive project of the self, intended to address the stresses and the strains of modern life through more-or-less self-conscious practices of cultural consumption, representation, and circulation. Gauntlett has suggested the metaphor of "self-narrativising" as a helpful way of understanding this process, one that is articulated into media and media consumption. He sees analysis within this framework as allowing the capture of the fluid and evolving identities around masculinity. Reflexive practice, in Gauntlett's view, routinizes ways of imagining that were once less self-conscious and interacts with media in new and different ways. Individuals are more empowered by their sense that media give them insights into the workings of social realms such as gender, at the same time that they provide important clues as to the nature of contemporary gender roles. Media, to Gauntlett, accomplish this in part through their being a shared context of common understanding of what is normative in contemporary culture (Gauntlett 2002: 103).

By extension, we can posit that a more descriptive and more relevant account might be made of the ways that women and men understand masculine identity through media practice. Such an approach would have the additional benefit of addressing an important lacuna in prior work on media and masculinity in the area of religion and spirituality. No studies thus far have specifically looked at the way that religious contexts, ideas, and meanings might relate to the broader cultural mediation of gender. This in spite of the fact that in the United States (where much of this research has taken place) religion persists as an important frame and dimension of private, public, and social life.

A number of scholars, however, have looked at the relationship between religion and gender. Wilcox points to three different perspectives in the sociological understanding of gender and religion: the "family modernization" perspective (2004: 7), the "'culture war' thesis" (2004: 8), and what Bartkowski called the "discursive tacking" perspective (2004: 53). Each of these perspectives seeks to understand the relationship of religion, particularly Christianity in the United States, to gender and to broader cultural discourses. The first perspective builds on the secularization thesis in religious studies by suggesting that the marginalization of religion goes hand-in-hand with the weakening of the family as an institutional force (Wilcox 2004). This thesis suggests that gender traditionalism will slowly give way to more egalitarian impulses as the cultural centrality of religion and family wane. The second perspective suggests that conservative religion is "at war" with broader cultural forces (especially the media) and that the "family is the primary battleground for this conflict" (Wilcox 2004: 8). This is a perspective that pits traditional male authority against feminist impulses thought to dominate the secular, cultural sphere. Finally, Bartkowski suggested that conservative Christian men, in particular, oscillate, or "tack," between authoritarian language and expressive egalitarianism in the construction of masculine identity.

What is most notable in these perspectives for our purposes is the largely unstated role of the media—one that is part of the feminist cultural impulse and that is providing the symbolic inventories that allow conservative Christian men to tack toward egalitarianism in an effort to "soften" their patriarchy. None of these perspectives considers polysemy or the patriarchal hegemony of the media sphere discussed previously. Instead, media are always simply cast within the egalitarian culture sphere that religious men must encounter and negotiate. To the extent that media are discussed at all in this literature, it is within the discussion of conservative, Evangelical media (e.g., Messner 1997; Bartkowski 2007; Gallagher and Wood 2005).

The literature engaging religion and gender moves in a parallel direction with the literature of masculinity and media by moving toward an examination of polysemy in official rhetoric while recognizing that varieties of meaning are often embedded in heteronormativity. What is surprising, then, is that the conversation about masculinity in religious studies rarely, if ever, extends beyond *religious media* to media more generally. If variety exists within official religious discourses, then we should not be surprised that a wider array of gendered narratives and symbols exists in the broader media sphere, even while that sphere tends to maintain patriarchy. This view of media challenges the three religious studies perspectives introduced above, which imply that media are fundamentally at odds with religion and that media are the driving source of the egalitarian impulse in culture.

The religious studies literature moves toward reception studies, particularly in the "discursive tacking" perspective outlined above (Bartkowski 2004). This move follows Hoover's suggestion (2006) that nuanced, narrative, and constructivist approaches are the only ones that adequately account for the complex, layered ways that religious ideas are articulated into and through media cultures. The remainder of this chapter will turn to such complexity to show the ways in which Evangelical and mainline Protestant men in the United States engage the symbolic inventories provided by media and religion.

Christian men, mediated meanings

Our interviews[1] demonstrate that Evangelical and mainline Protestant men are both reflexive about their own media practices and conversant with the dominant public scripts about media (see Hoover *et al.* 2004). At the same time, however, each of the men in our study was able to pinpoint *positive* examples of masculinity in relation to media that align with their religious ideals *and* that help them understand themselves as men.

For example, one respondent, who we've named "John," a student at an Evangelical seminary, discussed how the character "Jack" on the television series, *Lost*, represented positive values of leadership. He stated:

> Jack actually does take up a head position. He actually tries to lead people ... not just the women, the men as well. So he actually does show what leadership is about, caring for others, taking care, thinking of them first before himself.

Another respondent, "Will," a mainline American Protestant from the Upper Midwest, identified with "Coach Taylor," the protagonist on *Friday Night Lights*. He said:

> so he's got all this pressure on him to, uh, lead the [football] team to state every year, but he's kind of this interesting mix of coach, aggressive, self-reliant, very quick judgments, but also, um, whatever. Like he has a soft side too, you know? He's faithful to his wife ... I think the show dramatizes how he makes difficult decisions and a lot of times it's sort of consulting with his wife or like showing that it is a difficult decision that he has to make.

The men in our study identify with a range of media, and we have found that these identifications often articulate with their vocations or life course. Given the variety, if not diversity, of media messages, this should not come as a surprise. Yet, beyond this level of common identification, themes emerged in our study that both linked and separated Evangelical and mainline Protestant men in their use of media symbols as positive sources for masculine identity. Evangelical men focused on leadership, courage, strength, provision, and protection. Media examples of these themes, as expressed by the men in our study, include "Jack" on *Lost*, "Andy Taylor" on *The Andy Griffith Show*, "Mr. Ingalls" on *Little House on the Prairie*, and "Luke Skywalker" in the *Star Wars* films. Further, one of the most-cited role models thought to embody these themes is the actor/director Mel Gibson, particularly his role as William Wallace in *Braveheart*. "Clark", a pastor at a non-denominational, Evangelical church, best sums up this sentiment.

> Positive qualities of manhood. I think Mel Gibson has done a pretty good job ... You go to *Braveheart*, and you see a man who has a cause. He has a passion; he has something he is willing to die for. And I think that's probably—if you're going to say what's the core difference between a man

and a woman, a woman by and large will be protecting her children, and she may be willing to die to save her children. But she's going to try to do everything she can to protect her family whereas a man, he may be willing to die for a cause that he just firmly believes in, and that's kind of the *Braveheart* mentality.

In this quote, Clark expresses the selflessness of the (white) male hero, his courage in the face of death, and his commitment to a cause that is larger than himself and, even, his family. Wallace (and to a degree Gibson) is a warrior—unabashedly violent and unashamedly sacrificial if the "cause" calls for it.

Mainline Protestant men express similar narratives of their Evangelical counterparts and often draw on the same media texts. Their heroes, like Evangelical heroes, tend to be white, heterosexual men who are driven by purpose and calling and who have an abiding love for family and honor. If William Wallace was the exemplar for Evangelical men, then Tom Hanks's character, Captain John Miller, in *Saving Private Ryan*, would be the exemplar for many mainline Protestant men in our study. The differences between these choices are subtle, but telling. "Sam," for example, said:

So when they are just walking out along through the pasture and whatever and come across the machine gun guys and they capture the one German guy, and they all want to kill him—or most of them want to kill him because he killed their friend. And Tom Hanks lets him go, just says, turn around and walk, and they took off. You know, that—the moral character, whatever, of not just killing somebody just because, um, for revenge or whatever, and killing is obviously an extreme example. But, just the redeeming value of life, um, and, uh, so, what other examples? And, again, the fact that the whole plot of the movie that the mom has lost all her sons except one, and their whole mission is to get him home, to have, you know, keep some of the family. And that that—again, the call of duty ...

The similarities between Evangelical and mainline Protestant engagement with media as a positive resource is striking. In fact, the majority of men in our sample drew on media characters and narratives who embodied patriarchal ideals and who expressed powerful narratives of (white, male) protection, provision, and purpose. This echoes Hanke's sentiment that despite polysemy in media texts, alternative gendered ways of knowing are often marginalized by the patriarchal norm. Further, despite the potential availability of diversity in the media sphere, the men in our study, all of whom were religiously active, gravitated toward the norm. This engagement with mainstream media would seem to counter the sharp rhetoric of the "culture war" thesis and the modernization thesis that suggests cultural winds have shifted toward gender egalitarianism. Religious men (both self-styled conservatives and progressives) find ample positive resources in media culture with which to create aspirational, plausible narratives of essentialist masculine selves.

This striking similarity between these often rhetorically opposed groups should not close off different readings among them. First, mainline Protestant men tended to express more ambivalence toward some of the characteristics of the traditional American monomythic hero, who is violent and alone (Lawrence and Jewett 2002). Their ambivalence toward violence and the need for camaraderie can be seen not only in the choice of Captain Miller over William Wallace as an exemplar but also in the way violence is discussed as regrettable, but necessary. This ambivalence was also expressed through the embrace of Captain Miller- or William Wallace-type heroes and their antithesis, personified by Mr. Rogers, who was perceived by a number of mainline Protestant men as "gentle, and so, kind of, languid, peaceful," as one focus group respondent described him.[2] These expressions fit within "New Men" sensibilities, often ascribed to American mainline Protestant men who have taken a more accommodationist stance toward gender equality and masculine domesticity. American Evangelical men have also embraced their "softer" side but created brighter lines between affective softness and perceived weakness (Wilcox 2004). Thus, American Evangelical conversations about positive resources in media tend to be more concerned with maintaining authority and leadership and are less ambivalent about the male hero. Further, their conversations rarely, if ever, embrace a media character like Mr. Rogers, who is considered too soft, and, even, homosexual.[3]

Second, there was much more diversity of thought *within* American mainline Protestant men with regard to positive resources in media. This is indicative of a broader trend generally, in which, "almost half of active mainline Protestant married men identify themselves as theological conservatives" (Wilcox 2004: 196). Thus, it was more difficult to "pin down" a consistent mainline Protestant narrative since narratives moved in and out of "Soft Patriarch" and "New Men" expressions, depending on the person (Wilcox 2004). This was much less the case with Evangelical men. Only two within our Evangelical cohort expressed a decidedly different narrative from their peers, which suggests stronger narrative control within Evangelical social networks than with mainline Protestant social networks.

The power of this unified narrative within Evangelical social networks can best be described through respondents' discussions of Fred Rogers and Mel Gibson. Mainline Protestant men tended to embrace Rogers as a positive male figure, but this was not universal. Mainline Protestant men also tended to critique Mel Gibson's media characters, but a number of men pushed back against the critique or found another character, like Captain Miller, who would allow them to express Wallace-type characteristics, if only with a measure of nuance. Conversely, not a single Evangelical critiqued Gibson's role as William Wallace, and only one Evangelical embraced Rogers as an example of positive masculinity. In short, expressions of masculinity appear to be more "settled" within Evangelical settings than in mainline Protestant settings. Again, this is not surprising, given the range of religious discourses in American mainline Protestantism, but it is a compelling finding, particularly since Evangelical men are also much more likely to embrace the language of a "crisis of masculinity" (see Eberly 1999) than their mainline Protestant peers.

"Negative" media as resource for identity

In addition to incorporating positive media into their narrative constructions of gender, the men in our sample also draw on perceived negative male stereotypes in the media in their self-construction of gender. While these perceived negative references to media reinforce the public scripts about the damaging effects of media common in "culture war" narratives, these references also work constructively in men's identity narratives. Naming particular media examples as "negative" provides boundary markers for identity; they represent "male others" from which men want to distance themselves.

The most striking example of this in our Evangelical cohort was the "dumb dad" narrative. Respondents typically lament that fathers are depicted as socially challenged imbeciles juxtaposed against intelligent, hardworking, strong mothers. Among our informants, the most commonly cited examples of this stereotype are Homer Simpson, "Jim" in *According to Jim*, "Raymond" in *Everybody Loves Raymond*, "Tim Taylor" in *Home Improvement*, and "Al Bundy" in *Married with Children*. For example, "Harold," an Evangelical seminary student, said, "You've kind of gone from *Father Knows Best* to Bill Cosby but then from there to modern shows where the father is the doofus, you know?"

For Evangelical men, the "dumb dad" narrative challenged the theological notion of headship. In fact, of the nine Evangelical men who challenged the "dumb dad" narrative, eight of them also expressed how narratives like this challenged male leadership in the home. In talking about media, "Jeremy" said:

> You look at most of these shows now, and most of the shows play down the role of men in the household. You can really see that. Not that women can't be leaders within the household, but men are almost lacking any kind of leadership because the women. They're portraying the women as so dominant to men. The men are like unable or unwilling to take up their leadership role. I think that's playing into our culture.

Evangelicals are not alone in their lament of negative roles of the father in the media, however. Mainline Protestants also lamented the "dumb dad" role, as well as the "absent father" role. However, none of these men connected the "dumb/absent dad" narrative directly to the coded language of headship. "Jack," a stay-at-home dad, for example, said:

> Rarely do men on TV change a diaper without making a face or some overreaction or I think of the Mr. Mom with the apron and tongs and the

goggles and the gloves, and that's a fascinating 1980s look into the same stereotypes that are out there today, only more nuanced. Rarely do they portray fathers sitting down and reading or dancing on the floor like Catherine and I do. No physical contact like hugging or even mental contact. It's more manipulating the child for the comedy.

Evangelical men are also concerned about the "absent dad" narrative, parti-cularly in terms of material, emotional, and spiritual provision. In this regard, Evangelical and mainline Protestant men are very similar. But Evangelical men tend to interpret the "absent/dumb" father narrative as a direct threat to a patriarchal authoritative system set forth in their interpretation of the Bible, whereas mainline Protestant men (at least in some cases) tend to interpret this "absent/dumb dad" media narrative as *supporting* the dominant patriarchal narrative that suggests dads are inept in domestic space. Jack, for example, is not concerned with male headship in the home; rather, he is concerned with the media narrative that suggests that men cannot be primary caregivers to their children. What we see in either case is a re-casting of the same media symbolic inventory (and often the same television shows) into the terms associated with religious or moral discourses with which these men identify. In short, men in both groups engage perceived negative media portrayals *constructively*. That is, they position themselves against certain portrayals in the media sphere in ways that resonate with their religious and moral worldviews.

Discussion

It should be clear that the men in our study engage media reflexively. They incorporate what they perceive as "good" and "bad" media into their senses of self. As these excerpts from interviews illustrate, media resources and the values attached to them become the language through which men articulate ideals of masculinity, many of which are essentialist and patriarchal but which have notable differences and valences. Thus, rather than seeing media as unequivocally antagonistic to religion, it is more appropriate to understand media as *constructive* in masculine identity narratives. In response to various critiques of the media (as they relate to gender), it would be more productive to evaluate the ways that men engage media in their constructions of a gen-dered self than to think about media only in terms of "negative" influences. Such an approach would examine how men attach value to media products and how that valuation allows them to construct boundaries of self and to situate their narratives within what they perceive to be legitimated, social (gendered) spaces.

Religion is one of the filters through which men engage media and attach value to certain media symbols and narratives. It should be clear that the media symbols men select as "good" and "bad" are connected to their religious and/or moral worldviews. Evangelical men, for example, exist within a religious space that equips them to navigate "good" and "bad" media through the distinctive, theological narrative of headship. Mainline Protestant men lack such a guiding theological narrative of distinction, likely because of mainline Protestantism's attempts to accommodate cultural modernization rather than reject it, at least in the United States (Wilcox 2004). The differences between the symbolic inventories of Evangelicalism and mainline Protestantism in the United States create important distinctions between the two groups' notions of masculinity. However, given the strong impulse of heteronormativity within the self-selected media choices both groups made, the differences, while notable and important, were coupled with some striking similarities related to patriarchal notions of provision, protection, and purpose within the heterosexual family. Religion, it would seem, still has the capacity to mold the meanings ascribed to media symbols and narratives, particularly in the context of the United States.

Further, many media narratives do not have to be read "against the grain" to reinforce patriarchy, or, particularly, the "headship narrative." That is, Christian men—Evangelical and mainline Protestant—do not have to engage in much symbolic work to find media symbols and narratives in their symbolic inventories to support patriarchal points of view. It is much more difficult, it seems, for men with non-heteronormative gender sensibilities to find symbols and narratives both in religions and media. Certainly, there is evidence of what conservative critics would call "alternative lifestyles" in the media, but these alternatives are still largely marginal and, thus, do more to fuel the rhetorical "culture war" narrative essential to Evangelical identity than to actually challenge the power of patriarchy.

Thus, the intersections among religion and media are more complex than what religious studies or media studies have considered. And it is certainly the case that both media and religion still play a powerful role in how American Protestant men understand themselves *as men*. The way forward, we propose, is to maintain focus on plausible and aspirational narratives of self, which draw on the symbolic inventories through which religion and media circulate. Such an approach will afford a more robust understanding of how masculinities are constructed in the media age, which will move the conversations of media, gender, and religion beyond concepts of media representation and effects, on the one hand, and static (or non-existent) conceptualizations of religion, on the other.

Notes

1 This study involved interviews with 30 American households who situated themselves on both "sides" of the American Protestant-political "divide," that is, Evangelical and non-Evangelical. The interview process consisted of an initial interview with adults in the household and a follow-up interview with the adult male in the household. In accordance with human subject research protocols, all names have been changed in publication to preserve anonymity of our respondents.

2 Fred Rogers was a television host of the famous children's program *Mr. Rogers' Neighborhood*, which aired on American public broadcasting from 1968 to 2001.
3 One Evangelical respondent, "Jasper," mentioned Mr. Rogers as a positive model of masculinity. Jasper also suggested that this idea would make him an outsider in his Evangelical community because most Evangelical men, he thought, would think that Mr. Rogers was homosexual.

Bibliography

Bartkowski, J.P. (2007) "Connections and Contradictions: Exploring the Complex Linkages between Faith and Family," in Ammerman, N. (ed.) *Everyday Religion: Observing Modern Religious Lives*, Oxford: Oxford University Press.
——(2004) *The Promise Keepers: Servants, Soldiers, and Godly Men*, New Brunswick, NJ: Rutgers University Press.
——(2001) *Remaking the Godly Marriage: Gender Negotiation in Evangelical Families*, New Brunswick, NJ: Rutgers University Press.
Beynon, J. (2002) *Masculinities and Culture*, Buckingham, PA: Open University Press.
Butler, J. (1990) *Gender Trouble: Feminism and the Subversion of Identity*, London: Routledge.
Connell, R.W. (2003) "Masculinities, Change, and Conflict in Global Society: Thinking about the Future of Men's Studies," *The Journal of Men's Studies*, 11(3) (Spring): 249–266.
——(2000) *The Men and the Boys*, Sydney: Allen and Unwin.
Consalvo, M. (2003) "The Monsters Next Door: Media Constructions of Boys and Masculinity," *Feminist Media Studies*, 3(1): 27–45.
Craig, S. (1992) "Considering Men and the Media. Introduction," in Craig, S. (ed.) *Men, Masculinity, and the Media*, Newbury Park, CA: Sage, pp. 1–7.
——(1993) "Selling Masculinities, Selling Femininities: Multiple Genders and the Economics of Television," *The Mid-Atlantic Almanac*, 2: 15–27.
Eberly, D. (ed.) (1999) *The Faith Factor in Fatherhood: Renewing the Sacred Vocation of Fatherhood*, New York: Lexington Books.
Erzen, T. (2000) "Liberated through Submission? The Gender Politics of Evangelical Women's Groups Modeled on the Promise Keepers," in Claussen, D.S. (ed.) *The Promise Keepers: Essays on Masculinity and Christianity*, Jefferson, NC: McFarland and Company.
Faludi, S. (2000) *Stiffed: The Betrayal of the American Man*, New York: Harper Perennial
Farrell, W. (2001) *The Myth of Male Power*, New York: Penguin.
Fiske, J. (1997) *Understanding Popular Culture*, London: Unwin-Hyman.
Gallagher, S.K. (2003) *Evangelical Identity and Gendered Family Life*, New Brunswick, NJ: Rutgers University Press.
Gallagher, S.K. and Wood, S.L. (2005) "Godly Manhood Going Wild? Transformations in Conservative Protestant Masculinity," *Sociology of Religion*, 66(2): 135–160.
Gauntlett, D. (2002) *Media, Gender and Identity: An Introduction*, London: Routledge.
Giddens, A. (1991). *Modernity and Self-identity: Self and Society in the Late Modern Age*, Stanford, CA: Stanford University Press.
Gunter, B. (1995) *Television and Gender Representation*, London: John Libbey.
Hanke, R. (1992) "Redesigning Men: Hegemonic Masculinity in Transition," in Craig, S. (ed.) *Men, Masculinity, and the Media*, Newbury Park, CA: Sage, pp. 185–198.

——(1998) "Theorizing Masculinity with/in the Media," *Communication Theory* 8 (2): 183–203.

Hoover, S.M. (2006) *Religion in the Media Age*, London: Routledge.

Hoover, S.M., Clark, L.S., and Alters, D.F. (2004) *Media, Home, and Family*, New York: Routledge.

Justad, M.J. (2000) "Women's Studies and Men's Studies: Friends or Foes?" *The Journal of Men's Studies*, 8 (3): 401–406.

Kimmel, M.S. (1999) "Patriarchy's Second Coming as Masculine Renewal," in Claussen, D.S. (ed.) *Standing on the Promises: Promise Keepers and the Revival of Manhood*, Cleveland, OH: The Pilgrim Press.

Lawrence, J.S. and Jewett, R. (2002) *The Myth of the American Superhero*, Cambridge: W.M. Eardmans Publishing Co.

Macnamara, J.R. (2006) *Media and Male Identity: The Making and Remaking of Men*, New York: Palgrave Macmillan.

Mansfield, H.C. (2006) *Manliness*, New Haven: Yale University Press.

Messner, M.A. (1997) *Politics of Identity: Men in Movements*, Thousand Oaks, CA: Sage.

Nathanson, P. and Young, K.K. (2001). *Spreading Misandry: The Teaching of Contempt for Men in Popular Culture*, Toronto: McGill-Queen's University Press.

Obama, B. (2008) "Obama's Father's Day Speech," http://articles.cnn.com/2008-06-27/politics/obama.fathers.ay_1_foundation-black-children-rock?_s=PM:POLITICS (retrieved Dec. 2, 2011).

Saco, D. (1992) "Masculinity as Signs: Poststructuralist Feminist Approaches to the Study of Gender," in Craig, S. (ed.) *Men, Masculinity, and the Media*, Newbury Park, CA: Sage, pp. 23–39.

Weber, S. (2006) *Tender Warrior: Every Man's Purpose, Every Woman's Dream, Every Child's Hope*, Colorado Springs: Multnomah Books.

Wetherell, M. and Edley, N.E. (1999) "Negotiating Hegemonic Masculinity: Imaginary Positions and Psycho-Discursive Practices," *Feminism and Psychology*, 9: 335–356.

Wilcox, W.B. (2004) *Soft Patriarchs, New Men: How Christianity Shapes Fathers and Husbands*, Chicago: University of Chicago Press.

Chapter 11

Saving Grace

Television with "something more"

Diane Winston

In *Loving with a Vengeance*, a 1984 book on mass-produced fantasies for women, feminist scholar Tania Modleski argues that a "utopian sensibility"— the desire for something more than what everyday life offers—helps account for the abiding popularity of romance novels, gothic fiction and soap operas (Modleski 1990: 24). That something more, she wrote, is the desire for community, transcendence and female autonomy. In the 30 years since Modleski's book was published, social and cultural shifts have tweaked female fantasies, reconfiguring romance as chic lit and gothic as werewolf and vampire sagas. Soap operas, too, have changed (France 2011), morphing into primetime melodramas as a growing number of working women have sought content that reflects their 9-to-5 realities and altered viewership patterns. But notwithstanding these evolutions in style, the substance of "something more" remains constant.

Saving Grace, which ran on the cable network TNT from July 2007 to June 2010, exemplifies many of the changes and continuities in the form and content of female fantasies. Using Grace Hanadarko, the series' eponymous heroine, as a starting point, this chapter examines its representation of women as well as the "utopian sensibility" engendered among the series' viewers. The utopian sensibility reflects profound longings for identity, meaning and community— the matrix both for spiritual searching and religious teaching. Unlike most American television series, *Saving Grace* explicitly plumbs the human need for religion and spirituality. Moreover, Grace and her best friend Rhetta explore their spiritual calling and religious identity within a postfeminist context that emphasizes their very different subjectivities, life situations and responses to problems.

The subsequent discussion analyzes *Saving Grace*'s formations of gender and religion within the context of mediatization as the "ongoing, long-term process in which more and more media emerge and are institutionalized," thus causing media to "increasingly become relevant for the social construction of everyday life, society, and culture as a whole" (Krotz 2009: 24). Explaining mediatization's significance, communication scholar Lynn Schofield Clark writes: "Mediatization. refers both to the processes by which social organizations, structures, or industries take on the form of the media, and the processes by which genres of popular culture become central to the narratives of social phenomena" (Clark 2009: 87). Invoking mediatization thus raises key questions: Might media supersede institutional religion in telling religious stories, creating religious communities and facilitating religious encounters? What kind of religion does mediatization privilege? Does media logic—the "processes, formats and routines" (Stromback and Esser 2009: 212) deployed to capture consumers' attention—affect media representations of religion and gender? How do viewers use media to express religious feelings or to engage in religious experiences? How are ritual, re-enchantment and redemption experienced in a mediatized world?

In today's mediatized world, the conditions of television viewership and production are no longer fixed as they were before online opportunities created new feedback loops. Viewers can produce content, and producers can see and respond to viewer-created products such as fanzines, fan sites, website extras and YouTube. As a result, audiences once accustomed just to watching television shows now can interact with them. Moreover, they can enter alternate worlds through online gaming, augment and amplify stories through blogging and participate in affinity groups that they have had a hand in creating through electronic social networks. Producers of media can monitor the results and, in turn, respond to viewers by answering their questions online, integrating their ideas into scripts and developing transmedia products such as graphic novels or webisodes—short online episodes, which offer new dimensions to the original narrative.

The smaller communities that develop around particular aspects of a story—forums that speculate on alternative relationships between characters or YouTube collaborations that extend the narrative—bypass the constraints of media logic, which require producers to present stories that ensure the largest audience possible. During the heyday of analog television (1960s–1990s), media logic typically entailed hiring attractive actors, writing inoffensive scripts and providing happy endings. The goal was to appeal to the largest possible audience. With the advent of digitalization and the subsequent expansion of the cable universe, new networks jettisoned the lowest-common-denominator approach of analog media to serve an expanding array of niche audiences. New shows catered to viewers who valued gardening or animals or even anti-heroes. HBO, a cable pioneer in the US, promoted "quality" entertainment that differentiated it from traditional network fare. Its tagline boasted "It's not TV, it's HBO," and the network's series featured complex characters pursuing ambiguous ends. HBO thrived, feted for inaugurating a new golden age of television with shows such as *Oz*, *Six Feet Under*, *The Sopranos* and *The Wire*.

At the heart of many of these series were questions of meaning, identity and community. Yet rather than reflect a utopian sensibility—the desire for something more—they bespoke a dystopian world-weariness that seemed to ask, "Is this all there is?" *Oz*, *Six Feet Under*, *The Sopranos* and *The Wire* were all developed by men and anchored by male characters. Each had strong female roles, but women were not the heart of the drama (with *Six Feet Under* as a possible exception). At Lifetime, a cable channel aimed at women, female characters were central, but they tended to appear in traditional romantic and gothic scripts updated to fit contemporary realities.

In the late 2000s, several cable networks debuted shows with female leads who were as flawed and compromised as any ambivalent Mafia don. *Damages'* Patty Hewes, *Weeds'* Nancy Botwin, and *Nurse Jackie*'s Jackie Peyton are perverse characters. Their spiritual struggles are only glimpsed at the edges of their ambition, insecurities and narcissism. Grace Hanadarko is equally difficult but markedly different, her backstory darker, her persona edgier. Grace is an Oklahoma City police detective with a shocking secret: during her preteen years, her parish priest repeatedly molested her. Believing the priest died of cancer, Grace is unable to avenge the crime against her, but she seeks justice for others. Despite her dedication to her work, she is a nihilist seeking refuge, or maybe obliteration, in alcohol and sex. Grace's world shifts when she encounters Earl, her guardian angel. The series explores Grace's spiritual path as well as her police cases and evolving relationships.

Compounding Grace's problems is the producers' decision not to place her in the familiar terrain of melodrama or dramedy. Rather, *Saving Grace* unfurls in an unfamiliar mash-up of police procedural, magic realism and spiritual inspiration. Grace struggles neither for worldly success nor romantic love, but for the redemption manifest in accepting herself, loving others and recognizing a Higher Power. Nancy Miller, the series creator and executive producer, had wanted "to explore God, faith, religion and sin" and "do a show about a reluctant saint" (Miller 2011). She also wanted it to be about a strong woman.[1]

A new type of hero

Smoking, drinking and fornicating, Detective Grace Hanadarko blazed through the 2007 summer season. Following TNT's Monday night hit *The Closer*, *Saving Grace* similarly featured a sexy blonde cop with a thick Southern accent. But unlike the Los Angeles Police Department's Deputy Chief Brenda Johnson, or any other television law enforcement officer, Grace Hanadarko has a "last chance" angel named Earl, who suggests she change her ways. Some reviewers panned the supernatural twist, but many viewers related to Grace's dark night of the soul. That dark night deepened when, in the last scene of the season finale, Grace points her gun at the priest who had repeatedly molested her during her preteen years. But as she stands over her attacker, ready to fire, he whispers the same phrase Earl had spoken to her at their first meeting. In that moment, the priest becomes a divine conduit, reminding Grace that she is chosen and that she has a choice. In a moment of clarity, Grace apprehends her autonomy, her connection to others and her calling.

Gender roles are among the most ingrained aspects of religion, establishing men and women's relationship to spirituality, sexuality and power—shaping, in these arenas, what they can say, what they may do and how they define themselves. Within western Christianity, gender roles have been set by defining archetypes, and since the formation of the biblical canon, there have been two pre-eminent classifications for women: Madonna and whore. Even today, when women have penetrated the innermost circles of religious power, these deep-rooted typologies—harkening back to both the Hebrew Bible's stories of Eve and the matriarchs (Sarah, Rebecca, Leah and Rachel), and the New Testament's portrayals of the Virgin and Mary Magdalene—are culturally pervasive, reducing women to bodies for procreation or recreation.

The theological narrative that flows from Grace Hanadarko's life offers an alternative vision of a spiritual woman. Rather than accept traditional prescriptions of the holy woman's role, Grace is rambunctious and only begrudgingly open to God's call. She functions as a counterpoint to friends and family who follow more conventional paths to redemption, and she holds out hope and elicits empathy from viewers eager for fresh perspectives on both women and religion. At the heart of her story is an unsought and unwanted religious calling. A calling—the perception that a supernatural power has a special plan for one's life—is a staple of western religious literature. Yet there is no general agreement about what a call is, why it occurs or how to judge its authenticity. Given the uncertainty among real-life religious practitioners, how then to understand a fictional calling? One possibility is to contextualize the phenomenon within religious traditions, three of which—Judaism, Roman Catholicism and Protestantism—are most familiar to American television viewers as well as television series creators, producers and writers.

Judaism begins with a call: God tells Abram to leave his home for a new land where he and his descendants will prosper (Genesis 12: 1). Years later, God again calls Abraham, whose name has been changed by his divine encounter, and demands the ultimate sacrifice, his son Isaac. The Hebrew patriarch answers, "Hineni," or "Here I am" (Genesis 22: 1–2) and readies Isaac for slaughter. This unqualified acceptance of God's command became a touchstone for subsequent rabbinic discussions on whether blind obedience is always the correct response to God's demands.

In early medieval Europe, the Roman Catholic Church developed a different notion of calling. It required the discernment of a religious vocation that took one out of the everyday world and into a cloistered, celibate community. This notion of calling, more privatized and personalized than the mandates received by the Hebrew prophets and patriarchs, reflected both different theologies and historical circumstances, specifically the contrast between a nomadic, desert people and a hierarchal religious institution. The idea of calling evolved further after the Protestant Reformation. Both Luther and Calvin understood it to be a deeper commitment to life in this world. Among the ramifications of the doctrine of the priesthood of all believers was the conviction that all work could be a calling if performed with the right intentions. Instead of viewing membership in cloistered communities as the best and highest expression of the divine will, these new religious movements taught that believers could follow God's mandate and remain in the world.

Grace's calling borrows from all three. Hers is a direct call, private in nature, which has her stay in the world with a new intentionality. That intentionality demands that she treat herself with the same respect and compassion she shows to others. As Grace's best friend Rhetta tells her, she is the kind of person who loves everyone more than herself.

Grace's professional and personal dramas play out within the context of a close-knit police unit and a loose-knit family. Her deepest familial connection is with Clay, her young nephew whose mother (Grace's sister) died in the 1995 bombing of the Alfred P. Murrah Federal Building in Oklahoma City. Grace's brother Johnny, a priest who appears to be the "called" person of the family, predictably questions her wild life and atheism. Their sister Paige is less charitable in her disapproval of Grace's excesses, and four more brothers are amused by Grace's antics. Only Rhetta, a wife, mother and devout Catholic, knows about Earl and Father Murphy.

"Bring It On, Earl"

Life as Grace knows it ends when after a hard night of drinking she drives her Porsche into a pedestrian (*Saving Grace* 101). Trying desperately to revive him, Grace whispers to God to help her. When a scruffy, older man appears and announces God has sent him to help, Grace assumes he is crazy. But when he unfurls a great set of white wings to prove that he, Earl, is indeed an angel, Grace fears that it is she who has come undone. In this initial response and subsequent meetings, Grace makes it known that Earl's appearance is anything but the annunciation of "good news." Rather, it is the beginning of ongoing resistance as Grace rebels against the call of faith. That first night, when Grace questions whether Earl is the "real deal," he transports her to the Grand Canyon. There, Earl says she is going to hell unless she accepts God's love. When Grace refuses to admit she needs divine help, Earl stirs up a tremendous storm. Fearing for her life, she takes his hand and he wraps her in his wings. There she feels God's power, which her expression registers as sublime. Earl says that he, like FedEx, is just delivering the message, which is the same phrase Murphy uses in the first season finale.

Nancy Miller wanted the series to be about a woman because, traditionally, "women get short shrift and are victims of men" (Miller 2011). A Catholic who believes "deeply" in God, Miller hoped the show would explore the questions of faith that she feels are compelling. Yet despite a clear vision for the character and a commitment to the integrity of her story, Miller says she avoided over-thinking the tropes that define Grace, whether the Madonna/ whore dichotomy or the "woman warrior," a female challenge to the archetypal male warrior and his "reliance on violence and its concomitant objectification and exploitation of women and 'others'" (Early and Kennedy 2003: 3).

Rooted in pre-Christian mythology, the woman warrior fights for virtuous causes, often confronting wicked men who hurt women. The contemporary fictional ur-figure for the female fighter whose fierce determination is a result of male victimization is Xena, best known from the television series *Xena: Warrior Princess*.[2] After a swashbuckling career as a warlord and "destroyer of nations," Xena seeks redemption and becomes a protector of women. Grace is temperate in comparison to Xena, but her story echoes that of the warrior princess. Like Xena, her crusade against male oppression is a projection of her own rage. Unlike Xena, who periodically abandons her mission, Grace compartmentalizes her struggle, pursuing "good" in her police work while behaving badly on her own time. Even after Earl's admonitions, Grace succumbs to egregious impulses, including binge drinking, indiscriminate sex and compulsive risk-taking. Her anger, unlike Xena's, is turned inward, a psychological twist that reflects how the differences in their historical circumstances, the pre-Christian Mediterranean world and twenty-first-century Oklahoma City, shade their spiritual worlds. Xena lives in a time of gods whose desires, like hers, take shape in a physical world. Grace lives in a godless age when the individual psyche is a battlefield.

Grace's spiritual journey is hidden from those who judge her, and her interior life opaque to all but Rhetta. Yet she is continuously tested by her cases and by the puzzles Earl leaves for her. Earl does not explain God's purpose or his plan for her life; instead, he plants clues. Grace is drawn into a relationship with him because he intrigues her. He's a redneck, taco-eating angel. She takes a feather from his wings and a saliva sample from his taco so Rhetta, a forensic scientist, can test his DNA. As Grace comes to believe in Earl, she begins to believe in herself. Over the course of the first season, viewers see incremental changes in Grace. She tries to stop lying, she becomes more rigorous in her professional conduct and she refuses to be compromised by others' opinions. When a sleazy lawyer seeks to shake the detectives' commitment to a case by revealing hidden and embarrassing facts about their own lives, he parades a long line of Grace's lovers through the detectives' office. She laughs at the ruse and refuses to be shamed.

The characters of Grace and Rhetta mirror the Madonna/whore archetypes, but with a twist. It is the Magdalene not the Madonna who receives God's call. Yet Rhetta, the good wife and devoted mother, has no difficulty believing that Grace is visited by an angel. Neither postfeminist theory nor television criticism has paid much attention to religion, yet these characters redefine biblical archetypes for a postmodern landscape. Grace and Rhetta not only subvert essentialist conventions that demarcated women's roles for two millennia, but they also dissolve the differences that pit woman against woman, Madonna against whore. Grace and Rhetta reclaim religious space, as well as their own households and workplaces, as sites for battling oppression, whether constituted as inner demons or societal expectations.

The Madonna/whore distinction is never clear-cut, since Rhetta is dispassionate both at home and in the precinct while Grace displays a mother's zealous heart in her concern for family, friends and victims. But her maternal instincts are seen only intermittently. More common is her lusty bravado, which some viewers characterize as promiscuity. Short, tight-bodied and small-busted, Grace lacks affectation and rarely combs her hair. Her lack of feminine artifice and indifference to traditional gendered behavior transgresses social and television norms, angering some female viewers. But she radiates sexuality and never lacks for partners. At the start of the series, most of her encounters are one-night stands. But as her relationship with Earl progresses, the subtext of these couplings becomes clearer, seeding clues about the interconnection between sexuality and spirituality.

Initially, Grace approaches sex as uncomplicated fun, exemplified by her relationships with two colleagues in her squad. Butch Ada is single and ready to commit. Ham Dewey is married and emotionally unavailable. Grace prefers Ham with whom she enjoys a less demanding relationship. He allows her to dominate him; during one encounter, she ties him up and does tequila shots off his stomach and chest. Yet Ham is not her only bedmate. In "A Language of Angels" (*Saving Grace* 109) a one-night stand handcuffs her to the bed, sprawled backside up in a perverse tableau of a crucifixion. Ham, finding Grace with another man's name scrawled in lipstick on her posterior, refuses to free her. When Earl comes along, he too leaves her bound saying, "Well, what do you want to talk about? I finally have you for a change." Although staged for fun, the bondage tableau evokes Grace's past, a reminder that her sexuality was formed by a predatory relationship that physically, emotionally and spiritually immobilized her.

Another tryst with Ham alludes to themes of blood and atonement. In "Bring it On Earl" (*Saving Grace* 102) the two go hunting, and Grace shoots a deer with her handgun. Recounting how, at 12, she made her first kill, Grace tells Ham about a dream in which a deer with sparkly hooves trampled on her entire family. (Later in the season, viewers learn that Father Murphy stopped molesting Grace at 12, when she began menstruating.) Ham, having no knowledge of this history, suddenly feels aroused and in a strikingly primal scene begins foreplay with Grace alongside the dead deer. Grace touches a bit of blood to his face, foreshadowing a shooting later in the episode when Grace is splattered with blood. At the end of the show, Ham steps into the shower with Grace and helps wash the blood off her body.[3]

The theme of blood and water closely mirrors Christian themes of suffering, death and redemption. Viewers may wonder whether redemption will come through Ham's human love or Earl's spiritual healing, but Grace behaves as if sexuality is its own path to salvation. She tries to purge the memory of the past by fully immersing herself in the intensity of vigorous copulation. Sex replaces, or at least allows her to control, the pain and shame of earlier violations. Yet her post-Earl couplings reveal that sex, too, is part of God's plan and inextricably tied to her spiritual journey. Tellingly, it is in the "orgasmatron" of Earl's embrace (*Saving Grace* 101) that Grace feels something overwhelming, or as she puts it "better than sex."

"Better than sex"

In the final moments of the first season, the themes of atonement, sacrifice and salvation come together when Grace faces Father Patrick "Satan" Murphy. She has discovered that he is alive, comfortably ensconced in a nearby retirement home. Right before she leaves to find him, she despairs of God's mysterious ways, wondering why innocent babies die and Father Murphy tends roses.

Worked up to a righteous rage, Grace sneaks up on her nemesis, rouses him from bed and orders him to kneel before her. Having denied God and dismissed Earl, she can dispense justice and savor revenge. When Murphy begs her not to stain her soul with his murder, she is unmoved. Only when he repeats Earl's words, "I'm just Fed Ex trying to deliver a message," is her hand stayed. Her face registers shock, disbelief and wonder as the moment yields to the utopian sensibilities that Modleski describes as the heart of soap opera. Grace becomes the avatar for the audience's spiritual longings, as she perceives the "truth." God is real. Her actions have meaning because she, Murphy and the others she has met on her journey are linked through divine intentionality. Thanks to God's love, she has the freedom to choose and her identity emerges from the decisions she makes. It is a deeply religious, personally empowering vision of the unity between self, God and others.

It is also a canny rendering of gender issues and religious messages in a way that works perfectly for television. And it illustrates what media scholar Stig Hjarvard sees as mediatization's capacity to "change the very ideas and authority of religious institutions, and alter the ways in which people interact with each other when dealing with religious issues" (Hjarvard 2008). Analyzing the kinds of religion that "work" on television, anthropologist Elizabeth Bird argues that whereas programs that feature overtly religious characters and plots often fail, "the default position for TV drama is an assumption of faith, although leaving vague the question of exactly in what" (Bird 2009: 25). According to Bird, this "open-ended" religiosity allows viewers to engage with characters and become involved in their lives. It also reflects the experience of many viewers for whom religion "is more about getting through the day than debating the finer points of faith" (Bird 2009: 38).

This significant non-specificity poses a challenge to religious institutions that base their *raison d'être* on particularity. Nevertheless, Earl tells Grace that there are multiple roads to God and offers her totems from diverse traditions. Miller, despite her own attachment to Catholicism, never uses characters or plots to indicate that the Church is the one true way. In fact, her familiarity with Catholicism might explain why she roots Grace's trauma in the very real issue of Catholic clergy sexual abuse. But that type of specificity, pointing out the religious identity of wrongdoers, is prevalent on television. Bird notes that "true believers," extremists and hypocrites, are usually portrayed negatively and their religious affiliations are prominent. Often these are men whose religious identity masks their sexual predations. But there also are women, including "misguided" mothers, whose deep religiosity is suspect.

A living oxymoron

In the case of *Saving Grace*, the hypocrisy of the Roman Catholic Church, enabling and then sheltering Father Murphy, became a popular online topic, and in one forum a priest offered to be a sounding board for viewers.[4] Many posts, which can be as raw as the show itself, are from men and women who themselves were sexually abused. In a TNT thread titled "Salvation and Forgiveness," Phillip164 sees Grace's experience in light of his own stating,

> I can and have forgiven myself because I have and can accept God's forgiveness ... I have forgiven those who have hurt me. That said, I am not sure what I would do in Grace's position. The desire to pull the trigger would be oh so strong.
>
> ("Phillip164" 2007)

The online discussion, following the season finale, includes nine pages of responses on sexual abuse, forgiveness, parenting, marriage, finding God, the Bible and mental illness. For many, Grace's journey is a starting point for analyzing their own experience of abuse and its aftermath. An iconic figure, Grace embodies strength as well as pain. "Grace is a beautiful angel which fell from the heavens" ("fans1228" 2008) fans1228 writes and "The pain I feel for her makes me want to pull her in my arms." Deborah195 posts, "Grace is weak/strong and powerful/tender. A living oxymoron" ("Deborah195" 2008).

As an oxymoron, Grace polarizes viewers much as she does characters on the series. Posts fall one of two ways: writers love her or loathe her. Those in the latter category hate her "skanky hair," "potty mouth" and "bony" body. The TNT forum initially was flooded with Christians offended by the show's depiction of drinking, smoking, nudity and adultery. But others criticize the "Christian" response as strikingly un-Christian. In a defense of the series on GodTube, Charles RC wrote, "Christians attacking the show miss the point. The show is for people who need it ... If she were perfect she wouldn't need God's help ... The Pharisees complained that Jesus ate with the sinners. Exactly, that was the whole point" (GodTube 2008).

This perspective, echoed elsewhere online, treats the series as a morality tale that captures God's point of view. As one post at tv.com noted,

"God thinks she is worth saving so who wants to argue that point?" ("How'BoutThatSavingGrace?" 2008).

Other viewers, less concerned with the divine perspective, are pleased to see a very human character on television. "For those of us who once lived life in the fast lane, that needed to be helped. we love you Grace" ("How'BoutThat SavingGrace?" 2008). Female cops feel special empathy: "We cuss, we drink, we make stupid, risky sexual decisions. We find it impossible to commit because we find it impossible to trust. We doubt God is actually up there but so would you if you saw what we see" ("TenNinetySix" 2007). In closing, the post notes, "A vagina ain't a halo," a sentiment subversive of religious gender norms that assume that "good" women are angelic—virginal and submissive.

Some viewers decry a double standard that condemns Grace for behaviors that would be acceptable for men. "I've been wondering about the equality question for a long time. Why is Grace 'slutty,' but there are few comments about Butch or Ham, or any of the other men she has slept with?" ("TXJetSet" 2007). They welcome a sexually active woman at the center of a show: "GRACE is every woman. A part of her character exists in each of us. We all want to be loved. We all have felt desperate and alone at one time or another" ("Falcon T" 2007). Others underscore Grace's ability to care: "I think Mary Frances [Grace's sister that died in the bombing of the Murrah building] saw in Grace what I see in Grace – someone who loves the people around her more than she loves herself" ("A Shot at Redemption" 2007).

Not surprisingly, online viewer responses reflect conflicted attitudes toward female sexuality, especially when it is acted out within a religious context. But leaving aside negative "Christian" responses, most posts treat Grace sympathetically, if not empathetically. Her sexuality is accepted either as an understandable response to past abuse or as an expression of physical desire that would be appropriate or at least less inappropriate if she were a man. Comments also detach Grace's sexuality from her spiritual journey; her behavior is problematic because it is self-destructive rather than sinful. Removing morality from the discussion, viewers reject traditional religious teachings about women and sexuality, specifically the polarities of Madonna and whore. Instead they invoke a postfeminist perspective that takes into account Grace's subjectivity as well as her relationship to power. Grace's relationship to the Church and her search for a spiritual path are the context for her struggle against an oppressive patriarchy and for self-acceptance. Yet when feminist theorist Amanda Lotz lists the multiple axes (ethnicity, class, age, etc.) that position women in society and in relation to power, she omits religion (Lotz 2001: 115).

Grace's narrative speaks to viewers whose lives have spun out of control but who still hold out hope for redemption. Her story overcomes the divide between the Madonnas and the whores and, at the same time, draws attention to the subjectivities—Grace is white, working-class, middle-aged and single—that make each person unique. By smashing categorical boundaries yet insisting on the specificities of difference, *Saving Grace* invites viewers to use their own experiences to fashion a model of redemptive womanhood. Nancy Miller, the series creator, said that although she read the posts, they did not affect the development of the character, a different decision than, for example, the creators of *Lost*, who often took cues from online fans.

Saving Grace lasted three seasons. Dissatisfied with overseas and DVD sales, Fox, the studio that produced the series, canceled the show. TNT wanted to keep it even though its numbers had fallen from 6.4 million for the first season premiere to 3.5 million for season three. The show worked because its plots, themes and characters were sufficiently mainstream. Some viewers were appalled by Grace's casual bed-hopping, but others enjoyed seeing a buff, attractive blonde who was unabashedly sexual. Similarly, those who would have preferred to see a "good" character chosen by God (and a God clearly identified with Christianity) were matched by viewers who liked that spirituality trumped religion in Grace's metaphysical universe.

Grace's attractiveness and the open-ended nature of her spiritual quest underscore the impact of mediatization on television portrayals of gender and religion. These characteristics conform to the commercialization inherent in the entertainment media. If Grace were a frumpy hag or if Earl demanded that she don a burka and pray seven times a day, the package would be a harder sell. Similarly the series' depictions of ritual and re-enchantment, the deeper structures of religion, meet audience expectations of the possible and the desirable. Specifically, the rituals that enable the transitional time and space to engage other realities are experienced in the characters' daily lives rather than in religious institutions. A familiar chore like cooking becomes a time-out-of-time experience as Grace and Rhetta discuss the radical break that Earl has introduced into their world. A familiar place like Grace's living room becomes a ritual space when Earl fills it with religious objects. This exemplifies historian Jonathan Z. Smith's description of ritual as "a mode of paying attention" and "a process for marking interest." According to Smith: "A ritual object or action becomes sacred by having attention focused on it in a highly marked way. From such a point of view, there is nothing inherently sacred or profane. These are not substantive categories but situational ones" (Smith 1992: 103–104).

These situational categories are woven through everyday life. Historian Robert Orsi defines "lived religion" as experiencing the sacred through the rituals of daily life or, as he explains it, "religious practice and imagination in ongoing, dynamic relation with the realities and structures of everyday life in particular times and places" (Orsi 2002: xiii).[5] *Saving Grace* ritualizes quotidien realities as Grace encounters a world transformed by God's presence. That realization re-enchants the world for her and the audience. Rhetta, a scientist by training, has no problem reconciling Earl's appearance with her professional empiricism. In fact, she uses her scientific skills to test the clues that Earl leaves behind, and Earl's existence opens up a new realm of questions: What about the Virgin Birth, the Trinity, and Heaven? Rhetta believes there are mysteries that transcend everyday reality and that God is manifest in the world. Accordingly, when she examines Grace's "clues" (the feather from Earl's wings, a carved duck, the half-eaten taco), she interprets them scientifically (what is Earl's DNA like?) as well as spiritually (what is Earl's message for Grace?).

Rhetta's world is filled with signs, mysteries and miracles, and she challenges Grace—who has actual evidence—to see them, too. In the series' pilot (*Saving Grace* 101), they debate the possibility of miracles after Grace survives a fatal shooting. Grace wants hard and fast proof but Rhetta has none to offer, saying: "Why can't you believe it just happened? Miracles happen all the time you just have to believe."

Nearly 80 percent of Americans believe in miracles, according to a 2010 Pew Forum survey (Pew Forum on Religion and Public Life 2010). The same study also found that even among Americans who don't belong to a formal religion or who call themselves "secular," many still believe in miracles. *Saving Grace* exemplifies a new imaginary where shifting notions of religion, spirituality and gender can find empathetic audiences open to the miraculous in anyone's everyday life. But the role of commercial media as the site for such cultural experiments is vexed. On the one hand, consumers have become producers, developing transmedia vehicles that enable them to participate in story making and character development. Yet, on the other, the increasing monetization of the media rouses caution: Will sharp edges be dulled, subversive characters tamed, and radical behaviors blunted to ensure advertisers and secure large audiences?

Saving Grace speaks to viewers who believe but do not belong, or who belong but are not sure what or even if they believe. Its storytelling fills the gap between religious institutions with no room for doubt and secular venues with no room for belief. There is a growing chasm between institutional religion and the American public: although 16 percent of Americans do not adhere to a formal religion, the number rises to 25 percent when young adults are the focus of the survey (Pew Forum on Religion and Public Life 2007). This reflects the growing influence of media in our lives, specifically its challenge to traditional religious authority, structures and messages. *Saving Grace* illustrates this point—its protagonist's journey not only occurs outside the institutional church; it happens in spite of it. Grace finds redemption on her own terms, which probably seems just right to the million-plus viewers whose utopian sensibilities yearn for stories about strong women with deep friendships, healthy sex lives and a drive for "something else."

Notes

1 Miller also was executive producer of *Any Day Now* (1998–2002), a series about a longtime friendship between a black woman and a white woman in Alabama that Amanda Lotz cites as an example of postfeminist television (Lotz 2001:115).

2 Xena debuted in the 1995 television series *Hercules: The Legendary Journeys*. She also appears in an animated movie, a comic book and a video-game. Fans have re-cast her story in numerous blogs and fanzines.

3 Thanks to Anthea Butler for these insights. See Winston 2009: 259–286.
4 Posts about *Saving Grace* were accessed between 2007 and 2009 but have since been removed from forums. It is impossible to know if respondents used real names or changed their names for reasons of confidentiality. These sources are cited in the text with the respondent's name or the title and the year in which they were accessed (e.g. "Phillip164" 2007, or "How'BoutThatSavingGrace?" 2008). All available source information appears in the 'Online Sources Cited' section in the Bibliography.
5 For more on the gendered aspect of lived religion, see McGuire 2008.

Bibliography

Bird, E. (2009) "True Believers and Atheists Need Not Apply," in D. Winston (ed.) *Small Screen, Big Picture: Television and Lived Religion*, Waco, TX, Baylor University Press.

Clark, L.S. (2009) "Theories: Mediatization and Media Ecology," in K. Lundby (ed.) *Mediatization: Concept, Changes, Consequences*, New York, NY, Peter Lang.

Early, F. and Kennedy, K. (2003) "Introduction: Athena's Daughters," in F. Early and K. Kennedy (eds) *Athena's Daughters: Television's New Women Warriors*, Syracuse, NY, Syracuse University Press.

France, L. (2011) "Soaps are Hot, Just Not in the U.S.," www.cnn.com/2011/SHOWBIZ/04/19/soap.operas.telenovelas/index.html (accessed January 5, 2012).

Hjarvard, S. (2008) "The Mediatization of Religion: A Theory of the Media as Agents of Religious Change," *Northern Lights*, 6, 9–26.

Krotz, F. (2009) "Mediatization: A Concept with which to Grasp Media and Societal Change," in K. Lundby (ed.) *Mediatization: Concept, Changes, Consequences*, New York, NY, Peter Lang.

Lotz, A.D. (2001) "Postfeminist Television Criticism: Rehabilitating Critical Terms and Identifying Postfeminist Attributes," *Feminist Media Studies*, Vol.1, No. 1.

McGuire, M. (2008) *Lived Religion: Faith and Practice in Everyday Life*, New York, NY, Oxford University Press.

Miller, N. (2001) Telephone interview with author, December 9.

Modleski, T. (1990) *Loving with a Vengeance: Mass Produced Fantasies for Women*, New York, NY, Routledge.

Orsi, R. (2002) *The Madonna of 115th Street: Faith and Community in Italian Harlem* (second edition), New Haven CT, Yale University Press.

Pew Forum on Religion and Public Life (2010) "U.S. Religious Landscape Survey," http://www.pewforum.org/age/religion-among-the-millennials.aspx (accessed May 23, 2012).

Smith, J.Z. (1992) *To Take Place: Toward Theory in Ritual*, Chicago, IL, University of Chicago Press.

Stromback, J. and Esser, F. (2009) "Shaping Politics: Mediatization and Media Interventions," in K. Lundby (ed.) *Mediatization: Concept, Changes, Consequences*, New York, NY, Peter Lang.

Winston, D. (ed.) (2009) *Small Screen, Big Picture: Television and Lived Religion*, Waco, TX: Baylor University Press.

Online sources cited

"Deborah195," "Grace is a Beautiful Angel Which Fell From the Heaven," Online discussion board comment, TNT, http://forums.tnt.tv/jive/tnt/thread.jspa?threadID=15642&tstart=0 (accessed February 16, 2008).

"Falcon T," "The Best Show Ever," Online discussion board comment, TNT, http://forums.tnt.tv/jive/tnt/thread.jspa?messageID=31546&#31548 (accessed September 7, 2007).

"fans1228," "Grace is a Beautiful Angel Which Fell From the Heaven," Online discussion board comment, TNT, http://forums.tnt.tv/jive/tnt/thread.jspa?threadID=15642&tstart=0 (accessed February 16, 2008).

GodTube, www.godtube.com/CharlesRC/blog/view/605 (accessed February 16, 2008).

"How'BoutThatSavingGrace?" onlinediscussionboardthread,TV.com, www.tv.com/saving-grace/show/72393/ how-bout-that-saving-grace/topic/85990-845475/msgs html?tag=board_topics;title,7 (accessed February 15, 2008).

"Phillip164," "Salvation and Forgiveness," Online discussion board comment, TNT, http://forums.tnt.tv/jive/tnt/thread.jspa?threadID13642&start=0&tstart=0 (accessed December 19, 2007).

"A Shot at Redemption," MySpace, www.myspace.com.savinggracereport (accessed September 7, 2007).

"TenNinetySix," "It's About Time," online discussion board comment, TNT, http://forums.tnt.tv/jive/tnt/thread.jspa?messageID=22223&#22223 (accessed August 13, 2007).

"TXJetSet," "Re: The Character," Online discussion board comment, TNT, http://forums.tnt.tv/jive/tnt/thread.jspa?messageID=46415&#46415 (accessed November 30, 2007).

Chapter 12

Digital storytelling

Empowering feminist and womanist faith formation with young women

Mary E. Hess

In the last five years there has been an explosion of interest in, and research connected to, understanding religious identity in contemporary contexts. The National Study of Youth and Religion (NSYR), for example, offers us rich data to explore in relation to young people (Smith and Denton 2005, Christerson *et al.* 2010). Putnam and Campbell's book *American grace* (2010) offers a multi-faceted look at religion in the United States more generally. In more specific pastoral contexts, Martinson, Roberto and Black's study (2010) of exemplary youth ministry provides insight into the discrete elements that point toward ongoing youth involvement in Christian congregations, and the Inter-faith Youth Core's publications explore how shared service aligned with opportunities for exploration of faith can lead to enhanced religious identity (IFYC 2012). Yet even while there is much that is encouraging about these studies, in general they share at least one basic thread of observation: religious faith is on the ebb in the US, with more people identifying themselves as "spiritual, but not religious."

When we consider this research in terms of young women, the challenges are even greater. As Bischoff notes, "in the girls' studies literature, the primary location for academic discussions of girls' identities, consideration of the place of faith identity in the formation of female identity is almost completely absent" (Bischoff 2011: 38). Although there are a few published studies that suggest that "organized religious and other ethical institutions can offer girls important practical and psychological alternatives to the values conveyed by popular culture" (American Psychological Association as quoted by Bischoff 2011: 38), there is very little that actually offers advice on how to do so. Even explicitly feminist and womanist research has tended to focus on articulating theological frameworks, that is, scriptural inter-pretations that provide liberating foundations for religious belief, and liturgical resources for enacting liberative insights rather than concentrating on how feminist and womanist religious identity might be encouraged in younger women.[1]

Authority, authenticity, agency

At the same time, the birth of the web – and even more recently, of web 2.0 and social media tools – has dramatically altered the larger discursive terrain, creating a multitude of spaces which scholars describe as having characteristics of "participatory culture" (Jenkins 2009, 2006 Shirky 2008, Gauntlett 2008). There is some evidence to suggest that gender differences are less stark in some of the spaces present in digital culture – young women appear to participate in social media in about the same numbers as young men, for instance – but even with this participatory emphasis, research suggests that there are gender differences present here, too. Vedantham's careful research exploring the creation of online videos amongst undergraduates is particularly striking, finding that there are "significant differences in creation of online videos and roles played with video editing" (Vedantham 2011: x), with young men taking by far the more active roles in the process.

I have argued previously that three elements of religious identity are shifting particularly rapidly amidst media cultures: authority, authenticity and agency (Hess 2010, 2008). As these elements shift, new opportunities – and new challenges – arise for feminist and womanist faith formation that is attentive to the needs of young women. The crises of authority that have emerged as digital tools enter communities with clear hierarchical structures such as the Roman Catholic church, also create new possibilities for re-envisioning communal authority (Shirky 2008: 143–160). At the opposite end of the theological spectrum, amongst evangelical Protestant Christian communities, the vast reach and speed of digital tools create a similar crisis of authority (see, e.g., Eckholm 2011 on the recent controversy over Rob Bell's latest book),[2] with additional new opportunities.

At the same time, the question of what constitutes authentic faith has opened up new room for young women to assert their own conceptions of that term. Perhaps most striking is the reality that faith is no longer sustained and clarified primarily, or even generally, within religious institutions. The number of people who identify themselves as "spiritual, but not religious" is at an all time high. Indeed, the question of what constitutes authentic faith is increasingly being represented by, and contested within, popular culture contexts. Clark notes, for instance, that figures such as the late-night television satirist Stephen Colbert who "are positioned to serve as interpreters of religion's role in society, and whose views articulate those that are consensually accepted, thus emerge as authoritative figures in contemporary culture" (Clark 2011: 4).

These examples are drawn from the Christian context, where – at least in the US – there are still many vestiges of "established religion" to support faith formation. For other communities of faith, however, religious education develops in spite of the larger cultural surround, or even in active contestation with it. Imagine trying to raise healthy Muslim children in the midst of the current Islamophobia in the US, or trying to help your family celebrate Holi while contesting the representations of Hinduism in the *Simpsons*. Active engagement in practices of faith is the single most effective means of faith formation that scholars have identified, but how does one practice faith without a larger active community within which to do so?

These dynamic streams of authority and authenticity flow together into perhaps the single biggest challenge to faith formation in the US context: how we understand agency, or the active initiating, executing and controlling of one's actions in the world. Nearly every religious community has a theology of agency. In Christianity, for instance, God is understood as the primary Agent, with varying degrees of control (depending upon the theological perspective on free will, predestination and so on) over God's creation and God's creatures. There are even more complex articulations of the relationship between human agency and transcendence in Hinduism (Clooney 2010) and Buddhism (Makransky 2007).

In contrast to these religious frameworks, "agency" is generally understood in popular US contexts as originating individually with individual consequences. People have less and less ability to imagine organized collective action or action that is primarily group oriented. Although the advent of participatory digital media has begun to challenge this ideological dominance of the individual, that resistance is by no means widespread or hegemonic (Benkler 2006).

This challenge, where religious communities speak of agency as something that emerges within community and through community, and yet the wider popular culture represents agency almost wholly in individualistic terms, opens up room for young women to find ways to discover their own voices in the midst of community. As the dominant notions of religious authority – thoroughly permeated by centuries of patriarchal and sexist dynamics – begin to crumble, new experimentation emerges and young women can be encouraged to claim alternative understandings of religious authority, which are present in religious traditions but have often been marginalized or suppressed. Feminist and womanist approaches to faith, for example, often emphasize deeply collaborative, non-hierarchical and participatory forms of religious authority.

Yet coming to a sense of oneself as a person of faith *and* a female within any of the primary faith traditions in the US context requires a complex and difficult process that encompasses what Parker calls a dance of "realization, resistance, resilience and ritual" (2006b: 165). It is at one and the same time a dance into the heart of a community of faith, and to the edges of that same community. Young women – indeed, women of all ages – must find ways to hold within themselves the "tensegrity" of living amidst the destructive dynamics of religious cultures that privilege patriarchal dynamics and heterosexism, and yet at the same time also provide powerful narratives of resistance and deep traditions of transformation.[3]

Ironically, popular digital cultures and ancient religious traditions provide at one and the same time both resource and restriction for this tensegrity. Caught in the grip of this paradox, a group of creative feminist and womanist religious educators are working with young women in ways that help them to develop the critical stances and pragmatic practices that result in the very kinds of resistance and resilience that Parker (2003, 2006a, 2006b) promotes.

Digital storytelling offers one route into this pragmatic practice of faith formation with young women. Given the vast array of definitions that have accrued to the term "faith formation," I will note here that my use of this term incorporates two interconnected elements: religious education and spirituality. By "religious education" I mean a process of "making accessible the traditions of the religious community and the making manifest of the intrinsic connection between traditions and transformation" (Boys 1989: 193). Notice that this definition is not linked to a specific religious tradition: it could be used within Judaism, Christianity, Islam and so on. Notice, too, that it emphasizes "traditioning" as opposed to "traditionalism" (Pelikan 1984: 65).

I understand spirituality as:

> the unique and personal response of individuals to all that calls them to integrity and transcendence … . [it] has something to do with the integration of all aspects of human life and experience … . spirituality is that attitude, that frame of mind which breaks the human person out of the isolating self. As it does that, it directs him or her to another relationship in whom one's growth takes root and sustenance.
>
> (Schneiders 1986: 264)

These two components, when linked together, define what I mean by "faith formation" in this chapter. The former element describes the communal or collective character of faith formation, while the latter voices the more personal elements of that process. Faith formation, then, must take into account the historical and contemporary process of engagement with a community of faith collectively at the same time as it attends to the journey of individual persons as they seek to listen to and develop a relationship with transcendence: in Christian terms, to "know as we are known" (Palmer 1993).

In the case of working on feminist and womanist faith formation with young women, the whole process becomes a level more complex and challenging, given the patriarchal nature of faith communities through time, and the necessity of both finding one's voice within a tradition, but also of being an active agent of transformation for that tradition. Given what research has suggested is already a gendered divide between young men and young women in their sense of agency within the digital culture, finding ways to develop one's voice within a community becomes of significant importance in emerging digital cultures, yet – and this is precisely the heart of the challenge – feminist and womanist communities of faith are few and far between. Digital tools provide some possibility that such communities might be made more accessible, might even be developed in some way. As Clark notes, young people often experience practices that become possible through digital tools as "liberating and empowering, a way to manage risk and to direct one's own life course ... . an openness to possibilities rather than a limit" (Clark 2005: 218).

Digital storytelling

In this chapter I am working primarily within the tradition of digital storytelling that has been established by the work of Lambert, Weinshenker, and others associated with the Center for Digital Storytelling (CDS 2012). That process of telling stories using digital tools emerged from a community theater group which was deliberately focused on evoking and empowering personal "voice" and its sharing. Since 1993, the CDS has taught the elements of this process in a myriad of contexts, estimating that more than 12,000 stories have been created (Davis and Weinshenker 2012: 417). In contrast to some of what is labeled "digital storytelling" in current commercial media contexts, the CDS process is focused primarily on the storytelling part of that phrase. The digital tools might at first glance seem incidental or even merely instrumental to the primary learning. As Joe Lambert notes:

> What we know is that when you gather people in a room, and listen, deeply listen to what they are saying, and by example encourage others to listen, magic happens. The magic is simple. We do not have many safe places to be heard.
>
> (2006: 95)

There are, however, elements of the dynamics peculiar to digital tools and digital distribution that add a layer of learning outcomes that were originally unanticipated by the CDS, and at the same time lend themselves to powerful use when engaged in faith formation (Lambert 2006: 10–11, Gauntlett 2008: 256). So how might this additional layer be useful for feminist and womanist work with young women? To explore that layer I need to add two elements to this discussion that grow out of the work of Michael Wesch, Douglas Thomas and John Seely Brown.

The first element has to do with yet another paradox, this time one that Wesch, who is a cultural anthropologist at Kansas State University who works in the field of digital ethnography, has identified.[4] Wesch has observed that the medium of YouTube "vlogs" – a form of autobiographical self-presentation to the imagined community of YouTube – demonstrate an important experiential paradox. Their combination of "anonymity plus physical distance plus rare and ephemeral dialogue can equal hatred as public performance," and at the same time, "anonymity plus physical distance plus rare and ephemeral dialogue can equal the freedom to experience humanity without fear or anxiety" (Wesch 2008, time stamp 29:13).[5]

I believe that the "hatred as public performance" phenomenon is fairly well described, but much less attention has been paid to what it means to have the freedom to "experience humanity without fear or anxiety." That kind of experience, built upon the constructed or perceived intimacy of being able to stare directly at a close-up of a person baring their experience to a potentially global audience, is perhaps most analogous to the confessionalism previously encountered through spiritual autobiographies (Bondi 1987, 1991). It is this element of digital storytelling, with the context collapse which accompanies it, that offers new room for young women to walk into feminist and womanist identities, for it creates a space in which young women can become part of a visible community, or at least a collective arena, in which they have the freedom to explore an identity that is not constrained by institutional religious authorities, but is still embedded in something larger than themselves alone.

In addition, the CDS authors have noted that the creator of the digital story in many instances is "writing to the future" in a way that articulates an aspiration which, once having been articulated, draws the creator toward achieving it (Davis and Weinshenker 2012). While the spiritual autobiographies of times past most often were explicit in their address to God, or at least explicit about their author's desire to explore a relationship with God, what is most analogous here is not necessarily an explicit engagement with a Divine entity, but rather the baring of one's affective knowledge of self-in-relation, and the aspirational quality of the reflection that can arise from creating such a public disclosure. For young women exploring feminist and/or womanist identities, this room to practice an articulation of identity that is grounded in a community that cherishes (or at least is perceived as possibly cherishing) such an identity is a precious resource.

A further dynamic that Wesch observes comes in what he terms a "cultural inversion," where we are "craving connection but experience it as constraint" (Wesch 2008, time stamp 31:34). He notes three elements in particular — individualism, independence and commercialization — that we are immersed in, but which vlogs seem to want to counter by reaching out for, or at least expressing a desire for, community, relationships and authenticity. This "cultural inversion" directly invokes the elements I stated earlier as essential for faith formation, both in terms of community as well as in personal spiritual connection. Wesch notes that "Media do not just distance us, they connect us in new ways that can sometimes feel distant but sometimes that distance allows us to connect more deeply than ever before (Wesch 2008, time stamp 31:34) ... And new forms of community create new forms of self-understanding" (Wesch 2008, time stamp 32:10). Note that I am not ignoring that Wesch has also identified these new environments as allowing for "the public performance of hatred." I am simply recognizing a positive element of the paradox he has described.

These elements that Wesch is pointing to appear to be echoed in Thomas and Brown's observations in their recent book *A new culture of learning: Cultivating imagination for a world of constant change* (2011). In this book, most of which is an integrating argument based on the research coming out of the MacArthur Foundation Digital Media and Learning Project, Thomas and Brown argue that learning which emerges in media culture (particularly as observed in computer gaming and social media) is best understood as a process of "indwelling," with three key questions (What is my relationship to others? What am I able to explore? And how can I utilize the available resources?) constituting distinctive characteristics of learning today (Thomas and Brown 2011: 101–105). Note how the dynamic tensegrity of the communal/personal is described in this term of "indwelling." Note, too, that it is possible to see iterations of "authority, authenticity and agency" being voiced.

In digital spaces such as these, young women are learning to ask questions, and taking that practice into their engagement with their faith. In ways that encourage them to come to feminist and womanist responses, that invite them into the "resistance and resilience" so necessary to faithful and faith-filled identities, they ask, for instance: What is my relationship to a community of faith? What kinds of questions and concerns can I explore there? What resources exist within that community and tradition for the articulation of my own experience?

Indeed, one very fascinating and constructive film about religious identity recently created by a group of young women was made in the context of the organization TVbyGirls, rather than in a faith community. The film, *Undercover*, is an exploration by a group of diverse young women – Muslim, Christian, agnostic – of the practice of wearing *hijab*. In order to engage in this practice they found they needed to think about it through the experience of creating a film, rather than in their own specific communities of faith because they wanted to ask questions and to be in dialogue in ways not wholly possible in their communities, and in a manner which crossed faith borders (TVbyGirls 2012). People working in the field of faith formation who desire to foster feminist and womanist religious identities with young women need to enter into these processes with care and attention to the dynamics of authority, authenticity and agency. We must discern ways to apprentice young women into experiencing a freedom to observe humanity without stress or anxiety that moves them actively into the embrace of empathy – for themselves as well as for others (Hess 2011). At the same time, we need to find ways to help our learners weave their own stories into the larger story of the faith community through time, and at least in traditions where this matters, with God (or transcendence or the Divine) (Anderson and Foley 1998, Scharer, Hilberath, and Hinze 2008).

Pedagogies of digital storytelling

One very fruitful learning mechanism for doing so lies in the pedagogical design of digital storytelling, using story prompts that evoke connections to communities of faith. Because digital storytelling begins in learning to tell stories, and most frequently stories that have a personal foundation to them, the process is immediately congruent with the kind of faith formation process that seeks to sustain and develop spirituality. Further, in learning how to construct a story – learning the basic elements of a story, working in a story circle to refine and hone a story, multiple rounds of editing as various elements are placed into a digital framework – learners are brought into a more critically engaged relationship with their own story, as well as, potentially, the story of their community of faith. When the additional layer of distributing the story in digital format is added, the process can take on a deeply communal character (McQuistion 2007). That communal character takes shape around the individual learner's agency. As Erstad and Silseth write:

> Digital storytelling, then, both gives students the opportunity to learn how to use technology to make their own voice heard and the opportunity to use knowledge and experience acquired outside of school in the process of becoming citizens – a potential way to foster agency … . The democratic potential of digital storytelling lies both in the way people might learn to express themselves and the way it challenges traditional conceptions of formal vs. informal ways of learning.
>
> (2008: 218)

So far, there are only a few projects investigating digital storytelling in the context of religious education, but their findings are encouraging. Kaare and Lundby, for instance, in Norway, have been involved in studying one of the Norwegian church's pilot projects in new forms of faith formation. Their work on a project that engaged digital storytelling suggests that:

> By participating in the Story Circle, and negotiating how their stories should be constructed and interpreted, the young narrators are connected to the collective identity of the congregation. Identity in practice is defined socially not merely because it is reified in a social discourse of the self and of social categories, but also because it is produced as a lived experience of participation in specific communities.
>
> (2008: 117)

Similarly, in a DMin completed within the program at United Theology Seminary in Dayton, OH, where McQuistion used digital storytelling as the culminating project of a year-long confirmation program, there was consistent evidence that the young people involved in the program had very positive experiences in deepening their faith – a process which spilled over into the larger church community (McQuistion 2007: 146).

These same elements are being noted in the rare instances in which story-telling with digital media has been picked up as a constructive tool for feminist and/or womanist engagement with young women. Parker writes of developing a "faith, film and the feminine" series for young women (Parker 2003: 168).

Baker and Mercer describe using films as a way to help young women see "mutuality, distinctiveness, and community as central to the good life" (Baker and Mercer 2007: 93). Baker suggests that doing what she calls "girlfriend theology" invites young women to recontextualize and reframe the stories they pick up from the wider culture (Baker 2005). The most thorough research to date on this topic is Bischoff's dissertation on young women, narrative agency and religious education (Bischoff 2011). As she writes:

> Young women with strong imaginative faculties tell counterstories about female identity that challenge and serve to eradicate sexist master narratives. They work for social, political and religious change in the world, tapping into new ways of being, knowing, and acting to address troubling issues like poverty, addiction, ecological degradation, and war from new perspectives.
> (Bischoff 2011: 227)

Further, in each of the larger cases – the Norwegian project and the Ohio project – the primary challenge was in developing the story, *not* in the use of the technology to craft the story. Yet the lure of learning to use the technology added an element of energy and engagement to the projects, I believe at least in part because it drew on the "cultural inversions" Wesch describes, and promoted the "indwelling" of which Thomas and Brown write.

The most pressing challenge for feminist and womanist faith formation in these arenas is finding constructive ways to, as Kaare and Lundby put it, develop identity that "is defined socially not merely because it is reified in a social discourse of the self and of social categories, but also because it is produced as a lived experience of participation in specific communities" (2008: 117). Their research project did not focus specifically on gender, but had it done so it is hard not to imagine that the dynamics of "resistance and resilience" about which Parker (2006a, 2006b) writes would align themselves congruently with this "lived experience" participation of which Kaare and Lundby write.

The feminist, womanist and liberationist work that has been done in non-digital settings focused on storytelling in religious education is also helpful in this element of learning design. See, for example, Baker (2005), Bischoff (2011), Conde-Frazier (2007), Court (2007), Foster (2007), Irizarry (2003, 2008), Miedema and Roebben (2008), Parker (2006a, 2006b, 2003) and Selçuk (2008). Stories are at the heart of faith experience, they often form the primary content of faith practices that engage sacred texts, and they wind their way through liturgical and other ritual practices. Indeed, much of the more general literature in the field of Christian religious education in the last decade has centered on discussion of narrative in religious identity. See, for instance, the work of Avest, Bakker, and Miedema (2008), Dalton (2003), Everist (2000), Vail (2007), Gilmour (1997), Groome (1991), Kang and Parrett (2009), Mercer (2008), Parker (2003), Smith (2004) and Wimberly (1994).

The pace of change in our current contexts, particularly around emerging digital tools, is far too rapid to draw definitive conclusions about the impact and utility of such tools when used within faith formation. Yet experience to date suggests that there is a powerful and deeply constructive learning convergence at the intersection of digital storytelling, faith formation and gender dynamics. It is too late to think that we can simply do "what we have always done" in faith formation. Such methods no longer function well in our pluralistic, non-established religion contexts; furthermore, they take no account whatsoever of the delicate and dynamic dance of feminist and womanist religious identity construction. Yet all around us there are examples of experiential learning unfolding through the use of emerging digital tools (Watkins 2009). Why not draw on these experiments within religious learning? Digital storytelling may well be the most creative bridge we have to a future of vibrant faith communities. If we are able to help young women come to a richer sense of themselves as feminist and/or womanist people of faith, and at the same time give them access to creative production tools that increase their sense of personal and communal agency, why would we do anything less?

Notes

1 I distinguish here, and throughout the paper, between "feminist" and "womanist." "Womanist" is a term that entered popular usage through the work of novelist Alice Walker, and intentionally conveys attention to dynamics of racialization as they intersect with sexism. It is also a term that conveys a more full-bodied intersectional critique of theological sexism, and as such was first advanced by theologians Delores Williams and Jacqueline Grant. Some of the most interesting recent work with adolescent girls and the development of religious identity has been done by womanist theologian and scholar Evelyn Perkins.

2 Prof. Rob Bell is a younger evangelical pastor with a national reach, given his astute use of various forms of digital and social media. In 2011 he published a book, *Love wins*, which many across evangelical Protestant Christianity felt erred on the side of being too universalist in its theology. The book became a bestseller, and its widespread reception sent shock waves across the evangelical establishment.

3 "Tensegrity" is a term first coined by the architect R. Buckminster Fuller, who combined the words "tension" and "integrity" to describe the incredible stability of structures that are built out of competing forces that are held together with respect to their individual integrities.

4 Wesch and his students are rapidly becoming famous for their short videos exploring various aspects of digital culture. "The machine is using us," for instance, has been viewed more than 11,500,000 times as of March 2012. Perhaps even more surprising, given its length and scholarly subject, is Wesch's 55-minute lecture, "An anthropological introduction to YouTube," which has been viewed more than 1,780,000 times as of March 2012.

5 These quotations are taken from my personal transcription of the "An anthropological introduction to YouTube" video available here: www.youtube.com/watch?v=TPAO-lZ4_hU (cited on May 11, 2011). In all cases, the numbers in parentheses refer to time elapsed.

Bibliography

Anderson, H. and Foley, E. (1998) *Mighty stories, dangerous rituals: Weaving together the human and the divine*, San Francisco: Jossey-Bass.

Avest, I. and Bakker, C. (2009) "Structural identity consultation: Story telling as a culture of faith transformation," *Religious Education* 104 (3): 257–271.

Avest, I., Bakker, C. and Miedema, S. (2008) "Different schools as narrative communities: Identity narratives in threefold," *Religious Education* 103 (3): 307–322.

Baker, D. (2005) *Doing girlfriend theology: God-talk with young women*, Cleveland: The Pilgrim Press.

Baker, D. and Mercer, J. (2007) *Lives to offer: Accompanying youth on their vocational quests*, Cleveland: Pilgrim Press.

Bass, D. (2010) *Practicing our faith: A way of life for a searching people*, San Francisco, CA: Jossey-Bass.

Benkler, Y. (2006) *The wealth of networks: How social production transforms markets and freedom*, New Haven, CT: Yale University Press.

Bischoff, C. (2011) "Toward tensegrity: Young women, narrative agency and religious education," A dissertation completed in the Graduate Division of Religion, Person, Community and Religious Life, Emory University; Atlanta, GA.

Bondi, R. (1995) *Memories of God: Theological reflections on a life*, Nashville, TN: Abingdon Press.

——(1987) *To love as God loves: Conversations with the early church*, Minneapolis: Fortress Press.

——(1991) *To pray and to love: Conversations on prayer with the early church*, Minneapolis: Augsburg Fortress.

Boys, M. (1989) *Educating in faith: Maps and visions*, San Francisco, CA: Harper & Row.

CDS (2012) Center for Digital Storytelling (website). Available from: www.storycenter. org/ (accessed June 19, 2012).

Christerson, B., Edwards, K. and Flory, R. (2010) *Growing up in America: The power of race in the lives of American teens*, Stanford: Stanford University Press.

Clark, L. (2005) "The constant contact generation: Exploring teen friendship networks online," in S. Mazzarella (ed.) *Girl wide web: Girls, the internet and the negotiation of identity*, New York, NY: Peter Lang Publishing, pp. 203–221.

——(2011) "Religion and authority in a remix culture: How a late night TV host became an authority on religion," in G. Lynch, J. Mitchell and A. Strahn (eds) *Religion, media and culture: A reader*, London and New York: Routledge, pp. 111–121.

Clark, L. and Dierberg, J.(forthcoming) "Digital storytelling and progressive religious identity in a moderate to progressive youth group," in H. Campbell (ed.) *Digital religion: Understanding religious practices in new media worlds*, London and New York: Routledge.

Clooney, F. (2010) *Comparative theology*, Malden, MA: John Wiley & Sons.

Conde-Frazier, E. (2007) "Culture and the production of religious knowledge and interpretation," *Religious Education* 102 (2): 111–115.

Court, D. (2007) "Glimpsing God on the rocky road of culture," *Religious Education* 102 (2): 116–119.

Dalton, R. (2003) *Faith journeys through fantasy lands*, Minneapolis: Augsburg Fortress Press.

Davis, A. and Weinshenker, D. (2012), "Digital storytelling and authoring identity," in C. Carter Ching and B. Foley (eds) *Technology and identity: Research on the development and exploration of selves in a digital world,* Cambridge: Cambridge University Press, pp. 47–64.

Eckholm, E. (2011) "Pastor stirs wrath with his views on old questions," *New York Times,* March 4. Available from: www.nytimes.com/2011/03/05/us/05bell.html (accessed May 11, 2011).

Erstad, O. and Silseth, K. (2008) "Agency in digital storytelling: Challenging the educational context," in K. Lundby (ed.) *Digital storytelling, mediatized stories: Self representations in new media,* New York: Peter Lang Publishing, 213–232.

Everist, N. (2000) *Ordinary ministry, extraordinary challenge,* Nashville, TN: Abingdon Press.

Foster, C. (2007) "Cultures matter," *Religious Education* 102 (2): 120–123.

Gauntlett, D. (2008) *Media, gender and identity: An introduction,* New York, NY: Routledge.

Gilmour, P. (1997) *The wisdom of memoir: Reading and writing life's sacred texts,* Winona, MN: Saint Mary's Press.

Groome, T. (1991) *Sharing faith: A comprehensive approach to religious education and pastoral ministry,* San Francisco, CA: Harper.

Hess, M. (2005) *Engaging technology in theological education: All that we can't leave behind,* Lanham, MD: Rowman and Littlefield Publishers.

——(2010) "From ICT to TCI: Communicative theology(ies), pedagogy and web 2.0," in M. Scharer, B.E. Hinze and B.J. Hilberath (eds) *Kommunikative Theologie: Zugänge – Auseinandersetzungen – Ausdifferenzierungen* (Communicative Theology: Additions, Disputes, Differentations), Vienna: Lit Verlag GmbH & Co.

——(2011) "Learning religion and religiously learning amidst global cultural flows," *Religious Education* 106 (4): 360–377.

——(2008) "Responding to the challenges of religious storying in a digital age: Building new opportunities through feautor.org," in Y. Gächter, H. Ortner, C. Schwarz and A. Wiesinger (eds), in collaboration with C. Engel, T. Hug, S. Neuhaus and T. Schröder, *Erzählen – Reflexionen im Zeitalter der Digitalisierung / Storytelling – Reflections in the Age of Digitalization,* Innsbruck: Innsbruck University Press.

Hoover, S. (2006) *Religion in the media age,* New York, NY: Routledge.

IFYC (2012) Interfaith Youth Core (website). Available from: www.ifyc.org (accessed July 2, 2012).

Irizarry, J. (2008) "REA Presidential Address: Spaces of inter-cultural provocation for spiritual formation," *Religious Education* 103 (4): 396–408.

——(2003) "The religious educator as cultural spec-actor: Researching self in inter-cultural pedagogy," Religious Education 98 (3): 365–381.

Jenkins, H. (2009) *Confronting the challenges of participatory culture: Media education for the 21st century,* Cambridge: MIT Press.

——(2006) *Convergence culture: Where old and new media collide,* New York: New York University Press.

Kaare, B. and Lundby, K. (2008) "Mediatized lives: Autobiography and assumed authenticity in digital storytelling," in K. Lundby (ed.) *Digital storytelling, mediatized stories: Self representations in new media,* New York: Peter Lang Publishing, 105–122.

Kang, S. and Parrett, G. (2009) *Teaching the faith, forming the faithful: A biblical vision for education in the church,* Downers Grove, IL: InterVarsity Press.

Kosmin, B., Keysar, A., *et al.* (2009) "American nones: The profile of the no religion population," Hartford, CT: Trinity College. Available from: http://commons.trincoll.edu/aris/publications/american-nones-the-profile-of-the-no-religion-population/ (accessed May 11, 2011).

Lambert, J. (2006) *Digital storytelling: Capturing lives, creating community*, Berkeley, CA: Digital Diner Press.

Lynch, G., Mitchell, J., and Strhan, A. (2011). *Religion, media and culture: A reader*, London and New York: Routledge.

MacArthur Foundation (2012) Digital media and learning (website). Available from: http://tinyurl.com/2d74eb9 (accessed 19 June 2012).

Makransky, J. (2007) *Awakening through love: Unveiling your deepest goodness*, Somerville, MA: Wisdom Publications.

Martinson, R., Roberto, J. and Black, W. (2010) *The spirit and culture of youth ministry: Leading congregations towards exemplary youth ministry*, St. Paul, MN: EYM Publishing.

Mazzarella, S. (ed.) (2005) *Girl wide web: Girls, the internet and the negotiation of identity*, New York: Peter Lang Publishing.

McQuistion, R. (2007) "Digital disciples: Reconceptualizing adolescent confirmation instruction by combining biblical storytelling and digital media," a dissertation completed for the DMIN program at United Theological Seminary in Dayton, OH.

Mercer, J. (2008) *GirlTalk, GodTalk*, San Francisco, CA: Jossey-Bass.

Miedema, S. and Roebben, B. (2008) "The two contested concepts of culture and tradition in religious education," *Religious Education* 103 (4): 480–492.

Mitchell, J. and Marriage, S. (eds) (2003) *Mediating religion: Conversations in media, religion and culture*, New York: T.&t. Clark.

Nakamura, L. (2008) *Digitizing race: Visual cultures of the internet*, Minneapolis: University of Minnesota Press.

Palmer, P. (1993) *To know as we are known: Education as a spiritual journey*, San Francisco: HarperCollins.

Parker, E. (2006a) "Cultural studies meets religious education," *Religious Education* 101 (4): 462–465.

——(2006b) *The sacred selves of adolescent girls: Hard stories of race, class and gender*, Cleveland, OH: The Pilgrim Press.

——(2003) *Trouble don't always last: The sacred selves of adolescent girls*, Cleveland, OH: The Pilgrim Press.

Pelikan, J. (1984) *The vindication of tradition*, New Haven, CT: Yale University.

Putnam, R. and Campbell, D. (2010) *American grace: How religion divides and unites us*, New York: Simon and Schuster.

Ohler, J. (2008) *Digital storytelling in the classroom: New media pathways to literacy, learning and creativity*, Thousand Oaks, CA: Corwin Press.

Scharer, M., Hilberath, J. and Hinze, B. (2008) *Communicative theology: An introduction to a new theological culture*, Chestnut Ridge, NY: Crossroad Publishing Co.

Schneiders, S. (1986) "Theology and spirituality: strangers, rivals or partners?" *Horizons* 13 (2): 264.

Selçuk, M. (2008) "Who am I between 'us' and 'them?'" *Religious Education* 103 (5): 511–516.

Shirky, C. (2008) *Here comes everybody: The power of organizing without organizations*, New York: Penguin Press.

Smith, C. and Denton, M. (2005) *Soul searching: The religious and spiritual lives of American teenagers*, New York: Oxford University Press.

Smith, Y. (2004) *Reclaiming the spirituals: New possibilities for African American Christian education*, Cleveland, OH: Pilgrim Press.

Thomas, D. and Brown, J.S. (2011) *A new culture of learning: Cultivating the imagination for a world of constant change*, Lexington, KY: CreateSpace.

TVbyGirls (2012) (website). Available from: http://www.tvbygirls.tv/the_site/home.htm (accessed June 19, 2012).

Vail, G. (2007) *Stories in faith*, Boston, MA: Unitarian Universalist Association.

Vedantham, A. (2011) "Making Youtube and Facebook videos: Gender differences in online video creation among first-year undergraduate students attending a highly selective research university," a dissertation in the University of Pennsylvania Graduate School of Education.

Watkins, S. (2009) *The young and the digital: What the migration to social-network sites, games, and anytime, anywhere media means for our future*, Boston: Beacon Press.

Wesch, M. (2008) "An anthropological introduction to YouTube." Lecture given at the Library of Congress. Available from: www.youtube.com/watch?v=TPAO-lZ4_hU (accessed June 19, 2012).

Wimberly, A. (1994) *Soul stories: African American Christian education*, Nashville, TN: Abingdon Press.

Chapter 13

Media, religion and gender

Key insights and future challenges

Mia Lövheim

The film *The Matrix*, released in 1999, captured the hearts of a broad audience as well as of the scholarly community. It has been discussed and analyzed from a number of different perspectives, not least concerning its "post-modern" play with categories of religion, reality, science – and gender (see Irwin 2002, Freeland 2002). Trinity, the lead female character in the film, is no traditional woman. She is a skilled, cool, slick and purpose-driven computer hacker and martial arts expert. When the male hero, Neo, first meets her in what he then still believes to be the "real world" he surprisingly exclaims "I thought you were a guy!". Trinity's stoic reply – "most guys do" – highlights the double-sided nature of her as an exception to the norm, in films as well as the "real world". She is, on the one hand, an example of the non-traditional female characters that have become more frequent in films, television series and computer games during recent years (see Butler and Winston 2009: 260). On the other hand, she still features attributes and values that position her, in relation to the "guys", as a conventional female heroine: she is beautiful, slim, white, sexually attractive, caring and deeply in love with the male hero. And even though Trinity functions as Neo's spiritual guide and plays a crucial role for his ability to fulfill his mission, she in the end sacrifices her life while he goes on to save humankind.

The aim of this volume, as presented in Chapter 1, has been to address the "blind spot" of gender in research on media, religion and culture by showing how studies that, from different theoretical and methodological perspectives, take gender as their point of departure have contributed to the field. A further reason has been to inspire research that goes beyond "adding women" as an object of study toward using gender as a lens to highlight emerging transformations, raise new questions and critically evaluate the state of research. The example from *The Matrix* illustrates how contemporary media representations of gender and religion many times blur traditional attributes and roles ascribed to women and men within religion and society. However, the ambiguous mix of gender attributes and roles in the film also illustrates why an analysis that combines insights from religious studies and media studies with gender studies is necessary to understand a character like Trinity. Analyzing the meaning of

Trinity requires the scholar to take into consideration questions such as: from what understanding of gender do I analyze her potential as an alternative female heroine? From what perspective of the relation between media as a discursive and social structure and individual agency do I analyze her empowering qualities? How do I handle my own gendered and religious position and experience in the analysis? By evoking these questions the example of Trinity shows that an analysis that includes theoretical and methodological perspectives from gender studies is crucial for addressing key questions in current research on media and religion, such as the implications of mediatization for the public presence of religion in contemporary society, how the media works as a resource for individuals and groups in performing religious identity and social relations, and the implications of our research for the wider religious, cultural and political context in contemporary society.

This volume illustrates in various ways how this kind of analysis is under way in studies of media and religion, and how studies focusing on gender have contributed in the process. This final chapter will, first, present three key insights that studies of gender have brought to the field, exemplified through the case studies presented in the book. These insights also bring out what researchers within studies of gender and the media can learn from research on media and religion. Secondly, the chapter will address the increased interest in gender as a theme in research on media, religion and culture that has become visible over the last decade. This question actualizes the third and final theme of how the chapters of this book point to challenges for future research.

Key insights

The review chapters by Mia Lövheim and Lynn Schofield Clark and Grace Chiou highlight a number of issues raised and pursued in previous studies of media, religion and gender, which also intersect with shifts and debates in theoretical and methodological approaches to gender and media during the past two decades. Among these issues three themes in particular stand out: the widening of the category of religion to include experiences and expressions by women and other groups marginalized by religious establishments, an emerging critical analysis of media as a resource for individual meaning making and negotiations of values and identities mediated through religious institutions as well as the media, and a discussion of the position of the researcher with regard to the wider social and political context of our research.

With regard to the first issue, Pamela Klassen and Kathryn Lofton's chapter is an example that highlights how women throughout the twentieth and twenty-first centuries have found ways of expressing their knowledge, experiences and interpretations of religion through media. Examples such as Mary Lena Tate, Evangeline Booth and Oprah Winfrey show how women have played an active part in initiating the use of new media forms with Christianity. However, their analysis also underscores how gender, in particular relations between gender, access and power, has shaped this process. As Klassen and Lofton point out (see also Maddux 2010: 14, cf. Campbell 1989), women have often become pioneers in the use of new media forms because they were denied access to established religious and media channels and arenas. This theme of women's use of new media forms to find alternative ways to assert their voices is also developed in the chapters by Line Nybro Petersen, Anna Piela and Mary Hess, which show how women use new digital media to carve out spaces for expressing their ideas and experiences of religion.

These studies contribute to previous research by widening our understanding of mediated religion, in representation as well as use. There are recurrent themes in these accounts of Christian mommy bloggers acting as spiritual advisers, Muslim women discussing interpretations of the Qur'an online, and Danish teenage girls exploring the supernatural twist of love relations in *Twilight* on Facebook. One of these is how their religious beliefs are shaped not so much by formal authorities, as by experiences from their personal life and the social relations in which they are situated. This insight in itself is rooted in the work that has emanated out of the culturalist turn in studies of media, religion and culture with its focus on "lived religion" or religion as a form of cultural work shaped by personal experience and practice as well as texts and institutions (see Orsi 1997). However, what the analysis in the chapters in this book clearly shows is that religion as expressed outside of institutions is situated in particular social and historical contexts, where more informal social and cultural institutions structure experiences, subjectivities and social interaction not least with regard to gender. As shown by Klassen and Lofton, the common patterns across time in women's articulations of religiosity, such as the connection between the personal and the transcendent, are not so much shaped by a female "essence" as by the situatedness of these women. Women draw on the personal and intimate in their articulations of religion because the private sphere of home and family has situated and still to a large extent situates their lives more than men, but women's articulations of religion also – more frequently than men's – become associated with private life and bodily aspects when taken up in a broader cultural discourse. Para-phrasing McLuhan's device that "the medium is the message", Klassen and Lofton underline how when it comes to religious women's witnessing, "the matter of her body always haunts her words, staining their clarity and whatever channel transports them" (this volume, p. 72). How women's articulations of religion become interpreted as belonging to the private sphere is evident also in Joyce Smith's discussion of how women are represented as victims, or associated with sexuality, personal opinion, emotions and the private or domestic sphere in news coverage of religion. An additional dimension is how women's uses of media to reflect on and express religious experiences often become a sounding board for debates over boundaries between the authentic or deleterious character of mediated religion, not least when women's religious identities and stories are expressed in ways that border on popular media forms or intersect with commercial interests. This is evident in Klassen and Lofton's description of discussions over the legitimacy of the spiritual advice by Evangelical mommy bloggers, but also in discussions about the implications of young women's fascination with the *Twilight* films as presented by Nybro Petersen (see also Bode 2010).

The contribution of these studies to analyzing varieties of mediated religion is, however, not only to be found in adding the experiences of women to the picture, but also in the variety they uncover among women's mediated expressions of religion. This insight contributes to challenge essentialist understanding of women's and men's religiosity, and underlines how this variety is equally shaped by their social situatedness. The chapter by Anna Piela clearly brings out the differences among Muslim women's interpretations of Islam online, and how these challenge generalizing conceptions of "women in Islam" as well as of the relation between women and a certain feminist agenda. The varieties that exist in attitudes to male role models presented in media among Evangelical men is also a core insight in Curtis Coats and Stewart Hoover's chapter.

Highlighting gender thus contributes to understanding the variety of mediated expressions of religion. As pointed out above, studies such as those presented in this book exemplify different perspectives for analyzing the causes and implications of these varieties through highlighting the social and in particular gendered situatedness of mediated religion. With regard to media representations of religion and gender, several of the chapters in this volume exemplify how an analysis of the intersections of various social and cultural contexts, including religion and gender, can deepen an analysis of the implications of media logics or frames of reference for representing social events (see Klaus and Kassel 2005). Smith's chapter shows how the "beat" of certain news journalism genres shapes the representation of religion as either "foreign" news or "soft" issues. The combination of women *and* religion in a news event enhances the chance that it will end up in the "soft" areas, connected to clusters such as "social issues, minority issues, and personal relationships". Thus, the themes of gender *and* religion in combination seemingly reinforce the representation of such events as something "other" than the "hard" political, majority and public affairs of society.

Line Nybro Petersen and Diane Winston analyze the process of mediatization, or how religious symbols and stories become moulded according to the purpose of a certain genre, within entertainment media such as film and television series. As highlighted by Winston, the commercial dimension of this genre is crucial to understanding the representation of gender and religion. In the television series *Saving Grace* the media logic of the genre means that religion is presented in an "open-ended" form to make viewers engage with characters and, consequently, with the show. However, in a parallel to the example of Trinity in *The Matrix*, the media logic also demands that a "non-traditional" female lead character expresses attractiveness to conform to the demand of the entertainment media to appeal to consumers. Winston's chapter raises several important questions for further studies of the implications of this process: "Will sharp edges be dulled, subversive characters tamed, and radical behaviors blunted to ensure advertisers and secure large audiences?" (this volume, p. 166).

The focus on varieties in mediated expressions of religion between and among women and men brings us to the second contribution of applying gender perspectives to studies of media and religion: the critical analysis of media as a resource for religious meaning making. That symbols, values and stories circulated through media increasingly become resources for the construction of religious identities is a theme well developed in media, religion and culture research (cf. Hoover 2006). This research has had a strong focus on the agency of individuals and groups to make use of media symbols and narratives to negotiate their relationship to traditional religious discourses. As pointed out by Clark and Chiou the significance of the interpretive turn in research methodologies in the 1980s and 1990s for this development is crucial, and previous studies of religion and media in everyday life conducted at the University of Colorado at Boulder initiated a focus on wider cultural and ideological patterns that inform these processes. The chapters in this volume contribute to this research by making gender a primary focus and thereby enhancing a critical analysis of how this agency is situated and structured.

Several of these studies are set within a discussion of new forms of digital mediation. Nybro Petersen and Piela argue for the potential of new media forms to allow young women and Muslim women to contribute to the construction of religious identities, imaginaries and to develop new social relationships around these. Boutros', Winston's and Klassen and Lofton's chapters contribute to this picture through bringing the body and sexuality into the analysis. These chapters show clearly how material dimensions and their gendered implications do not disappear with digital mediation but rather become even more complicated and contested. The power of traditional (male) authorities to control expressions of gender and sexuality and their implications in terms of inclusion or exclusion from a religious community or from divine grace might be weakened but norms regulating appropriate gender and sexual behavior still structure these interactions. Michele Rosenthal's chapter in particular shows that new media can become powerful tools for religious communities to sanction certain forms of piety that reinforce obedience to traditional, strongly gendered, authorities and strictures. The chapters by Alexandra Boutros and Anna Piela also remind us of how online negotiations of religious texts and rituals are situated within histories of power relations between Western countries and their former colonies, and illustrate how conceptions of and boundaries around sexuality and gender are a fundamental part of these histories.

The final key issue where perspectives from gender studies contribute to developing studies of media and religion concerns the position and role of the researcher. As pointed out by Clark and Chiou, the aims of feminist theory and research methods challenge the role of the researcher and participant in traditional research paradigms and also the goals of research as confined to the norms of the scholarly community. Feminist approaches, they argue, bring out the importance of self-reflexivity on behalf of the researcher and point to new directions, such as participatory, collaborative and reflexive research. Among the authors in this book, Lynn Schofield Clark and Grace Chiou, Anna Piela and Mary Hess in particular incorporate reflections on the implications of their own experiences and position as a researcher *vis-à-vis* those that they study for their research. Along with Joyce Smith they exemplify how research can be used for addressing the concerns of feminist researchers, journalists and teachers of to increase mutual engagement with the subjects of research and teaching and with media audiences in general. Through raising questions about how the researcher's position in terms of gender shape his or her research, and how our research might empower or stigmatize particular groups in society, these chapters address in an important way the relation between research on media and religion and the wider social and political context in which they are situated.

As Lövheim's and Clark and Chiou's chapters show, post-colonial perspectives and Third World feminisms have been important in developing all of the key insights presented above. These perspectives will continue to be important in increasing our attention to context in various intersections of religion and media, such as the historical landscape, the political economy of media, and the position of various audiences and discourses with regard to gender, class, nation and family.

Finally, researchers working with feminist and gender analysis of the media can also learn something from current research on media, religion and gender. One point of learning, exemplified in the chapters by Boutros and Piela is how studies of religion, gender and media challenge assumptions in media and cultural studies about "traditional" or conservative religious discourses and communities, in particular, as connected to oppression of women as well as heteronormativity. Studies of these issues through the lens of gender reveal how the meaning of media discourses are subject to negotiations in these communities, and con-tribute to knowledge about the complexity of agency in the construction of religious subjectivities through media practices. Put differently, being religious does not disqualify women and men from being active and critical participants and "produsers" (cf. Bruns 2006) of new symbols, practices and discourses on gender and religion through their media use. Another point of learning con-cerns, as described earlier, how research on media and religion contributes knowledge about how religion intersects with the gendered mechanisms of media logics and the conventions of certain genres, as described in by Smith, Winston and Nybro Petersen.

A new interest in gender?

This volume represents an example of an increase in published works on gender, media and religion during the last decade, which is also noticeable in the growing amount of papers and panels addressing gender at the two latest Conferences on Media, Religion and Culture held in Toronto, Canada (2010) and Eskisehir, Turkey (2012). Can this be interpreted as a growing awareness of gender issues within research on media, religion and culture? If so, what might be the reasons behind this interest? One possible reason can be traced to changes in the public visibility of religion as the main subject of research in this field. As pointed out by, among others, Stewart Hoover (2008) media reporting on religion in the wake of events such as the attack on the Twin Towers in New York on September 11, 2001 and the London Underground on July 7, 2005 has come to focus on the persistence and resurgence of religion as a national, regional and global force (Toft, Philpot and Shah 2011). As pointed out in recent work by feminist scholars such as Aune, Sharma and Vincett (2008), Duits and van Zoonen (2006) and Göle (2006) issues of gender and sexuality, such as Muslim women's lifestyle, dress and bodies, often become focal points of interest in debates. Another example concerns the media interest in sexual abuse within traditional religious institutions, most prominently the Catholic church (Lynch 2012), and a third example is the "culture war thesis" in the US context described by Coats and Hoover (cf. Wilcox 2004: 8), where the family and issues of sexual morality are seen as a primary battleground for a conflict between conservative religion, primarily articulated in the form of traditional male authority, and feminist impulses thought to dominate the secular, cultural sphere. This connection of religion and gender, family and sexuality within news and entertainment media during the last few decades has probably contributed to the placing of gender higher on the research agenda of studies in media, religion and culture.

There are also reasons that relate to changes within the research field of media, religion and culture. One of these reasons can be found in the growth of the area of media, religion and culture studies during the past decades which has contributed to a more interdisciplinary and international character of the field (see Lynch. Mitchell, and Strhan 2011). The interaction between researchers and the intersection of perspectives from different disciplines, from media producers and from religious organizations of various kinds, can enhance the potential of a critical awareness of and dialogue about "blind spots" and dominant patterns in research. This reason must, however, be connected to another change: the growing numbers of researchers and larger interdisciplinary character of the work presented has also enhanced the potential for a new generation of researchers to enter the field, of which a larger share than before are female and/or from non-US or non-Western origins.

These reasons do not bring about changes in the perspectives and focus of a research field on their own. They are intrinsically connected to whatever space and encouragement are given to new and previously marginalized issues, perspectives and participants. The growing plurality of the field represents a resource but also a responsibility and a challenge for the constant process of critical reflection on the theoretical and methodological foundations of research on media, religion and culture.

Furthermore, the lingering question raised by Clark and Chiou about why research on women's experiences and by scholars working from a feminist and gender perspective has been less frequently cited as central to the field remains to be answered. Are feminist and gender studies growing mainly as a sub-area within research on media, religion and culture, or to what extent are the insights and questions raised by this work also becoming integrated in mainstream studies? A continued dialogue across disciplinary, religious and national boundaries, as well as inclusion of the voices and perspectives of people outside of mainstream research traditions, is needed in order to take advantage of this momentum for gender issues in the field.

Challenges for future research

The influence from feminist and gender theories and methodologies revealed in the chapters by Lövheim and Clark and Chiou in this volume is in several ways connected to the shift of focus in the late 1990s in media studies and religious studies toward the contexts and practices of everyday life, followed by the focus on how intersections of globalization and local cultures shape these practices brought by Third Wave feminism and post-colonial theory. The chapters in this book have, as pointed out above, shown how this development has continued and how studies focusing on gender have contributed to the process. However, as underscored in these chapters, there is also a great deal of room for further research development building on the contributions and insights from feminist and gender theories and methodologies.

At the beginning of the twenty-first century many of the issues raised in the formation of the research area of media, religion and culture remain important, but changes within religion as well as media have also brought new challenges. Building on the insights of recent work in sociology of religion (Woodhead 2012) and religion and media studies (Hoover 2008, Hjarvard and Lövheim 2012, Lynch, Mitchell, and Strhan 2011) we can outline some tendencies in this moment that bring out new challenges for further research. Linda Woodhead argues that the "new visibility" of religion in the public sphere, primarily in a European context, to a large extent is driven by new forms and actors of religion that emerge outside the control of states and religious institutions and in relation to new opportunities of market and media. This means that forms of religion previously deemed as "latent" or implicit, in contrast to official and collective religion, have become a strong feature of religion also in the public sphere. As these forms have previously often been associated with private and female spheres such as the home, family, the body, emotions and personal life, this underscores the importance of gender as an analytical category. As argued by Heidi Campbell (2012, cf. Hoover 2008) the media, not least digital media, play an important part in shaping and articulating these shifts in contemporary religion. Mediated religion brings out how religion today is becoming more popular and more personal, located in narratives of self and in personal networks rather than in dogmas and institutional form, and practiced in many, intersecting sites which challenge formal religious authority and institutional control. As shown by Clark (2011) this development also goes together with a discourse that emphasizes empowerment and authenticity through new, digital media as enabling the formation of agentic subjects that choose and produce their own religion.

In understanding what this situation means for religion as an individual resource and a social and cultural force in contemporary society, and how the media shape this process, three crucial challenges for future research emerge: how to analyze context, how to analyze change, and the question of power. As the history of feminist and gender research shows, gender is a core aspect of each of these questions. As argued by Clark and Chiou, part of the reason why feminist and gender thought has not been a focus in media and religion is skepticism toward gender as a theoretical approach that is too particular. Placing gender in the wider picture of religious change in contemporary society rather shows the value of gender as lens to highlight core aspects of these transformations and the role played by the media in them (Lövheim 2012).

The first challenge concerns the importance and complexities of analyzing the contexts of mediated religion. As contemporary religion cannot so easily be located within the traditional context of religious institutions, the researcher is faced with mapping and tracing individual and sometimes collective trajectories of interaction with religion across several contexts, where media in various forms become central sources of information and arenas for articulating religion. An important question for further research becomes to analyze how these contexts are structured by gender. This is not least important in evaluating if, how and when religion through mediation is becoming more of a public matter or rather something more private and individualized. Different communicative spheres and genres are not only deemed public or private, but also as "masculine" and "feminine". What does this mean for the articulation of new forms of religion in the media? Furthermore, how does the gendering of various contexts structure the possibility for the transition of religious messages and identities across contexts? Finally, how does gender structure the intersection of different contexts with regard to the possibilities to act out various religious identities?

As pointed out by Clark and Chiou acknowledging the goals of feminist scholarship to embrace this complexity requires increased labor. A full contextual analysis, taking into account historical, political and economic aspects of various intersections of religion and media, as well as the positions of audiences and discourses regarding not just gender, but also class, ethnicity and sexuality, is challenging. However, the current situation shows that it is also fundamental for making valid research claims about the interplay between media, religion and culture in contemporary society.

The question of context also brings out issues of inclusion and exclusion. As this volume shows studies from a feminist perspective have contributed to the inclusion of women in research on media and religion, but – as pointed out by Clark and Chiou – the question of which populations have become invisible and marginalized in studies of media and religion is still persistent. As Lövheim's chapter shows, studies of white, US-based Protestant Christian middle-class culture and religion still dominate many research themes. Furthermore, there is a clear dominance of female scholars and work on women and religion in the field. The new questions and challenges for feminist media studies introduced by masculinity, queer and post-feminist perspectives have just started to be addressed in studies of media, religion and gender. The growing awareness of the experiences of gay, lesbian, bi- and transsexuals within religious communities shows that a further development of these perspectives is urgently needed.

The challenge of analyzing change in new forms of mediated religion highlights the question illustrated by the example from *The Matrix* in the introduction. It is important not to overemphasize the transformations happening through new media and media cultures. As exemplified in this volume, studies focusing on gender show that attributes, norms and roles that assign women and men different positions, value and agency become re-enacted in new and complex ways in contemporary media representations of religion. An important challenge for future research is a further analysis of how processes of mediatization are structured by gender. The chapters in this volume has shown examples of how the media logics of news media and television series for representing religion intersect with frames, tropes and roles used to portray gender, but further analysis of these mechanisms and how they structure the characters and narratives of gender and religion also in other media genres are required. A related challenge concerns a critical reflection on the concepts and theories used for identifying change and agency in the field of media and religion. This concerns the tendency to deem stories of religion mediated, for example, through personal and popular media forms traditionally seen as the domain of women as less significant for political and civic participation. Furthermore, the critique from researchers drawing on a feminist post-colonial perspective that research on media and religion equates equality and agency with Western ideals of individual choice, bodily self-expression and sexual freedom calls for a development of theories that are open to various forms of religious agency. Finally, these questions underline the challenge for researchers working toward the understanding of the potential of digital media for media production raised by Clark and Chiou: even in a culture of increased participation in the process of mediating religion, not all communities and members have equal access and ability to take part. Gender is a key aspect of these barriers, and feminist critical perspectives can contribute to a further analysis also of the struggles and conditions of other underrepresented groups.

This brings us to the final challenge of how to analyze power in contemporary forms of mediated religion. If the culturalist turn implied a strong focus in studies of media and religion on how media is reflexively consumed by audiences and on individual agency, a focus on gender brings the question of power firmly back on the agenda. The complexity of power and agency in new media culture challenges several theories previously used to analyze power in media studies as well as feminist studies. On the one hand, changes in the social forms of religion and in media structures from institutional control to a plurality of actors in a "symbolic marketplace" erode the power of traditional authorities to enforce norms and control expressions of gender and sexuality. On the other hand, neo-liberal political discourses and the rules of the capitalist market introduce new regimes of power. How to analyze the potentials of new digital media for a more broadly dispersed agency with regard to the production, circulation and use of mediated stories of religion is one part of this challenge. Another part concerns how to interpret the potential for agency in uses of parody and play within contemporary media cultures presented by post-feminist perspectives.

These issues are parts of a wider challenge to engage further in developing theories and concepts for analyzing intersections between media, religion and gender building on the specific contributions of feminist and gender theories in previous research. One of the questions raised described by Clark and Chiou concerns generating dialogue between the need for the development of theoretical frameworks accounting for continuities and connections across cases, and the emphasis on variety and complexity. In facing this task, researchers in media, religion and culture can learn from several theories in gender studies. One is the analysis of gender in queer theory as performed or enacted within a range of possibilities and norms conditioned by historical, social and religious conventions (Butler 1990). The focus on the stability as well as instability in these theories can be fruitful for critical reflection on the relation between categories of religious identity, gender and sexuality, and how the affordances of various media structure or enable the performance of religious and gendered subjectivities.

Another insight comes from studies of intersectionality. As argued by Nina Lykke (2005), in order to reveal recurrent patterns of inequality, domination and oppression within the complexity and diversity of intersecting contexts this analysis needs to start out from a choice of a certain "asymmetry of power". The examples in this book show how gender can be a valuable lens for revealing recurrent and remaining structures and mechanisms that shape the way individuals negotiate and reformulate religious identities in interaction with the symbolic resources circulated through various media, as well as how and when the complex web of intersecting social and cultural contexts contribute to empowering them in the process.

The question of power, finally, connects to the challenges concerning the role and ideals of the researcher raised by Clark and Chiou. As they argue, to take seriously the ideals and goals of feminist and gender studies of contributing to empowerment and advocacy of those marginalized by religious institutions and academic hierarchies challenges some disciplinary norms and objectives, as well as those of publishers and funding bodies of our research. Thus, bringing gender into studies of media and religion not only means challenges for how we analyze the interplay between religion and media in the contemporary world, but also how researchers can contribute to the roles played by religion and media in politicals and social transformation.

The insights from research conducted so far and the growing awareness of the perspectives and issues raised by feminist and gender studies show that we have come further on the way toward addressing these crucial issues, but also that there are still things to do. It is our hope that this book will inspire scholars from many different contexts, experiences and perspectives, to continue this important work.

Bibliography

Aune, K., Sharma, S. and Vincett, G. (eds) (2008) *Women and Religion in the West: Challenging Secularization*, Farnham: Ashgate.

Bode, L. (2010) "Transitional Tastes: Teen Girls and Genre in the Critical Reception of Twilight", *Continuum: Journal of Media and Cultural Studies*, 25 (5): 707–719.

Bruns, A. (2006) *Blogs, Wikipedia, Second Life, and Beyond: From Production to Produsage*, New York: Peter Lang.

Butler, A. and Winston, D. (2009) "' A Vagina Ain't a Halo': Gender and Religion in *Saving Grace* and *Battlestar Galactica*", in Winston, D. (ed.) *Small Screen, Big Picture: Television and Lived Religion*. Waco, TX: Baylor University Press, pp. 259–286.

Butler, J. (1990) *Gender Trouble: Feminism and the Subversion of Identity*, New York: Routledge.

Campbell, H. (2012) "Understanding the Relationship between Religion Online and Offline in a Networked Society", *Journal of the American Academy of Religion*, 79 (1): 1 –30

Campbell, K.K. (1989) "Introduction", in *Man Cannot Speak for Her. Volume I; A Critical Study of Early Feminist Rhetoric (Contributions in Women's Studies)*, New York: Praeger.

Clark, L. S. (2011) "Considering Religion and Mediatisation through a Case Study of J+K's Big Day (The J K Wedding Entrance Dance): A Response to Stig Hjarvard", *Culture and Religion*, 12 (2): 167–184.

Duits, L. and van Zoonen, L. (2006) "Headscarves and Porno-Chic: Disciplining Girl's Bodies in the European Multicultural Society", *European Journal of Women's Studies*, 13 (2): 103–117.

Freeland, C. (2002) "Penetrating Keanu: New Holes, but the Same Old Shit", in Irwin, W. (ed.) *The Matrix and Philosophy: Welcome to the Desert of the Real*. Chicago and La Salle, IL: Open Court, pp. 205–215.

Göle, N. (2006) "Islam in European Publics: Secularism and Religious Difference", *The Hedgehog Review*, 8 (1–2): 140–145.

Hjarvard, S. (2011) "The Mediatization of Religion: Theorising Religion, Media and Social Change", *Culture and Religion*, 12 (2): 119–135.

Hjarvard, S. and Lövheim, M. (eds) (2012) *Mediatization and Religion: Nordic Perspectives*, Gothenburg: Nordicom.

Hoover, S.M. (2008) *Media and Religion*. A White Paper from The Center for Media, Religion, and Culture, University of Colorado at Boulder, USA. Online: http://cmrc. colorado.edu/cmrc/index.php/white-papers (accessed 06.06.2012).

Hoover, S. (2006) *Religion in the Media Age*, New York: Routledge.

Irwin, W. (ed.) (2002) *The Matrix and Philosophy: Welcome to the Desert of the Real*, Chicago and La Salle, IL: Open Court.

Klaus, E. and Kassel, S. (2005) "The Veil as a Means of Legitimization: An Analysis of the Interconnectedness of Gender, Media and War", *Journalism* 6 (3): 335–355.

Lövheim, M. (2012) "A Voice of Their Own: Young Muslim Women, Blogs and Religion", in Hjarvard, S. and Lövheim, M. (eds) *Mediatization and Religion: Nordic Perspectives*. Gothenburg: Nordicom.

Lykke, N. (2005) "Intersektionalitet – ett användbart begrepp för genusforskningen", *Kvinnovetenskaplig tidskrift* nr 2–3.

Lynch, G. (2012) *The Sacred in the Modern World: A Cultural Sociological Approach*, Oxford: Oxford University Press.

Lynch, G., Mitchell, J., and Strhan, A. (2011) *Religion, Media and Culture: A Reader*, London and New York: Routledge.

Maddux, K. (2010) *The Faithful Citizen: Popular Christian Media and Gendered Civic Identities*, Waco, TX: Baylor University Press.

Orsi, R.A. (1997) "Everyday Miracles, The Study of Lived Religion", in Hall, D. (ed.) *Lived Religion in America: Toward a History of Practice*. Princeton, NJ: Princeton University Press, pp. 3–21.

Toft, M.D., Philpott, D. and Shah, D. (2011) *God's Century: Resurgent Religion and Global Politics*, New York: W.W. Norton and Company.

Wilcox, W.B. (2004) *Soft Patriarchs, New Men: How Christianity Shapes Fathers and Husbands*, Chicago: University of Chicago Press.

Woodhead, L. (2012) "Introduction", Woodhead, L. and Cato, R. (eds) *Religion and Change in Modern Britain*, London and New York: Routledge.

Index

Please note that page numbers relating to Notes will have the letter 'n' following the page number.